# Law in Cameroon: A French Tradition

Moye Godwin Bongyu

# Law in Cameroon: A French Tradition

Moye Godwin Bongyu

W. B. Sheridan Law Books

Washington – London
Academica Press

Library of Congress Registration Information
Names: Bongyu, Moye, author.
Title: Law in Cameroon : A French tradition / Moye Bongyu.
Description: Washington, DC : Academica Press, 2020. |
Identifiers: LCCN 2020932836 | ISBN 9781680531923 (hardcover : alk. paper)
LC record available at https://lccn.loc.gov/2020932836

# Dedication

Students of the Faculty of Law and Political Science
Researchers in Governance Matters
Practicing Public Administrators
Good Governance Disciples

# Contents

**Acknowledgements ............................................................ xxi**

**Preface........................................................................ xxiii**

**Abbreviations and Acronymes .......................................... xxvii**

**General Introduction ..............................................................1**

I. The Concept of Public Administration................................................ 2
A. Perspectives of Public Administration................................................ 2
B. Distinctiveness of Public Administration ........................................... 3
II Distinction between Public and Private Laws .................................... 5
III. The Origins of *Droit Adminstratif* in France .................................... 7
IV. *Droit Administratif* and Administrative Law .................................... 8
V. Foundations of Administrative Law ................................................. 11
VI. Comparative Approach ................................................................. 13
VII. Organization of the Book.............................................................. 14

**Chapter One**
**Administrative Law, Law of the Administration.............................15**

1.1 Administrative Organization ........................................................... 15
I. The Administrative Organization of the State...................................... 16
A. Theory of Administrative Centralization............................................ 16
B. Theory of Administrative Deconcentration ........................................ 18
II. The Theory of Administrative Decentralisation ................................. 19
A. The Theory of Territorial Decentralization: Local Government ....... 19
1. Types of Decentralization.................................................................. 20
2. Autonomy of decentralized entities.................................................... 21
a. Political Autonomy ........................................................................... 22
b. Administrative Autonomy ................................................................. 22
c. Financial Autonomy ......................................................................... 23
B. The Theory of Technical
Decentralization: Specialized Institutions ............................................. 24
III. Relationships between the Administrative Techniques................... 25

1. Coexistence of Centralization–Decentralization ............................... 25
2. Coexistence of Deconcentration and Decentralization....................... 27
Differences between deconcentration and decentralization .................. 27
3. Hierarchical and Supervisory Control ................................................ 28
1.2 The Control of Administrative Power ............................................ 30
I. Specificities of the public administration and its law......................... 31
A. Wide administrative powers ............................................................ 31
B. Limitation of Power ......................................................................... 33
II. The Concept of Administrative Justice ............................................. 35
A. Sovereign Immunity to Rule of Law ................................................ 36
1. Judicial Self Restraint or Activism? .................................................. 37
2. Jurisdictional duality or monism?...................................................... 38
B. The Reviewability of Administrative Actions .................................. 39
1. Scope of Review ............................................................................... 39
2. The Principles (Doctrines)
Governing Administrative Litigations.................................................. 40
3. Obstacles to Obtaining Review ......................................................... 41

**Part One**

**French Administrative Law ............................................................43**

**Chapter Two**

**Administrative Organization in France .........................................45**

2.1. The Administrative Organization of the State ............................... 45
I. Central Administrative Authorities .................................................... 45
A. Administrative Attributions of the President of the Republic .......... 45
B. Administrative Attributions of the Prime Minister........................... 46
C. Ministers as Mangers of Administrative Action ............................... 47
II. Deconcentrated Services.................................................................. 49
A. Prefect of the Department................................................................. 49
B. The Prefect of the Region ................................................................. 51
2.2. Territorial Entities in France ........................................................... 52
I. Decentralized Local Organs ............................................................... 54
A. The election and mandate of local assemblies.................................. 54
B. Designation and mandate of local executives ................................... 54
II. The Attributions of Territorial Local Collectivities.......................... 55

III. The control on local collectivities ........ 56
A. Tutelage on the person ........ 56
B. Tutelage on the act ........ 56
2.3. Reorganization of Communal Administration ........ 57

**Chapter Three**
**Administrative Action in France ........ 59**

3.1. The Provision of Public services ........ 59
I. The public service as source of legitimacy ........ 59
II. The different categories of public services ........ 60
A. The domains of intervention ........ 60
B. The legal classification ........ 61
III. Management organs ........ 62
A. Direct management by a public authority ........ 62
B. Public establishment ........ 62
C. Delegated management to a private body ........ 63
IV. The nature and applicable law ........ 63
A. Administrative Public Services (SPA) ........ 64
B. Industrial or Commercial Public Services (SPIC) ........ 64
C. Services under the management of private bodies ........ 64
V. The 'laws' of public service ........ 65
A. The principle of continuity ........ 65
B. The principle of adaptation ........ 66
C. The principle of equality of users before the public service ........ 66
3.2. The Administrative Police Powers ........ 66
I. The domain of administrative police ........ 67
II. The holders of administrative police powers ........ 68
III. Conditions of exercise of administrative police ........ 69
A. The prerogatives attached to the police ........ 69
B. The rights of persons who are the objective of the measures are protected ........ 69
3.3. Administrative acts ........ 70
I. Unilateral administrative acts ........ 70
A. Regulations ........ 70
B. Individual decisions ........ 71

II. Administrative Contracts ... 72
A. The criteria of administrative contracts ... 72
B. The legal regime of contracts ... 73
III. The rules applicable to administrative acts ... 74
A. The hierarchy of norms ... 74
B. The legal framework of acts ... 75
1. The general principles of administrative procedure ... 75
2. The obligation of transparency ... 76
3.4 The Administrative Justice in France ... 76
I. Jurisdictional organisation ... 77
A. Jurisdictional duality ... 78
B. Tribunal of Conflicts ... 78
1. Conflicts of attribution of competence ... 79
2. Conflict of decisions ... 80
II. The structure of administrative jurisdiction ... 81
A. Organisation of the Council of State ... 81
B. Reforms on competences ... 82
C. The attributes of the Council of State ... 82
III. The competence of judicial judge on administrative matters ... 83
A. Reasons of a constitutional order ... 83
B. Exceptions resulting from court rulings ... 83
C. Where the solution to a dispute depends on another question ... 84
IV. The general rules of litigation procedure ... 84
A. Applications to the courts ... 84
B. Conditions of admissibility of recourse ... 85
1. The interest to act ... 85
2. Recourse prescription period ... 85
3. The procedure of recourse examination ... 85
C. The effects of the recourse ... 86
V. Litigations against abuse of power ... 86
A. The fields of recourse ... 86
B. The means of annulment ... 86
C. Control intensity ... 87
D. The consequences of recourse ... 87
VI. Litigations on responsibility ... 87

A. The bases of responsibility .......... 88
1. Responsibility with fault.......... 88
2. Responsibility without fault .......... 89
B. Conditions of enforcement of responsibility.......... 89

**Part Two**
**Administrative Organization in Cameroon ..........91**

**Chapter Four**
**The Administrative Organization of The Cameroonian State .........93**

4.1 Administrative Centralization:
Central Administrative Authorities .......... 93
I. The President of the Republic and Attached Services .......... 93
A. The Administrative Attributions of the President.......... 94
1. Regulatory Acts.......... 94
2. Individuals Acts.......... 94
B.The Presidency of the Republic .......... 94
II. The Prime Minister Office and its Services.......... 95
III. Ministerial Departments .......... 96
A The Number of Departments .......... 96
B Hierarchy and Structure of Departments .......... 97
C The Functions of the Minister.......... 99
IV. Coordination at the Central Level .......... 99
A Coordination at the Summit.......... 100
B Ministry of Public Service and Administrative Reforms.......... 100
C Ministry in charge of Finance .......... 101
4.2 Administrative Deconcentration:
External Services of the Central Administration. .......... 102
I. Governor of the Region.......... 103
A Attributions of the Governor .......... 103
B Services of the Governor's Office .......... 104
II. The Senior Divisional Officer of the Division.......... 105
A. Attributions of the Senior Divisional Officer .......... 105
B Services of the Senior Divisional Office .......... 106

**Chapter Five**

**Administrative Decentralisation in Cameroon ............................107**

5.1 Territorial Decentralization: Local Government ........................... 107
I. The Legal Environment of Decentralization..................................... 108
A Constitutional Provisions on Decentralization ................................ 108
B The Orientation of Decentralization ................................................ 110
1. Devolution of Powers ...................................................................... 111
2. Organization and Functioning of entities ........................................ 112
3. Supervision and monitoring entities ................................................ 112
C Rules Applicable to Councils .......................................................... 113
1. Management of council property..................................................... 113
2. Powers devolved upon councils ...................................................... 114
3. Council Organs................................................................................. 114
a The Municipal council...................................................................... 114
b Council executive ............................................................................ 114
i. Duties of the Mayor.......................................................................... 115
ii. Assistance to council executive....................................................... 116
c. Suspension and termination of duties .............................................. 116
4. Special Regime applicable to Urban Centres .................................. 116
a City Council (Communautés Urbaines)........................................... 117
b The Sub–divisional councils............................................................ 117
5. Inter–council Cooperation and Solidarity........................................ 118
D. Rules applicable to Regions ........................................................... 118
1. Regional Organs.............................................................................. 119
a. Regional Council ............................................................................ 119
b. President of the Regional Council.................................................. 119
2. Financial provisions for regions ..................................................... 120
E. Financial Regime of Decentralized Territorial Entities .................. 120
1. Elaboration of the budget ............................................................... 120
2. The execution of the budget ........................................................... 121
3. Control of the budget...................................................................... 121
II. Challenges to Territorial decentralization....................................... 122
A. Causes of Local Governments Crises ............................................. 122
1. Excessive Centralization ................................................................ 122
2. Financial Problems ......................................................................... 123

3. Mismanagement Problems ... 123
4. The Democratic Challenge ... 123
B. Attempted Solutions to the Crises ... 124
1. Combination of Local Governments ... 124
2. Financial Improvements ... 125
3. Personnel Training ... 125
4. Evaluation and enhancement ... 126
5.2 Technical decentralization: Specialized Institutions ... 127
I. Types of technically decentralized entities ... 127
A. Public Establishments ... 128
B. Establishment with public utility ... 128
II. Rules of Creation ... 128
III. Legal Regime of Specialized Institutions ... 129
IV. The Rules of Organization and Functioning ... 129
Conclusion of Part two ... 130

**Part Three**
**Administrative Action in Cameroon ... 131**

**Chapter Six**
**Ways of Administrative Action ... 133**

6.1 The Provision of Public Services ... 133
I. Scope of the public service ... 134
A. The Criteria of public service ... 134
1. The Finalist element ... 134
2. Organic element ... 134
3. Legal element ... 135
B. Creation, Extension and Suppression of Public Services ... 135
C. The domains of intervention ... 136
1. The regalia functions ... 136
2. Economic functions ... 136
3. Social functions ... 137
D. The Legal classification ... 137
1. Administrative public services ... 137
2. Public services of industrial and commercial character ... 137
II. Ways of Managing the Public Services ... 138

A. Direct Management (*Le système de la régie*) ........ 138
B. System of public establishment ........ 138
C. System of Assignment ........ 139
III. The Public Service Laws (Principles) ........ 140
A. The Principle of Continuity ........ 140
B. The Principle of Adaptation ........ 141
C. The Principle of Equality ........ 142
IV. Legal Situation of the User
(Public) of an Administrative Public Service ........ 142
A. Users' Legal Nature ........ 143
B. Content of Users' Situation ........ 143
6.2 The Administrative Police Powers ........ 143
I. Administrative Authorities vested with Police Powers ........ 144
A. Criteria for distinction of the types of police power ........ 144
1. Geographic Criterion ........ 144
2. Organic Criterion ........ 145
3. Material Criterion ........ 145
B. Cameroonian Authorities holders of the powers ........ 145
C. Coexistence of police authorities ........ 145
II. Target of Administrative
Police Powers: Maintenance of Public Order. ........ 146
A. The Evolution of Police Powers ........ 146
1. Classical Conception ........ 146
2. Modern Conception ........ 146
B. Administrative and Judicial Police Powers ........ 147
III. Particularities of the Regime of Administrative Police Acts ........ 147
A. The obligatory unilateral
character of administrative police acts ........ 148
B. The seemingly discretionary
character of administrative police acts. ........ 148
IV. Conditions for the Exercise of Administrative Police ........ 148
A. Prerogatives of the Administration
in matters of Administrative Police ........ 149
B. Protective Measures against Administrative Police ........ 149

## Chapter Seven
## Procedures of Administrative Action ......151

7.1. Unilateral Administrative Acts ...... 151
I. The Criteria of Identification ...... 151
A. Definition of administrative
act in the general theory of administrative law ...... 151
B. The criterion of the
unilateral act held by the Cameroon judge ...... 152
1. The unilateral administrative act is a legal act ...... 152
2. It emanates from the administrative authority ...... 152
a. The case of private persons ...... 152
b. The case of non–administrative public persons ...... 153
3. The Unilateral administrative
act creates rights and obligations for particulars ...... 153
C. Unilateral act and public law ...... 154
II. General Conditions of
Legality of Unilateral Administrative Acts ...... 155
A. The Rules of Competence ...... 155
1. Criteria of Competence ...... 155
2. Delegation of competence ...... 156
3. Expressions of competence ...... 156
B. Rules of procedure ...... 157
1. Consultative procedure ...... 157
2. Contradictory procedure ...... 157
C. Rules of Form ...... 158
1. General presentation of the act ...... 158
2. Visas ...... 158
3. Motivation ...... 159
III. The Effects of Administrative Acts ...... 159
A. Entry into Force ...... 159
B. Execution of Administrative Acts ...... 159
1. Provisional Execution ...... 159
2. Forced Execution ...... 160
C. Disappearance of Administrative Acts. ...... 161
1. Abrogation (Non retrospective effect) ...... 161

2. Retreat (Retrospective withdrawal). 161
7.2. Administrative Contracts 162
I. Generalities on Administrative contracts 163
A. Types of Administrative Contracts 163
B. Criteria to Determine Administrative Contracts 163
1. Public Person as co–contractor 163
2. Target as public service execution 163
3. The presence of exorbitant clauses to common law 164
II. The Formation of Administrative Contracts 164
A. Choice of the Contractual Partner 165
1. Contracts awarded to the tenderer who makes the lowest offer (*adjudication*). 165
2. Contracts awarded by invitation to tender (*appel d'offres*) 165
3. Contracts awarded by mutual agreement (*marché de gré à gré*) 165
B. Elaboration of contract terms 165
1. Different types of charges documents (*cahiers des charges*) 166
2. Characteristics of charges Documents 166
C. Conclusion of the contract 166
1. Determination of competent Authorities 166
2. Validity of contractual terms 166
III. The Execution of Administrative Contracts 167
1. The prerogatives of the administration 167
a. Power of unilateral modification 167
b. Right of Direction and Control 168
c. Power of sanction 168
d. Power of unilateral termination 168
2. Rights accorded the co–contractors 168
a. Theory of administrative action *(La théorie du fait du prince)* 169
b. Theory of unforeseen (la théorie de l'imprévision) 169
c. Theory of unforeseen subjection (*La théorie des subjections imprévues*) 169
IV. Termination of Administrative contracts (extinction). 170
A. Annulment by the Administration 170
B. Annulment by the judge 170
Conclusion to part three 170

**Part Four**
**Control to Administrative Action in Cameroon ............................171**

**Chapter Eight**
**Specific Administrative Law .........................................................173**

8.1 Sources of Administrative Law ..................................................... 174
I. International treaties and accords ..................................................... 175
II. The Constitution ..................................................... 175
A. Constitutional provisions ..................................................... 176
B. The constitution and its preamble ..................................................... 176
III. Legislative/Executive Sources ..................................................... 177
A. Laws stricto sensu ..................................................... 178
B. Regulations. ..................................................... 178
C. Ordinances ..................................................... 178
IV. Case Law ..................................................... 178
A. Establishment of general rules ..................................................... 179
B. Establishments of general principles of law ..................................................... 179
V. Administrative Acts ..................................................... 180
A. Unilateral Acts ..................................................... 180
1. Types of Acts ..................................................... 180
2. Hierarchy of Administrative Acts ..................................................... 180
B. Contractual acts ..................................................... 181
8.2 Respect of Hierarchy of Acts ..................................................... 181
I. Control of constitutionality ..................................................... 181
II. Laws as shield to administrative acts? ..................................................... 182
8.3 The Principle of Legality ..................................................... 184
I. From legality to Juridicity? ..................................................... 184
II. The State of Law– A contradiction? ..................................................... 186
8.4. Theory of Exceptional Circumstances and Increase of Powers..... 187
I. The Hypotheses of Exceptional Situations ..................................................... 188
A. State of emergency (*L'état d'urgence*) ..................................................... 188
B. State of siege (*L'état d'exception*) ..................................................... 188
II. The legality of exception ..................................................... 189
A. Controversy on relationship
between exceptional circumstances and legality ..................................................... 190

1. Positions of Legal writers ..... 190
2. Positions of the Judges ..... 191
B. The control by the judge ..... 191
1. The Domains of control ..... 191
2. Limits of legal control of the measures of crisis ..... 192
8.5 Control of the Administration ..... 192
I. Controls by actors inside the administrative system ..... 192
A. Administrative controls of the administration ..... 192
B. Financial controls of the administration ..... 193
1. Control exercised by the Minister of Finance ..... 193
2. Control by the Supreme State Audit Services ..... 194
II. Controls by Actors outside the Administrative System ..... 196
A. Socio–Political Controls of the administration ..... 196
1. Societal Controls ..... 197
2. Legislative Controls ..... 197
B. Judicial Controls of the Administration ..... 198
1. Cases of Annulment: Abuse of Powers
(*recours pour excès de pourvoir*) ..... 199
a. Internal and external illegality ..... 200
b. Effects of the appeals ..... 201
2. Cases of Responsibility:
Payment of Damages (*plein contentieux*). ..... 201
a. Responsibility for Fault and without fault ..... 201
b. Responsibility for the payment of damages ..... 202
c. Private and public systems liability ..... 204

**Chapter Nine**
**Administrative Litigations ..... 207**

9.1 The Evolution of Administrative Jurisdiction in Cameroon ..... 208
I. Administrative Jurisdiction before 1972 ..... 208
A. *Le Conseil du Contentieux Administratif* (CCA) ..... 208
1. The Organization of the CCA ..... 208
2. Attributions of the CCA ..... 209
B. *Le Tribunal d'Etat* (TE) ..... 209
1. Organization of T.E ..... 209

2. Procedure before the T.E ........ 210
C. *La Cour Fédérale de Justice* (CFJ) ........ 210
1. The CFJ as Supreme Federal Institution ........ 210
a. Competencies of the CFJ ........ 210
b. Composition of CFJ ........ 211
2. Contribution of CFJ to Cameroonian Administrative Justice ........ 211
a. Positive Opinion ........ 211
b. Negative position ........ 212
II. Replacement of CFJ by the Supreme Court in 1972 ........ 213
A. The Structures of the Supreme Court in Administrative Matters ........ 213
B. Competence of the Supreme Court in Administrative matters. ........ 214
9.2 The Competent Judge in Administrative Matters ........ 214
I. The General Rule of Competence ........ 214
A. Rule determination based on Parties ........ 215
B. Rule determination based on Object ........ 215
II. The Distribution of Competences in Matters of Administrative Litigations ........ 216
A. Administrative Judge; principal judge in administrative matters ........ 216
1. Constitutional provisions ........ 217
2. The Provisions of Law No 2006/016 ........ 217
3. The Provisions of Law No 2006/022 ........ 218
4. Extension of Competence of the Administrative Judge ........ 219
B. The Competence of the Ordinary Courts in administrative matters ........ 221
1. Disputes regarding administrative violation of fundamental and property rights ........ 221
a. Irregular administrative dispossession of immovable property ........ 221
b. Grave violation of fundamental liberties and property rights ........ 222
2. Interpretation and Appreciation of legality of administrative acts ........ 223
C. Resolution of Conflicts of Jurisdiction ........ 224
D. Exemption from administrative jurisdiction: Acts of government ........ 224
9.3 The Procedures Governing Administrative Jurisdiction ........ 226
I. Pre–Trial Complaint ........ 227

A. The Compulsory Nature of Pre–litigation complaint ...................... 228
B. Competent Authority for Pre–litigation Complaint ......................... 229
C. Time Limits for Pre–litigation complaint ........................................ 229
D. Assessment of Pre–trial petition ...................................................... 230
1. Information of the administration..................................................... 230
2. Linkage to the litigation................................................................... 230
3. Blockage of litigations...................................................................... 231
II. The Procedure before the Court ...................................................... 231
A. The Introduction of the Litigation ................................................... 231
1. Personal dimensions of the petition.................................................. 231
a. Capacity to sue................................................................................ 232
b. Interest to act .................................................................................. 232
c. Quality to sue................................................................................... 232
2. The temporal dimension of the petition............................................ 233
a. Time limit varies in function of administrator's attitude.................. 233
b. Extension of the time limit .............................................................. 233
3. The Material dimension of the petition ............................................ 234
B. The Examination of the Petition in Court........................................ 234
1. Investigations and Judgement........................................................... 234
2. Urgent procedures of judgement ...................................................... 236
C. Petitions against Court Rulings........................................................ 237
D. The Content of the Judgement......................................................... 237
9.4 Assessment of the Cameroonian Administrative Jurisdiction ........ 238
I. Autonomy of Administrative jurisdiction in relation to active administration.................................. 238
II. Autonomy of Administrative jurisdiction in relation to the French .................................................. 239
III. Scarcity of petitions on administrative matters ............................. 240
Conclusion of part four......................................................................... 241

**General Conclusion .........................................................................243**

**Bibliography ....................................................................................245**

Published Books .................................................................................. 245
Articles ................................................................................................. 248
Official Documents .............................................................................. 250

Case and Text Commentaries .......... 252
Unpublished Works .......... 253
Websites .......... 254

**About The Author .......... 255**

## Acknowledgements

First, I would like to appreciate my Administrative Law teachers notably Professors Kandem Jean Claude (The University of Yaoundé, Cameroon) and Odunsi Bennet (Jackson State University, Jackson, Mississippi, USA) for their lessons and inspiration.

Secondly, I sincerely recognize the inputs of my students of the Universities of Dschang, Bamenda and The Pan African University (PAU) for their interactive discussions in class and research works, may this work serve as guide to future research.

Thirdly, I greatly thank Doctors Nkweche Vitalis, Mbetiji Mbetiji, and Ndoh Nsoh, Kiven Gabriel for correcting grammatical errors and making significant suggestions.

More especially, I am grateful to my family for their perseverance, cordial and warm environment that served as a booster to the completion of this work.

**Moye Godwin Bongyu**
**The UBa, UDs**
**June 2019**

# Preface

This work is a combination of my experiences as a student, teacher and researcher. My public law, political science, and public policy backgrounds have been very instrumental. I have had the opportunity of researching, learning and/or teaching some pivotal subjects of public administration notably: Administrative Institutions and General Principles of Administrative Law (*Institutions Administratives et Droit Administrative Générale*), Financial Institutions and Public Finance (*Institutions Financières et de Finances Publiques*), Local Public Law and Political Life (*Droit Public Local et Vie Politique*), Local Governance and Democracy (*Gouvernance Locale et Démocratie*), Law of Decentralization (*Droit de la Décentralisation*), Public Personnel Law (*Droit de la Fonction Publique*) and Administrative Justice (*Contentieux Administrative*).

This work focuses on the transfer of administrative technology especially laws from the French to the Cameroonian systems.. I was also motivated by specialized works on American Administrative law especially those of Warren Kenneth, Jacobini H.B., Rosenbloom David and renowned French authors of *Droit Administratif* notably Debbasch Charles, Laubadere André de, Rivero Jean, Waline Jean and Chapus René. The works of Cameroonian authors particularly Kandem Jean Claude, Joseph Owona, Nlep Roger Gabriel, Kamto Maurice, Biyoum Joseph, Tchapnga Keutcha Célestin, Djuitchoko Sietchoua Célestin, Bilong Salomon, Eric Herman Nforbin and Folefack Ernest on the relationships between the administration and the law were very influential to the realization of this work.

In contemporary world, the Administrative Law challenge is balancing societal and individual rights even if the approaches differ. In the United States, Administrative Law typically involves the growth of administrative power, authority delegation, political control of the agencies, acquiring and disclosing information, protecting administrators, procedural due process, formal adjudications, procedural shortcuts, rulemaking / ordermaking, agency hearings and obtaining judicial review. Jacobini *et al* thus defines Administrative Law as a branch of Public law which consists of those norms establishing and governing public agencies and officials, the rules that such agencies themselves make, and the court rulings that circumscribe agencies and their rules. Much of the process is set forth in basic national and State procedural laws, usually known as the Administrative Procedure Acts (APA).

From the French tradition, *Droit Administratif* involves essentially, Administrative Organization (centralization, deconcentration and decentralization laws), the principle of legality, Ways of Administrative Action (the public services and administrative police powers) Procedures of Administrative Action (unilateral administrative acts and administrative contracts) and Administrative Justice or litigations. The French orientation due to colonialism has inspired the Cameroonian 'administrative law'. This importation or transplantation of foreign models at times poses the problem of environmental suitability.

The legal approach has been adopted for many reasons. The study of structures, institutions, general principles and laws is a starting point *par excellence* of more profound studies. From this stand point, the theory can easily be compared to the practice. The administrative environment is multi–dimensional with political, economic, social, cultural and legal aspects; however it is the legal environment that provides fundamental guidelines and sanctions for violations. The administration possesses legal personality with rights and obligations, consequently can sue and be sued. Therefore administrators, law students and researchers have to possess basic knowledge regarding the fundamental laws that govern the political system.

Since the 1990s, many public administrators especially those of developing countries have witnessed the impact of globalization and democratization tendencies. These have been after the pre–colonial, colonial and Cold War eras which influenced governments in various ways. With the new tendencies, African countries have engaged or have been imposed administrative reforms in order to meet with new political, economic, and social exigencies. Cameroon in particular passed through political and economic crises and has been part of the Structural Adjustment Programmes (SAPs) and the Heavily Indebted Poor Countries Initiative (HIPC) Programme. As a response to these and to meet the exigencies of more liberal environments, the starting point has been the revision of laws that hitherto governed the administration. Needless to say, law as a discipline is a dynamic subject that needs frequent updates. Logically, article 67 of the 1996 Cameroon Constitution states that the new institutions provided shall be set up progressively.

This work is expected to fill a vacuum in the Cameroonian literature on public law and political science. It is the first to adopt a holistic view of the administrative system. It is expected to provide students, teachers, researchers, administrators and anybody interested in public administration the laws governing the system. It attempts to deal with the often wrongly translated notions and concepts. It is expected to give future researchers the theoretical foundations for more profound research. As an introductory work, it provides the basics of each of the parts for future detailed studies and analyses. It should not be forgotten that the public administration is pivotal to the development of any society, and enacting and implementing good rules is a *sine qua non* for an effective and efficient public administration.

**Prof. Moye Godwin Bongyu**
**PhD, Public Administration and Policy**

# Abbreviations and Acronymes

| | |
|---|---|
| AP: | Assemblée Plénière |
| APA: | Administrative Procedure Act |
| CA: | Chambre Administrative |
| CAY: | Chambre Administrative de Yaoundé |
| CCA: | Conseil du Contentieux Administratif |
| CE: | Conseil d'Etat |
| CEFAM: | Centre de Formation pour l'Administration Communale |
| CFJ: | Cour Fédérale de Justice |
| CGCT: | Code Général des Collectivités Territoriales |
| COR: | Cameroun Oriental |
| CS: | Cour Suprême |
| CSM: | Conseil Supérieur de la Magistrature |
| ENAM: | Ecole Nationale d'Administration et de Magistrature |
| FEICOM: | Le Fonds Spécial d'Equipement et d'Intervention Intercommunale |
| GAJA: | Grands Arrêts de la Jurisprudence Administrative |
| HIPC: | Heavily Indebted Poor Countries |
| ISMP: | Institut Supérieur de Management Public |
| MAPS: | Administrative Procedure Manual |
| NPG: | National Programme on Governance |
| Ord: | Ordinance |
| PM: | Prime Minister |

| | |
|---|---|
| RDP: | Revue de Droit Public et de Science Politique |
| RFC: | République Fédérale du Cameroun |
| RGP: | Recours Gracieux Préalable |
| SDO: | Senior Divisional Officer |
| SIGIPES: | Système Informatique de Gestion Intégrée des Personnels de l'Etat et de la Solde |
| TC: | Tribunal des Conflits |
| TE: | Tribunal d'Etat |

# General Introduction

The colonial era played a fundamental role in the African history. It led to the importation or better still imposition of the State structures and administrative systems of the colons on the indigenous people. This was more so by the French who practised direct rule and the assimilation policy in their colonies. It is from this backdrop that the French applied their administrative systems or models with corresponding laws and this tradition basically continued after independence. The French *Droit Adminstratif* which is different from the Anglo–Saxon Administrative Law became part of the Cameroonian legal system, where there is clear distinction between public and private jurisdictions.

On independence, metropolitan powers bestowed or imposed on the colonies their institutions. The early forms of governments and legal systems were imposed on African societies regardless of national realities. The Europeans notably French transmitted the centralized nation State founded on the myth of national homogeneity to Africa.[1] The transplantation of this uniform, rigid and centralized State with slogan as "one and indivisible" is not apt for Africa where the society is heterogeneous, and allegiance is more to the micro–group than nation–state.[2] In many African countries, the centralized State provokes and always entails a profound divorce between the official and real situation. With the failure to pass from "death State" to an "internal State", the African State has become according to G. Nicholas one with "variable polarization." There are multiplicities of poles, fighting for the Central power which leads to rampant conflicts.

This situation is aggravated by the triumph of laws providing for rigid bureaucratic systems of administration. In a continent where underdeveloped structures, problems of communication, illiteracy, are

---

[1] Michalon Thierry, *Quel Etat pour L'Afrique*? (Paris : L'Harmattan, 1984), 19.

[2] Michalon Thierry, : ibid., 8 (préface de G. Conac) Bayart (j.f.): *L'Etat en Afrique: La Politique du ventre,* (FAYARTD, 1989), 315.

common currencies, the rigid application of imported models can be dysfunctional. The "imported State" and its administration do not really fit in Africa, where underdevelopment is still a chronic problem. The situation of the legal system is not different. Laws in general have been imported and at times copied word verbatim with minimal modifications. It is from this backdrop that it is germane to discuss the concept of public administration, the distinction between public and private laws, the origins of *droit administratif*, its relationship with administrative law, its foundations and the comparative approach.

## I. The Concept of Public Administration

The concept of the public administration can be captured by analysing its perspectives and distinctiveness.

### A. Perspectives of Public Administration

Public administration can be viewed from the broad and narrow perspectives. In the widest sense, it is used to mean the activities of the government.[3] These include the legislative, executive and judiciary, and in addition non–central, international authorities and forces of law and order. It involves all the actors and activities of the policy process. From this standpoint, it is seen as all the activities carried out by State organs charged with the satisfaction of general interests as defined by the government, with the possibility of using public power.

A stricter definition is from Dean Goerges Vedel, in what is termed the constitutional law approach. He views it from a negative respective, by providing three delimitations of what it is not. The first delimitation is that of the organic character which excludes from the administration what emanates from the parliament and the judiciary. The second delimitation is material, the exclusion from the administration of international relations. The third delimitation is legal, by its exclusion from the rules of private law. The administration is thus defined as '*the totality of the activities of the government and decentralised authorities,*

---

[3] Goodnow, Frank J., *Comparative Administrative Law Am Analysis of the Administrative Systems, National and Local, of the United States, England, France and Germany*, (Washington DC, Beard Books, 1903, 2000), 1.

*excluding the conduct of international relations and the relations between public powers, under the regime of public power'.*

According to Dean Vedel, public administration can be viewed from a double perspective[4]. From the functional point of view, it is the totality of activities which under the authority and control of the government tends to maintain public order and ensure the satisfaction of general interest. From the organic point of view, the administration is the totality of physical and moral persons who accomplish the administrative function. In the same line, Molitor holds that the public administration is first a public organism which receives from the political power the competence and necessary means for the satisfaction of general interest.[5] It is an apparatus for the management of public affairs comprising of the sum of public services whose smooth functioning permits the realization of objectives defined by the political power[6].

In the narrowest sense, which is the most appropriate to administrative law, it is the implementing or accomplishing side of government which comprises therefore the totality of the activities of the executive officers exclusively. Each of these approaches adds something to the clarification of the administrative concept. From the legal perspective therefore, the public administration is made up of specific organs that achieve well–defined functions with the approval of the political power.

## B. Distinctiveness of Public Administration

In order to perform its functions effectively, the public administration is bound to have some special features. These are the distinctive characteristics of the public administration or service that renders it different from private administration and politics. These

---

[4] Beget, Jean–Marie. *Les Institutions Administrative (* Paris: Economica, 1985),1.

Kandem, Jean .Claude. Institutions Administratifs et Droit Administratif ( UNIYAO, F.D.S.E, T1, 1988 – 1989, Cours Polycopie), 8 –9.

[5] Molitor, André.: *Les Sciences Sociales dans l'Enseignement Supérieur: Administration Publique* (Paris: UNESCO, Imprimerie Atar SA Genève, 1958), 17–18.

[6] Debbasch, Charles. *Science Administrative: Administration Publique* (Paris: Dalloz, 5e éd., 1989), 1.

specificities can be seen from a double perspective, notably the goal (general interest) and functioning.

As regards the goal, general interest renders the public administration different from the private because it is supposed to stand for public good. It is this "legal competence and finality of general interest that the public administration is different from others whose characters are not clear–cut."[7] The legitimatizing ideology for the administration in particular and the State in general is the concept of public interest. This is the conviction that "there is something called the interest of the realm, the public common or national interest, the general good, the public welfare..."[8], which is higher and broader than particular, narrow, self, group and individual interests. It is true that in practice nearly everything is self–interest and general interest is largely an illusion, "but the ideology of common interest does serve as a social sanction or norm to impel members to substitute for their own private or particular wants..."[9].

The functioning of the public administration is characterized by monopoly, competence, continuity, impartiality, hierarchy and accountability. The State's services are completely, or almost completely monopolies. There is no direct price for service rendered or a direct *guid pro quo*[10] for value received as in the private sector. Alternative supplies are rarely found in the public service. Besides the public administrators have some privileges, rights and obligations which are exorbitant to common law. Further, if legitimacy in the political sphere is based on elections, in the case of the administration it is competence.[11] Recruitment in the public service is based on educational qualifications. Moreover, the public administration is continuous, mindful of the importance of State services; they have to be regular and permanent even in political instability. Further, it is expected to be impartial. The public servants have

---

[7] Molitor, 17 – 18.

[8] Easton, David. *A Systems Analysis Political life (*New York: John Willey, 1965), 312.

[9] Easton, 314 – 315.

[10] Something given or returned as the equivalent of something else.

[11] Chevallier J..J. et Loschak D. *Science Administrative, Théorie Générale de l'Institution Administrative* (Paris : LGDJ, T1, 1978), 538.

the right to belong to any legalized organization but have to be neutral in the treatment of others. They have to be objective, impersonal and indifferent; to avoid favouritism and victimization. The last two features are common to public, private sectors and politics though at different spheres. In line with the principle of hierarchy, to ensure authority in the administration, the personnel are usually classified in grades, on the basis of their qualifications. In addition, the public servants are expected to be accountable and responsible for their deeds. They should be responsive, answerable and work for the general public.

Nevertheless, in the contemporary world especially with the globalization tendencies as observed by Barry Bozeman, there is an increasing 'publicization' of the private sector and 'privatization' of the public sector. As the public administration deals with power relations, the politics–administration dichotomy is put to question. However, the starting point in the examination of these relationships is through the laws that govern the public administration.

## II Distinction between Public and Private Laws

Man is by nature a social being, and is condemned to live in the society. In a state of nature, there is the law of the jungle and the survival of the fittest: a dangerous situation for the enjoyment of liberties. In order to ensure the protection of liberties, there must be public order. The members of society must edict and obey rules which render cohabitation possible. It is the totality of these rules that is qualified as "law" which seeks to balance the demands of power and liberties.[12] Law can be seen therefore as the sum of rules obeyed by the members of the community under the control of an authority endowed with the powers of constraint to enable the survival of the group possible. It is in this light that it is the sum of precepts of obligatory conduct aimed at ensuring the balance between authority and individual rights. It therefore governs, regulates the relations between individuals and those that concern the society as an entity.

In contemporary world, there is agreement on the distinction between public and private laws, but the content of the respective laws is

---

[12] According to the Roman statesman Cicero, "We are all servants of the laws in order that we may be free."

contentious in civil and common law jurisdictions. The distinction between public law and private law dates back to Roman law at the beginning of the nineteenth century. It spread to the countries of civil law tradition, and to common law countries. Understandably, with the diversity of applicable jurisdictions,[13] there have been controversies regarding the demarcation between public and private laws in content and aspects. As such theories have been formulated in order to establish the borderline between the two, which, however, have limits and are not exhaustive or mutually exhaustive.

The interest theory developed by the Roman jurist Ulpian holds that public law concerns State interest and private law the individual interest. But then some private relations affect the public and even so public interest is not clearly defined. The subjection theory explains the distinction by emphasizing the subordination of private persons to the State. Public law is supposed to govern unequal relationships, whereas private law is considered to govern equal relationships. However, inequality exists in some aspects of private law and in the State of law there are relations where the State appears as equal to a person. The subject theory concerns the position of the subject of law in the legal relationship in question. If the public person is concerned, public law applies, otherwise it is private law. One can deduce the misconception that private law is the rule and pubic law the exception.

The judges have not been silent on this issue. The Federal Court of Suisse uses four criteria to determine whether an issue is of private or public law: the theory of interests, the theory of subjects or persons concerned, the theory of relationship (equality or inequality), and the theory of sanctions. Consequently an issue can be mixed law having dimensions of both public and private laws.[14] These theories can be used in combination depending on the situation but there are some guidelines for separation.

---

[13] There is confusion where subjects like criminal law, human rights law and employment law should be placed.

[14] Zufferey, J.B.Cours de Droit Administratif Général, Documents d'Appui (Université de Fribourg: Faculté de droit, Suisse, Année académique 2010 – 2011), IX.

Private law, *(lat. jus privatum)* on the one hand, is the situation where individuals and/or private groups on their capacities as family members, businessmen, customers, employers or employees voluntarily exercise their activities. The relationships are essentially private and the intervention of public powers is simply to fix general guidelines, and legal framework for the contracts or accords. The main subjects of private law include: Civil Law, Law of Torts, Commercial law, Law of Contract, Family Law, Law of Succession, Social law and Private International Law.

Public law (lat. *ius publicum*) on the other hand deals with the rules which regulate relations between the private and public persons or institutions or between the latter themselves. It deals essentially with the State and its relations with other States, groups and individuals. The main subjects of public law include: Administrative Law, Decentralization Law, Public Personnel Law, Public Finance Law, Constitutional law, and Public International Law. However, with the interpenetration between the public and private sectors, the strict public–private law dichotomy is blurred and with various intersections there is the need to rethink the boundaries. That notwithstanding, public law is essentially asymmetric and unequal, and the public administration from its origins is based mainly on it.

## III. The Origins of *Droit Adminstratif* in France

The submission of the administration to a particular law has many historical and constitutional foundations. The emergence of administrative law in France was an attempt to ensure the separation of powers, and the separation between administrative and judicial authorities. There was an evolution from retained to delegated justice which finally led to the birth and institution of administrative jurisdiction. Thus, Article 15 of the French Declaration of the Rights of Man and Citizens of 26 August 1789 challenged sovereign immunity and declared that, "the society has the right to request for an account to all public agents of their stewardship." A year later, Law 16–24 August 1790 on Judicial Organization (still in force) confirmed the necessity of specific law for the administration on the basis of the "principle of separation of administrative and judiciary authorities." This was reiterated by the Law of 16 Fructidor Year III, which holds that administrative action, when exercised as public power, should not be judged by judicial tribunals.

Consequently in year VIII there was the institution of specialized bodies distinct from courts to judge the cases of the public administration This was notably Councils of the Prefecture (*conseils de préfecture*) (replaced in 1954 by administrative tribunals) and Council of State (*Conseil d'Etat*).[15] These jurisdictions assured the resolution of administrative litigations on the basis of rules that are different from those of private law and adapted to the particularity of the activities of public power.

The discipline needed to be consecrated with a legal status, by giving it official expression. This was done by the judgement pronounced on February 8, 1873, not by the Council of State, but by the Tribunal of Conflicts (*Tribunal des Conflits*), which has the exclusive powers to sovereignly hear difficulties that may arise from the sharing of competences between the administrative and judicial jurisdictions. In the French celebrated case Arrêt *Blanco*, the Tribunal of Conflicts laid the cornerstone for the construction of the edifice. It announced the substantive rule that: the administration – (public power) '*cannot be regulated by the principles which are found in the Civil Code, for the regulation of the relationship between private individuals*'; '*it has its special rules which vary according to needs of the service and the necessity to reconcile State authority and individual rights.*' The rules applied are "neither general nor absolute."

It is for this reason that contrary to the Anglo–Saxon legal tradition, when the French administration stands–in for public management, it applies specific rules; exercises specific jurisdictional control, the administrative jurisdiction, which is of a specific legal regime, the administrative law.

## IV. *Droit Administratif* and Administrative Law

There are a series of definitions most of which describe rather than define it confirming its eclectic nature. The definition and scope of administrative law differ from the Anglo–Saxon and French perspectives. In the United States, classically, the *Black's Law Dictionary* defines administrative law as the "body of law created by administrative agencies

[15] Supreme Court of the Public Administration.

to implement their powers and duties in the form of rules, regulations, orders and decisions." *Daniel Oran's Law Dictionary* sees it as "Laws about duties and proper running of an administrative agency that are handed to agencies by legislatures and courts. Rules and regulations set out by administrative agencies."

Renowned American administrative law scholars have their own points of view. Kenneth Culp Davis defines it as "the laws concerning the powers and procedures of administrative agencies, including especially the laws governing judicial review of administrative action."[16] Warren after a synthesis of various definitions observes that broadly speaking administrative law deals with "how power is transferred from legislative bodies to administrative agencies, how administrative agencies use power and how the actions taken by the administrative agencies are reviewed by the courts."[17] After a comparative approach, Goodnow synthesizes that administrative law is "that part of public law which fixes the organization and determines the competence of the administrative authorities and indicates to the individual remedies for the violation of his rights."[18] Jacobini *et al* thus defines Administrative law as a branch of Public law which consists of those norms establishing and governing public agencies and officials, the rules that such agencies themselves make, and the court rulings that circumscribe agencies and their rules. Much of the process is set forth in basic national and State procedural laws, usually known as the Administrative Procedure Acts (APA).[19] In the United States, therefore, administrative law typically involves the growth of administrative power, authority delegation, political control of the agencies, acquisition and disclosure of information, protection of administrators, procedural due process, formal adjudications, procedural shortcuts, rulemaking/order–making, agency hearings and obtaining judicial review.

---

[16] Davis, Kenneth C. *Administrative law Treatise*. (USA: San Diego, 1979), Chapter 1.

[17] Warren, Kenneth F. *Administrative Law in the Political System* (United States of America: Westview, 2004), 23.

[18] Goodnow, Frank J. 8–9.

[19] Jacobini, H.H., Melone, Albert and Kalvelage, Carl. *Research Essentials of Administrative Law*. (USA: Palisade Publishers, 1983) ,3.

From the French tradition, *Droit Administratif* is the branch of public law which deals with the legal requirements on the organization, powers and duties of administrative authorities, their relationships with the administered and the remedies available to those wrongly affected by administrative action. At the end of the XIX century, schools of thought emerged, thesis were advanced and discussed. There are two classical schools of thought which still have their interest or followers. The *public service school*, founded by Leon Duguit (1859–1928), Dean of the Faculty of Law, at the University of Bordeaux. The other school, is the *public power school*: it is the school of Maurice Hauriou (1856–1929), Dean of the Faculty of Law, at the University of Toulouse. The two schools of thought oppose each other, as one emphasizes on goals and the other on means.

As regards the notion of public service, as conceived by Duguit, what is important is the finality: an activity is qualified as public service, if it is destined to provide the best service for the general interest. According to the public service school, the means is of lesser importance. Where there is a public service, the rules of administrative law and the competence of administrative jurisdiction are applicable. It is by the notion of the public service that other notions of administrative law are and can be defined.

According to the public power school, it is the means employed that is important. It is likened to the procedures through which the administration accomplishes its missions. The rules of administrative law and the competence of administrative jurisdiction are applicable, when the public service employs public management procedures. In the definition of diverse notions of administrative law, the intervention of the public power is the distinctive factor.

Arguably, there should simultaneous consideration of the notions of public service and public power. There is undeniable existence of the link between the means and the end. And, since it is normal that the means be directed to a particular finality and to occupy a second place in respect to it, it is right to define administrative law firstly, as the law of the public service, and then as that of public power. It involves essentially, Administrative Organization (centralization, deconcentration and decentralization laws), ways of Administrative Action (the Public Services and Administrative police powers) procedures of Administrative Action (unilateral administrative acts and administrative contracts), and Administrative Justice or litigations. The French orientation has inspired the Cameroonian administrative law.

## V. Foundations of Administrative Law

In contemporary world, the administrative law challenge is balancing societal and individual rights even if the approaches differ.[20]The administration having a privileged position on society (executive privilege, resources, and use of force), administrative law has as fundamental finality the protection of citizen from power abuse or arbitrariness. The danger is, if rules are not respected the wide administrative powers can lead to despotism and dictatorship.

As regards the object of administrative law, there has been controversy between two schools of thought. The public service school spearheaded by the masters of the Bordeaux School notably Leon Duguit, Gaston Geze, Roger Bonnard and Andre de Laubadere. This entails that the distinctiveness and prerogatives of the administration is based on its goal of public service or general interest. The public power school led by Maurice Hauriou, George Vedel and Laferrière holds that the administration benefits prerogatives due to public power. They are founded on sovereignty invested to the executive. Surprisingly, this notion talks of prerogatives neglecting the obligations. As the public power is the means of achieving the goal which is the public service, it implies that one school emphasizes on the means and the other the end. It is both the public power and the public service that distinguishes the public administration from the private.

This justifies the use of rules derogatory to ordinary law. As Debbasch, Charles observes in «Le Droit Administratif, Droit Dérogatoire au Droit Commun?», the rules governing the administration are said to be exorbitant, derogatory to common law, because they confer to it privileges

---

[20] René Chapus, *Droit Administratif* (Paris, Montchrestien, 1992), 128–129. States that administrative law fulfills a double function rendering administrative action more effective and protecting the rights of the administered.

or rights and equally inconveniences or obligations which are contrary to the rules of ordinary law. Thus as Maurice Hauriou declares, 'administrative law, is law between unequal persons."

Administrative law has specific characteristic and is related to but autonomous from private law, constitutional law and administrative sciences. As consecrated in *Blanco case/ruling* the administration is submitted to special rules different from those of private. But it is not the 'law of exception' and that is a derogation from the norms or principle which is the application of "common" or private law. Woodrow Wilson declared that political science should concentrate on how governments are administered. This is so because, as he précised, "It is getting harder to run a constitution than to frame one." From this standpoint, the relationship between administrative law and science has caught the attention of some theorists. According to Mr. Vivien in 1845 – vice president of Council of State in "Etudes Administratives"; "The science (administrative) does not remain out of law nor law from it; but each of the two occupies a specific sphere... The science questions social phenomenon more than the written laws, it is more general in its views and more liberal in its orientations. It has a more extended horizon..."[21] While administrative law deals with what ought to be *(sollen)* administrative science deals with what is (*sien*).

In addition, administrative law uses laws and regulations no doubt, but is fundamentally judge–made. In France, the absence of a code on administrative law, analogous to the Civil Code, that is to say, defining the principles and notions of this law, has been, and continues to have as natural consequence, that it remains for the most part, the work of the judges. It is supposed to depend mainly on court rulings, despite a contemporary doctrinal tendency favouring written laws. Instead of having a general coherent code, there are many depending on the subject matter. There exist 'codes' which are practical working instruments, such as those public contracts, urban planning and territorial entities. There are collections of stipulations defining a particular regime or notion which have inspired the Cameroonian legislator.

---

[21] in Molitor, Andre; 31.

## VI. Comparative Approach

Environmental diversities and wide variations between governments make comparison problematic and complicated. Besides, under the heading "Century in a Quandary", Nicolas Henry described the field of public administration, as heterodoxy rather than orthodoxy. However, like political systems, administrative systems no matter their conceptions, ideologies, and contexts, perform the same functions, even if done differently.[22] Robert Dahl emphasizes that, the comparative approach gives credence to scientific study of public administration. Comparative research is a combination of descriptive (what), explanatory (why) and prescriptive (how) approaches. Its method can be inductive or deductive. The comparative method is imperative with colonization, globalization, growing interdependence, State failures, exportation and universalization of administrative values, techniques and models.[23] Comparative government emphasizes on administrative environment or ecology. It is on the basis of this that the importation of foreign laws to Africa can prove to be problematic in its application.

Comparatively as regards laws in general, the "African law" in francophone countries is predominately the development of French administrative and civil law. The principles and techniques of administrative law in particular are copied from France. In 1972, Bipoun–woum (J.) observed that an examination of decisions taken by administrative jurisdictions in Cameroon shows that they use in a spontaneous manner the principles of French administrative law. The one time president of the Cameroonian Supreme Court, Mr Nguini affirms the great influence of conceptions inspired by the French Council of State on francophone African systems. Bipoun–Woum continues that in the actual

---

[22] According to Gabriel Almond, the common functions of political systems are: Input functions (interest articulation, interest aggregation) and output functions (rule making, application, adjudication, and communication). The administrative functions are rule application, public law and order and general interest.

[23] Ferrel Heady. *Public Administration: A Comparative Perspective* (New York: Marcel Dekker, In. 4th ed. 1995). Farazmand,Ali. *Handbook of Comparative and Development Public Administration* (CRC, 2001).BakeR Randall. *Comparative Public Management: Putting U.S Policy and Implementation in Context* (Praeger, 1994).

state of affairs, contrary to what happened in the formation of French administrative law, the rules of law applied to the administration, are in African States of French expression, above all of legislative elaboration. Administrative law in these States is more legislative than judge–made more receptive than innovative.[24] The fundamental principles are those found in the French texts.

## VII. Organization of the Book

After the introduction, the book begins with a preliminary chapter that lays down the foundation by discussing the theoretical framework of the law of administration. It is further subdivided into parts and chapters. Part One examines summarily the French *Droit Administratif* model which involves essentially administrative organization and action, and has inspired the Cameroonian. Part two deals with the laws relating to administrative organization involving central and non–central entities in Cameroon. Part Three is on the laws governing Administrative action. It comprises the ways and procedures of administrative action. Part Four focuses on the control to administrative action. It examines the submission of the administration to specific law, and rules and procedures of administrative justice in Cameroon.

---

[24] KamdeM J.C. Contentieux Administratif, Université de Yaoundé, Cours polycopie T, 1988–1989, pp. 32–34.

# Chapter One
# Administrative Law, Law of the Administration

The administration is submitted to a law that regulates its organisation and its activities and by the same law, its relationship with the administered, which is its raison d'être and tends to satisfy the needs by the exercise of activities of general interest or to be more precisely, by public service activities.

As for the means by which it exercises its activities of public service, it is of a variable nature. The administration, which is invested with the prerogatives of public power, acts through the methods of 'public management'. At times and exceptionally, it proceeds with the use of private rules applied in 'private management'. From these standpoints, it can be discussed from the organizational and control perspectives.

## 1.1 Administrative Organization

To Dean Vedel, it is unconceivable that administrative law be defined independent of constitutional considerations, which is the source of the national legal order. Besides, the constitution provides "power maps" and relationships of the different organs of the State and the rights and freedoms of the citizens that need to be protected. The balance between authority and rights is ensured organizationally by the principle of separation of powers. Power separation can be horizontal or vertical. As regards horizontal separation James Madison argued that, "The holding of all powers–legislative, executive, and judiciary – in the same hands, whether by one person, a few, or many, and whether hereditary, self–appointed or elective, is the very definition of tyranny."[25] He described

[25] Edited by Mary E. Webster, *The Federalist Papers: In Modern Language Indexed for Today's Political Issues (Merril Press/Bellevue, Washington, 1999) (Federalist #47), 197.*

vertical separation as that between distinct governments. As such, the citizens are doubly protected.[26]

Politically and administratively State structures have to be organized in different ways in order to ensure coherence, authority, coordination, participation and performance. Politically, when the constitution divides competences between many levels like the case in the United States and Germany, there is the federal form of State. On the contrary, if the political competences are concentrated at the central level so that there is only one centre of power impulsion, the State is said to be of the unitary form. Administratively, the technique depends on the distribution of administrative competences between the State levels, central and non–central.

Centralization, deconcentration and decentralization are the key words of administrative organization. The imperative of bringing the administration nearer to the people renders the use of deconcentration and decentralization inevitable. Each administrative technique has corresponding administrative authorities, individuals or groups of individuals who have the competence to act in the name of administrative entities. Although the legal approach is adopted it is worth mentioning that the literature of decentralization, deconcentration and devolution is confusing and at times inconsistent. Some authors use the terms interchangeably, and to others devolution and deconcentration are part of administrative decentralization. For the purposes of this study, the French approach is adopted which clearly distinguishes the concepts.

## I. The Administrative Organization of the State

All States with different degree of successes attempt to centralize the management of the public service. Power flows from the summit through the non–central authorities or external services to the bottom.

### A. Theory of Administrative Centralization

To André de Laubadere, the central administration "is constituted of all the authorities who form the executive power, and who besides their political role, exercise an administrative role, being placed at the head of

---

[26] Edited by Mary E. Webster, *ibid, (Federalist #51), 212.*

the country's administration". Debbasch adds more to this by defining the central administrative organization as constituted of State services installed in the capital which direct the administrative actions of the state for the whole territory.[27] It is the concentration of power of decision with the authorities placed at the summit of the administrative hierarchy. It equally entails the concentration of compulsive power and public power to the benefit of the central authorities, authority–subordination relationships, and in this case, the state as unique moral person.

Centralization is a technique of arranging administrative power, which permits the central administrative authorities to direct all administrative affairs of the State with no other intermediaries than simple agents of execution. There are two types of centralization, which are geographical and technical centralization. Technical centralization is when power is centralized in the hands of the central authorities. Geographical centralization is the concentration of power in a particular geographical area. When there is centralization, there is the concentration of decision–making powers at the centre. The concentration of administrative services at the centre is known as concentration.

According to Surazus A Wisla, the components of a strong centralized government include:

a) Central control and distribution of resources,
b) The existence of professional administrative personnel with an unambiguous allegiance to the centre,
c) Stability that will allow for political consolidation of the center combined with broad scale, acceptance of central authority at all levels of government and within the populace.

Additionally, centralization as technique of administrative organization is credited for coordination, unity of command, unity of direction, provision of roadmaps and coherence. However, it faces challenges including slowness in decision–making, acting from blind

[27] Tsessue, D. Droit Administratif (Yaounde: National School of Administration and Magistracy, Cours polycopie, 1981) , 6–7.

spots, excessive bureaucratization, complicated administrative procedures, negligence of local realities and alienation of local actors.

## B. Theory of Administrative Deconcentration

In this system, authority is given to local representatives of the central government to take decisions of local interest in the name of the central government which supervises their action. The non–central (local) authorities are no longer simple agents of execution like in the case of integral centralization. They are given a certain margin of initiative notably the power to make certain decisions without consulting the central power.

There is deconcentration when the power of decisions which is held by the higher authorities is transferred to the lower ones within the internal hierarchy of the institution. In simple terms, deconcentration is the redistribution of power of decision by decreasing the original concentration at the centre in favour of non–central powers. The null–sum of power remains same but is redistributed in favour of local agents. It should be noted that under deconcentration, the administrative services belong to one administrative person, the State. In other words, deconcentration is a modality of centralization where there is restricted distribution of power to non–central organs. There are two types of deconcentration: territorial (horizontal) and technical (vertical). Territorial deconcentration consists on conferring the powers to competent non–central authorities over a portion of the national territory called administrative circumscription (region, division). Technical deconcentration is the transfer of power to non–central specialized authorities of services which remain under the control of the central authority ( e.g external services of ministries)

Deconcentration has as advantages: decongestion of the central power, increasing administrative rapidity and efficacy; taking the administration nearer to the administered and solution of local problems based on local realities. But there is the risk that with the scattering of power, national unity can be compromised. There can also be incoherence in the national policies.

According to Kamdem J.J for deconcentration to effectively exist, at least three essential conditions have to be met: It must be done globally (all the phases of the decisional process) profoundly (according larger powers to deconcentrated authorities) and generically (suppressing all central services whose attributions have been transferred to the local level). Deconcentration attenuates the rigours of centralization but does not destroy it. The local authorities remain subject to the hierarchical authority of the central powers that can cancel, suspend or reform their decisions.

## II. The Theory of Administrative Decentralisation

Decentralization is a technique of administrative organization where there is the process of devolving political, administrative and fiscal powers (autonomy) from the central to autonomous non–central governments under the supervision of the former. It is a system of organization where the State transfers its attributions to institutions (territorial or not) legally distinct from itself and benefiting under the supervision of the State, a certain autonomy in management. There exist two forms or variants of decentralization: territorial (geographical, horizontal) and technical (vertical, functional or by service) decentralization.

In a decentralized State, the functions of public administration are exercised by State authorities and multiplicities of public law bodies notably the 'self–governing' local government. With decentralisation, there are two moral persons, the State and the decentralized body. In order to ensure control and coordination between the administrative entities, there exist hierarchical and supervisory (tutelage) controls. The decentralized body is not submitted to direct hierarchical authority or control but simply to supervisory control.

### A. The Theory of Territorial Decentralization: Local Government

Territorial decentralization is the transfer of power from the central to the non–central entities which enjoy high level of autonomy within an administrative jurisdiction or part of the territory.

This administrative technique especially with local governments has four main types and some conditions have to be fulfilled for it to be effective.

## 1. Types of Decentralization

There exist four main types of decentralization: political, administrative, fiscal, and economic decentralization.

*Political decentralization* is democratic governance at the local level, the transfer of political authority, management and responsibility from the central to local governments. This entails organic autonomy (legislative and executive organs), the election of public bodies and authorities at the sub–national level by the local electorate. It aims at strengthening opportunities for local control over local services and to expand opportunities for electoral accountability, political representation and civil society engagement. The citizens and their representatives are given greater say in the formulation and implementation of local policies. In fact, unlike deconcentration, territorial decentralization is not a simple technique of administration, it has political significance.

*Administrative decentralization* is the transfer of bureaucratic decision making authority and managerial responsibilities from the central to the sub–national levels. The day to day management is the responsibility of professionals or experts. These bureaucrats have become powerful and crucial actors of urban politics due to their competence, stability and resources. The non–elected officials include secretary general, municipal treasurer, council managers, chief administrative officer, government employees, departmental heads etc. The bureaucratization of the local government raises many concerns. Firstly, critics argue that bureaucrats are not democratically elected and consequently do not respond to the needs of the people. Secondly, it is also argued that "budget maximization bureaucrats" use their superior information about requirements of implementation to pressurize elected officials to expand the government beyond what is efficient. Thirdly, it is claimed that bureaucrats are largely responsible to the needs of businesses. The bureaucrats need to be made accountable by limiting their discretion, institutionalization of competition through privatization and the creation of political and legal controls.

*Fiscal decentralization* means the ownership and transfer of some forms of resource allocation by giving sub–national units the authority over local resources and spending. That is, independence in the possession of resources (financial, natural, infrastructural) and the management of those resources to finance local expenditures. They have autonomous budgets which follow budgetary procedures different from the state budget.

*Economic or Market Decentralization* is the transfer of responsibility wholly or partially from the public to the private sector. This entails economic liberalization and market development policies which are usually characterized by privatization and deregulation. According to the World Bank privatization can range in scope from leaving the provision of goods and services entirely to the free operation of the market to "public–private partnerships" in which government and the private sector cooperate to provide services. Deregulation is the process of reducing the legal constraints on private participation in service provision or allows competition among private suppliers for services that in the past were provided by the government or by regulated monopolies. The bottom line of market decentralization is that functions that hitherto were primarily or exclusively the responsibility of government are carried out by businesses, community groups, cooperatives, private voluntary associations, and other non–government organizations. [28]

However, the autonomy of local governments is not absolute, to ensure coherence, the central government intervenes in various ways to contribute and control the local governments. Especially with the increasing responsibility and diminishing resources of local governments, they have to seek additional resources from national and international sources but then the various interventions should not affect the raison d'être of the local collectivities.

## 2. Autonomy of decentralized entities

In order to have effective decentralisation, it should be real and complete and some conditions have to be fulfilled. It entails a high degree of autonomy characterized by the existence of public person and award of legal personality. Kamdem Jean Claude makes a succinct discussion of what it takes for this to happen, which entails that the decentralized entities have to be autonomous.

---

[28] http://www.ciesin.org/decentralization/English / General/Different_forms.html assessed on 02/09/2017.

### a. Political Autonomy

Political autonomy entails the election of local representatives who are accountable to the population to satisfy local needs. Jean Rivero holds that a veritable decentralization presupposes "the election of the local organs by the collectivity, which substitutes their appointment by the central power." Territorial decentralization is nothing more than "democracy applied to the administration." It implies the choice of local authorities "in" and "by" the locality. The local collectivities will not seem to be administered externally, but by themselves, by their own organs.

Andre de Laubadere summarizes it all when he writes; the administrative interest of decentralization is that as regards the local affairs and the local needs, it is advisable that agents charged with their management know the local conditions, have interest to handle and defend the local interests and that they have confidence of the administered. This can only be the case when the authorities have a strict personal attachment to the locality, being chosen by the inhabitants, and possessing in their management a sufficient margin of autonomy, in a word when they are decentralized.

It is necessary to accept diversity and even desire it. A decentralized administration is necessarily a diversified one. It is done mindful of the local needs and realities which are peculiar to each entity. From this perspective, local debates have to be permitted. The elected officials have to discuss about their plans and realizations. National decisions do not necessarily fit the local realities, debates and solutions should be organized at the local level, which should be done with some sovereignty. Diversity of regimes and conditions must be accepted, and debates permitted

### b. Administrative Autonomy

The decentralized institution must have a legal personality distinct from that of the State (as all other institutions). Administrative autonomy entails the possession of enough personnel and technical means. The law should clearly define the nature and limits of the decentralized administration. They must have political, administrative, economic, social and cultural objectives. Supervision on persons must follow specific conditions and procedures.

To make this possible power must be determined by the law. The national and local domains should be clearly defined. There should be no confusion between hierarchical and supervisory powers. The reciprocal rights and obligations between the local and national levels should be precisely brought out.

### c. Financial Autonomy

The decentralized entities need to have sufficient material resources. This autonomy is demonstrated by the existence of an autonomous budgetary system, and specific resources and expenditures. The Council has property:– markets, cemeteries, museums, monuments, real estate etc. and subventions from the State should come only when these are insufficient. If the council is not financially autonomous there is the danger of financial subordination to the State. The risk is that local governments can be victims of temptations and manipulations. No entity can claim to be autonomous if it cannot count on its own resources. With the lack of resources, they can lose their capacity of being moral persons and simply become deconcentrated entities. They need the means to do their politics.

Decentralization is the division of the country into smaller entities which have some degree of autonomy, but this autonomy is not absolute. These structures have some autonomy and are only indirectly controlled by the central government. With decentralisation, there are two moral (corporate) persons, the State and the decentralized body. The decentralized body is not submitted to direct hierarchical authority or control from the center, but simply to supervisory control.

Under appropriate conditions and where it works effectively decentralization can be a catalyst of development. Administratively, it enables the de–congestion of the central power. It can alleviate the bottlenecks in decision making that are often caused by central government planning and control. It helps to cut complex bureaucratic procedures of the central government. More so, local problems are solved mindful of the local realities and the officials sensitivity to local needs is increased. From the socio–economic viewpoint, local government should serve as poles for development. It favours more creative, innovative and responsive programmes by allowing local "experimentation."[29] Politically, it leads to greater democratization, participation and representation of groups, inclusive administration to ensure the participation of the local people in the management of their affairs. It can lead to more political stability and national unity.

But decentralization has some risks and challenges. Politically, decentralization can lead to fruitless competition, more channels of corruption, and accentuate discriminations on the bases of party or other group belongings. From the administrative perspective, it may not be appropriate for routine, network–based and standardized activities. It may destroy; administrative unity and the central government may face problems of coordination and control of policies and resources which have become more complex. As localities are differently endowed, those with weak administrative capacities may become ineffective, consequently the inequitable distribution of services. Economically, the enjoyment of economies of scale will diminish, and it can also lead to wastage and financial disorder. At times, responsibilities are transferred to local governments without adequate resources which lead to financial stress.

## B. The Theory of Technical Decentralization: Specialized Institutions

Technical decentralization is a technique of administrative organization which entails the transfer of powers to specialized institutions or bodies without geographical basis. In an introductory work, it is difficult to exhaustively discuss on technical decentralization because of the diversity of legal regimes and the multiplicity or better still proliferation of specialized institutions governed by individualized laws.

One may say that the definition of technical or service decentralization depends on the institution concerned. However, technical decentralization which comprises of specialized administration can be seen from a double perspective. Professionally, it is a system that permits a totality of persons to ensure the management of affairs corresponding to

---

[29] http: // www.ciesin.org/decentralization/English/General/Different_forms.html 02/09/2017.

the specialty of the institution through the intermediary of their representatives normally elected e.g. professional orders. Administratively it is when the public powers deem it necessary to place some services in a situation of autonomous management or involve the private sector in public utility e.g public enterprises. In spite of the diversity, the specialized institutions have some common rules: They are all moral persons, aim at achieving general interest, submitted to the minimum rules of public law as regards their organization (creation, modification, dissolution); and submitted to supervision by public authority.

The concept of specialized public person is different from territorial collectivity (council, region) in that: while the territorial collectivities have an activity of the general administration limited to geographical circumscription, the specialized persons have an activity limited to particular tasks concerning a determined category of the administered. The specialized administrative entities are of different types, with different reasons for creation, organization and legal regime but are all submitted to state supervision.

## III. Relationships between the Administrative Techniques

The picture of the relationships can be examined by discussing the extremes of the continuum of the administrative techniques, the rapports between techniques of transfer of powers to the local levels, and controls to ensure coordination between the levels.

### 1. Coexistence of Centralization–Decentralization

Centralization and decentralization are not absolutes, they are relative. The two administrative methods are "either–or" but complementary. Excessive centralization can lead to rigidity and sluggishness. So too, excessive decentralization can lead to anarchy. Consequently, the need to strike an appropriate balance between them is essential to the effective and efficient functioning of government.

As observed by the Decentralization *Thematic Team* of the World Bank, not all functions can or should be financed and managed in a decentralized fashion. Besides, even when national governments decentralize responsibilities, they often retain important policy and supervisory roles. They must create or maintain the "enabling conditions" that allow local units take on more responsibilities. Central authorities often have crucial roles to play in promoting and sustaining decentralization by developing appropriate and effective national policies and regulations for decentralization and strengthening local institutional capacity to assume responsibility for new functions.[30] The success of decentralization frequently depends heavily on initiating and developing effective regulations at the central level, nonetheless, with indispensable local inputs.

The central administrative organs cannot ensure the accomplishment of tasks everywhere in the country; some of the powers have to be delegated to peripheral authorities. Consequently, two seemingly contradictory exigencies have to be taken into consideration. On the one hand, a minimum homogeneity must exist in administrative action throughout the territory, if not national unity becomes an illusion. On the other, the existence of particular aspirations in the various areas within the territory, and taking the administration nearer to the users. This exigency is in line with the need to marry the imperatives of unity with those of diversity and protection of the indigenes.[31]

From this standpoint, the preamble to the 1996 Constitution states that the State shall ensure the protection of minorities and shall preserve the rights of the indigenous populations (*autochthone, allogène*) in accordance with the law. As regards Regional Councils, Kamto pinpoints rightly that when representatives are elected by universal suffrage, the sociological configuration will not be preliminarily determined.[32] But then, as Olinga observes, the exigency of taking into account the sociological composition of the circumscription constitute an institutional counterweight to absolute numerical hegemony, and as such a factor of appeasement, a measure of confidence, of public security for all. This entails tempering the potentially devastating political and psychological

[30] http://www.ciesin.org/decentralization/English/General/Different_forms.html accessed 10/10/2017.

[31] Debbasch, 221–222.

[32] Kamto, Maurice, «Dynamisme Constitutionnelle du Cameroun Indépendante» *Revue Juridique Africaine*, numéros 1, 2,et 3,(1995), 45.

effects of the mechanical application of the principle of majority, a democratic principle *par excellence*; it entails ensuring that the democratic adventure, should be a national collective adventure, thus no one should be excluded *a priori*. This implies the construction of consensus democracy, which is not governmental but rather national ensuring civil and political peace.[33] The judicial consecration of this exigency to protect the indigenes Sindjoun observes is the consequence of logical reasoning but also the officialization of the unsaid, the implicit.[34]

## 2. Coexistence of Deconcentration and Decentralization

There are notable differences between deconcentration and decentralization. These can be viewed as regards their frameworks, degree of autonomy, controls, accountability, source and extent of appeals:

### Differences between deconcentration and decentralization

| | **Deconcentration** | **Decentralization** |
|---|---|---|
| Framework | Only one moral person, the State | Two moral persons, State and local entity. |
| Political Autonomy | Low | High |
| Administrative Autonomy | Low | High |
| Financial Autonomy | Low | High |
| Control | Hierarchical control | Supervisory control |
| Accountability | Upward Accountability | Downward Accountability |

[33] Olinga, Alain– Didier. «L'Exigence de la Prise en Compte des Composantes Sociologiques de la Circonscription en Droit Electorale Camerounaise» ,*Juridis Périodique,* No 23, Octobre–Décembre (1996), 67–68.

[34] Sindjoun, Luc. «Identité nationale et 'révision constitutionnelle' du 18 Janvier 2006: Comment Constitutionnalise–t–on le 'Nous' au Cameroun dans l'Etat Post–unitaire?» *Polis,* Vol. 1, Février (1996),19.

| Source | Common Law (full right) | No supervision without text, no supervision outside the text. |
|---|---|---|
| Extent of Appeals | Control of legal regularity and opportunity | Control of legal regularity |

Conceived by the author

These differences notwithstanding, though decentralization and deconcentration are not similar, they have some commonalities and interpenetrations. They have in common the fact that they are attempts to take the administration to the administered and the authorities have the powers to take certain important decisions without the direct intervention of central powers. Besides, both are brought together by controls which ensure coherence, effectiveness and legality.

### 3. Hierarchical and Supervisory Control

Central control is necessary, and deconcentration appears to be a useful, even a necessary corollary of decentralization. In the management of their affairs, the non–central authorities need interlocutors, to ensure coherence and legality. It should be noted that many non–central authorities play a double function. They represent not only their institutions but also the State.

In the administration, the exercise of authority is indispensable. The deconcentration of the administration and the specialization of tasks pose numerous problems of communication and coordination. The superordinates have enormous powers in the management of state resources. These powers are not ends in themselves but means to ends, which are administrative goals. The actions of the state personnel as a whole do not have only to be coordinated but also controlled. The authorities have to control others and be controlled according to the administrative goals.

In order to ensure coordination, the peripheral authorities are submitted to hierarchical control by the central organs. The role of deconcentrated organs becomes fundamentally the reception of instructions and transmission of information. Despite the devolution functions, the administration always remains to an extent centralised, as decisions are taken in the name of the State. The authorities in the various "administrative subdivisions" of the territory are subordinates to and are sent by the central organs. These authorities have to give account to the central authorities about their administration (stewardship). Generally, the hierarchical authority is more compulsive than supervisory authority that is why there is both control of regularity and opportunity (without a determined cause).

The hierarchical control can be viewed from a double perspective, means and characteristics. As regards the means, the hierarchical power can be exercised on persons as well as on decisions. It is the power which permits the superior authority that holds it to intervene in the activities of the subordinates. As regards persons, the superior authority has the power to appoint and dismiss. As concerns acts (decisions) the hierarchical power can be exercised in three ways (components): power of instruction, which entails giving general or particular orders or circulars of service; the power of annulment which implies canceling the decisions of the subordinate with retrospective effects; the power of reformation which entails that the hierarchical superior can replace the decision of the subordinate by his own (effects not retrospective). The characteristics are that hierarchical power exist without a text and the subordinates have an obligation to obey except if the order is "manifestly illegal" and can gravely compromise public interest (see C.E 1 Nov. 1994 *Langueur).*

The self–governing bodies, local government decision–making centers with their own policy–making processes, do not stand aside from the State legal order; they are not "States within the State". State supervision is accordingly the "natural counterpart" to the right of self–government of local authorities. It would not be in accordance with the rule of law if local authorities were able to act unlawfully without the possibility of intervention by the State. State supervision of local government authorities, is therefore a requirement of the rule of law. It has its means and characteristics. The means are on persons and acts. The control on persons is restricted since the authorities are elected and that of acts through approbation, annulment and substitution. Regarding the features there is no tutelage without text and the controlled public person can oppose the measure.

The authorities are required to control, advice and support local government authorities. Supervision at various state levels takes place first, as legal supervision, which only includes the supervision of legality in matters of the municipality's original competence, and second, as functional supervision that also supervises expediency in matters transferred by the State. The legality principle (intervention in all cases) is modified by the expediency principle (where control extends to municipal discretion). However, where municipalities consider that the supervisory measures, whether legal or functional, violate their rights of self–government, they have the right of recourse to the courts.[35]

In fact, neither the system of centralization, that of deconcentration nor that of decentralization should be used exclusively. They are means of achieving general interest, they should be dimensions and none should be exaggerated. In normal circumstances, they should be balanced. But at times, there is disequilibrium in favor of centralization (France/Cameroon) or decentralization (Britain, Swiss)). In administrative organization, each technique has its merits and demerits. Further, the administrative techniques are distinct but complementary.

## 1.2 The Control of Administrative Power

The administrative action is not done anyhow; it has the obligation to respect certain rules of law. Broadly speaking administrative law is defined as the totality of juridical rules which are conceived to regulate administrative organs and activities. More precisely, it constitutes the totality of legal rules which are derogatory to common law that regulate internal relations within the administration and the external relations towards the administered. This is in application of the concept of the "State of law" which is one in which the rule of law is applicable, where rules have to be respected. The laws governing the administration have their raison d'être and relevance. The peculiarities of the administration, can be seen through wide administrative powers and their limitations

---

[35] Jürgen, Harbich, State Supervision of Local Government Authorities, Bayerische Verwaltungsschule, UDK: 351.9(045), harbich□bvs.de, 53–56.

## I. Specificities of the public administration and its law

The submission of the administration to a particular law has many historical and constitutional foundations The administration having a privileged position on society (executive privilege, resources, and force), administrative law has as fundamental finality the protection of citizen from power abuse or arbitrariness. The danger is, if rules are not respected the wide administrative powers can lead to despotism and dictatorship.

### A. Wide administrative powers

The relevance of the law governing the administration has increased with the expansion of the public administration. There are many societal problems handled by governments in spite of the globalization trends. This entails widespread use of the administrative bodies to intervene for public interest. Increased regulation of the socioeconomic life has resulted in a massive number of laws in the broad sense that need to be respected by the public. The influence of bureaucrats is also due to their great numbers. Besides, the governments' responsibilities have increased quantitatively and qualitatively. In order to discharge these responsibilities, a wide variety of government units and programmes are created which enjoy great durability, and hardly disappear. No doubt much power is delegated to the administrative authorities by the elected officials. Besides, the bureaucratic power is enhanced by its expertise, permanence and discretion.

Bureaucrats, says Herbert Kaufman are major players in government. In the policy process, bureaucrats are generally found at implementation stage where ideals meet reality. Bureaucrats have the possibility to shape policies directly. First bureaucrats have official powers which include legislative, executive and adjudicative powers. These powers in aggregate exceed those of legislatures and executives. Second, derivative powers which entail influencing the meaning of policies by the way they go about their duties (friendly or hostile, rigid or flexible). Third, most administrators enjoy significant legal and procedural protections against unrestricted removal and sanctions.

Bureaucrats also influence other State organs that give them their powers and tell them what to do. They possess this influence because they are seasoned and knowledgeable "old hands" who have cumulated much experience. Besides they have other resources based on their technical and professional know–how and the fact that they are seen as impartial and experts. Further, public officers are citizens and voters. One more weapon in their armamentarium is that many officials are members of unions and professional organisations. Finally administrative units have constituencies. They generally develop ties with the interest they serve. [36]

Another important resource for bureaucracies is that they have considerable latitudes and discretion. If the exigencies are extended to all administrative actions, the administrators will be passive, there will be automation or robotization, which deprives the administrators from all liberty of appreciation and all spirit of initiative. This can certainly lead to the sclerosis of the administrative apparatus. More so, this will be disastrous for the opportunity of certain decisions cannot be appreciated in advance by general rules, but in contact with facts. Consequently, there is the necessity to leave a margin and liberty of administrative appreciation. Discretionary powers give the possibility to choose between solutions mindful of prevailing circumstances; actions are not dictated in advance by the rules of law as with the case of bound competence. According to Kenneth C. Davis, a public administrator "has discretion whenever the effective limits of his power leave him free to make a choice among possible causes of action or inaction."[37] In fact, when making decisions even under the most formalised or structural decision making situations, complete adherence to formal procedures is both impossible and undesirable. However the most awesome discretionary power is the "omnipresent power to do nothing" since checks are designed mostly to cope with abusive action not abusive inaction. Discretion has always been a challenge to law and the risk is that where law ends tyranny begins.

---

[36] Kaufman, H. "Major Players: Bureaucracies in American Government.". *Public Administration Review,61 (2001):*18–42.

[37] Davis, Kenneth C. *Discretionary Justice: A Preliminary Inquiry* (Westport: Greenwood Press, 1980), 4.

However, discretionary powers do not imply administrative arbitrariness; actions must be in favour of the law and general interest. It was affirmed in the *Essiane Aka'a Jean* Vs the *State of Cameroon* (1968) that discretionary powers does not avoid all legal controls, as powers must be exercised in line with general interest and following the limits fixed by the law. In the *Baba Youssoufa Vs the Federated State of East Cameroon Case*, (1968) it was ruled that the power of appreciation is implied in view of safeguarding general interest. Therefore, discretionary powers do not imply contradiction to the principle of legality. However in contradiction with bound competence where there is control of regularity (maximal control) the control of discretionary powers is more of opportunity than regularity, even if the judge examines the conditions of validity.

The worry, therefore is that bureaucracy can possess threats to the state of law, to human rights and freedoms. The influence and the degree of autonomy bestowed upon and acquired by public officials nationally and internationally alarm some commentators. Advocates of bureaucracy argue that modern society with its complex economic, political and social institutions requires a substantial degree of stability of the state only offered by bureaucracy. Critics think that bureaucrats, are "out of control" "unresponsive" and perhaps even moving towards domination of every political system. They warn against "The new despotism" and "our wander land of bureaucracy."[38] However, there is no reason to panic because bureaucracy is subjected to control, especially during the implementation process, thus the importance of administrative law.

## B. Limitation of Power

The constitution provides the national legal order; constitutional law and administrative law are closely linked. It can be said that administrative law has as base the constitution. The constitution regulates the relationship between the administrators themselves, and between the administrators and the administered. In modern constitutions, precautions are taken to avoid the concentration of powers and the rights of the citizens are declared.

---

[38] Kaufman, 18–42.

The separation of powers, between the three main State organs – the legislative, the executive and the judiciary renders power abuse difficult. Montesquieu declared that if the legislative power is united with executive power in the hands of one person, or of any one body of officials, there can be no liberty; nor can there be any liberty if the power to judge is not separated from the legislative and executive powers. The essence of the principle of separation of powers is that power should be limited or controlled. There should be constitutional checks and balances between state organs. Also the existence of democratic institutions like the Constitutional Council and Audit Bench can help to limit the arbitrary exercise of power.

The simple fact that the administration in its decisions must follow some rules provides some sense of security. In the preamble as well as in the body of modern constitutions, the rights and freedoms of the citizens are proclaimed. Benjamin constant summarizes it all when he says that the citizens possess certain rights independent of all, and any authority which violates these rights becomes illegitimate.

The famous French Universal Declaration of the Rights of Man and Citizen of 26 August 1789 states in its article 16 that "Every society in which the guarantee of rights is not assured and the separation of powers determined, has no constitution."

As MacIver puts it, the State is both child and parent of law. The State creates law, uses it to maintain public order and satisfy general interest. The State itself created by law has to act within the limits set by law and respect individual freedoms. MacIver further observes that "there is the law which governs the state and there is the law by which the state governs".[39] In other words, as Pailip J.C confirms "law is both an instrument for governing and a device for protecting the citizens."[40] This brings to mind the state as a legal personality with rights and obligations. One also thinks of the theory of auto–limitation of the state. The rule of law do not only define the prerogatives of organization but also and above

---

[39] MacIver, 250.

[40] Pailip (J.C): Public Law and Public Administration: The State of the Union in Lynn. N.B. and Widavsky A. eds: *Public Administration. The State of the Discipline* (New Delhi: East–West press (EWP) pvt Ltd, 1992), 258.

all the constraints of the administration. This is in line with the principle of legality which holds that the submission of the administration to all pre–established rules of law, is a *sine qua non* for the State to be qualified as "State of law". With this, there is a possibility of legal redress of official infractions of law or maladministration. Gierke's formula holds that "The Rechtsstaat is a state which sets itself not above the law but within it".[41] This guarantee should be inside and outside the administration for Finer holds that "as the civil service can abuse its powers *vis–a –vis* the ordinary citizens, so may the higher civil servants do to the lower."[42]

## II. The Concept of Administrative Justice

In contemporary world, the suing of government and public officials has been subject to much debate. Arguably, officials can find themselves in chains for decisions always hurt someone. This can lead to too much caution, administrative inefficiency and ineffectiveness. Indeed, given the pervasive and all–powerful nature of contemporary public administration, it should be held responsible for blatant neglect, exploitative and malicious actions. There are many formal and informal mechanisms of administrative control, but the judicial system is expected to provide the best authoritative vehicle or last hope for checking administrative abuses. The issue is that the scope of administrative acts is controversial for negatively it is defined as all acts that are not legislative, governmental, judicial or private.

Administrative justice is the totality of legal rules that govern the solution of administrative litigations or disputes by jurisdictional means. It comprises all the means and rules of law used to contest administrative decisions or actions. This definition implies the existence of a contestation, administrative action and application of public law. In addition, there should be specific organization, rules of procedure and competent judge. It consecrates the theory of the state of law and the principle of legality. There is therefore a shift of paradigm from sovereign immunity to rule of law with particular procedures and the extent of the role played depending on the personality of the judge.

---

[41] The Rechtsstaat entails maximum possible legality of the administration.
[42] Finer, 915.

Public management provokes the submission of the administration to specific rules of public law and in principle, the disputes that may arise, to the competence of the administrative jurisdiction. Contrariwise, private management permits the application of rules of private law in the administration, and eventually disputes are judged by tribunals with competence to adjudge private matters.

## A. Sovereign Immunity to Rule of Law

According to Warren, sovereign immunity doctrine holds that the government is sovereign, and, consequently cannot be held liable for its actions. This implies the impossibility to sue the government without its permission.[43] This doctrine rests on the medieval tradition that the King is sovereign and cannot do wrong. In modern administrations, however, there is distinction between governmental and official immunity.

The emergence of constitutional democracy has favoured the primacy of law. Under the system of rule of law, no one or entity is supposed to be above the law. As such, no public official has immunity simply because she works for the government. In democratic societies, public servants are like any other ordinary citizens, and are, subjected to legal equality under the law.

Administrative justice fulfils three fundamental goals in the modern society. It protects the citizens from administrative arbitrariness and provides them with some security. It contributes to the guarantee of human rights and freedoms. It renders administrative action more efficacious so as to defend the general interest in the best conditions.

In order for administrative justice to be autonomous, it must fulfil three conditions: First, a domain, field, a certain number of matters or specific litigations. Second the existence of a competent judge, in this case the trained administrative judge. Third the application of special rules different from the principle in private law. Warren defines judicial review as the legitimate sphere of judicial scrutiny of administrative actions and the methods that courts employ to consider the propriety of administrative behaviour.[44] This power is given to the courts enabling them to declare

---

[43] Warren, 457.

[44] Warren, 402.

acts illegal making them null and void. However, it depends on the place, time and judges. Particularly, there are situations of judicial self–restraint and activism, and question of competent judge.

## 1. Judicial Self Restraint or Activism?

Self–restraint or conservatism implies that the judge is passive, weak, meek and exercises power with caution. Psychologically, they are tamed by the principle of separation of powers. Besides, their appointments and promotion depends on other state organs. Further, courts depend on other officials for the enforcement of their decisions. Moreover, the courts do not operate in societal vacuums; they have to respond to environmental (political, economic, social and cultural) pressures. Indeed, the classical argument is that the role of the judge is to "discover" or "interpret" not to "make" law.

Judicial activism has been favoured by societal evolution towards liberalism. It implies that judges have to use above all their consciences and when need be, have to act with audacity, be combative, make laws and even act beyond the laws. Judges do exercise enormous discretion which enables them to create laws especially when these laws are ambiguous or have loopholes. In the now reputed United States case of *Marbury Vs Madison*, Judge John Marshal argued that, despite the fact that the constitution does not authorize explicitly, the courts have the right to overrule the acts of other branches of government as unconstitutional.

This activism tendency has been mainly due to the societal evolution from liberal (police) via interventionist (welfare) to the neo–liberal (global) State. Consequently, the transition from the court's classical to modern role. In the classical model, the court was supposed to settle legal disputes between individual litigants. In recent times, there have been both quantitative and qualitative increase in administrative caseloads. This has been due to increasing education, access to legal services, surplus of lawyers and economic progress. As such courts have become pervasive, "society handymen" hearing a broader range of cases, shaping government processes and substantive policies, in fact societal life. Depending on the situation, law can play fundamentally three functions: progressive and revolutionary where it seeks to transform the society, conservative where it maintains the society as it is, and illusory or better still incantatory function.

## 2. Jurisdictional duality or monism?

There is controversy in theory and practice whether the judicial and administrative jurisdictions should be separated or should form a unified system. While the Anglo–Saxon countries favour unified systems where the ordinary judge decides on all cases, on the other hand France, Portugal, Germany, Italy and Greece use administrative courts. The degree of unity or duality is measured by the level of personnel, textual, organic and functional autonomies between the jurisdictions. In the case of duality, the courts should be manned by personnel with specific training, following specific laws, submitted to distinct organs and principles.

Lewis Mainzer notes that "British and American observers worry deeply about the divided jurisdiction of the civil and administrative courts, and argue that there is great value in a single, unified system of courts." Harold H. Bruff voices the same concern, arguing that the development of an administrative court system could cause the "loss of the generalist perspectives." He believes that this is a serious loss because the wisdom of generalist courts is the exposition to diverse problems. Arguably also, the specialized courts are particularly susceptible to political pressures and can be "captured" by politicians, pressure groups and regulatory agencies.[45]

The administrative courts have their own merits; they help to decongest and reduce the caseload problem of the ordinary courts. Administrative judges can better adjudicate in administrative matters because of expertise knowledge on how the administration functions. Arguably, as seen in the unilateral administrative acts, administrative contracts, and liability issues the administration has special privileges and obligations which are not seen in relations between individuals. Besides, the civil judge is not expected to undo his training; there is the risk and temptation of applying private law principles in administrative matters.

In the Anglo–Saxon countries, jurisdictional monism is applicable where the judicial judge is competent to rule on all cases. In France, there

---

[45] Warren, 377–370.

are three types of courts; criminal, civil and administrative. The *Tribunal de Conflits* exist to solve conflicts between ordinary civil courts and administrative courts. The French practice jurisdictional duality where different jurisdictions handle public and private law matters. There is dichotomy between two court orders, *les jurisdictions de l'ordre administratif* and *les jurisdictions de l'ordre judicaire* with corresponding two types of trials le *contentieux administrative* and *le procès civil*. There is a Supreme Court (*Cour de Cassation*) for private law matters and another (*Conseil D'Etat:– Administrative Supreme Court*) for public law matters. Sure, different rules and procedures may be applicable; however there exist commonness of finality which is justice, mutual influences and interactions as what divides them is not a line but a zone. In normal circumstances, reciprocal or concurrent intervention should be authorized by texts. The peculiar status of the State, and the rules that forbid the judiciary tribunal to hear the acts of the administration, justifies the necessity to have a particular law and specialized jurisdiction.

## B. The Reviewability of Administrative Actions

The fundamental idea is that those who are harmed by administrative action should have the opportunity to challenge the legality of the action in court, as long as the action is legitimately reviewable. The fundamental question is whether the court has the jurisdiction to review. Once the issue is outside the legitimate competence of the court, it becomes un–reviewable. Reviewability is determined by what the law says, whether the plaintiff is eligible and if the case is timely. The fundamental issues are: the competent court, the scope, principles of and obstacles to reviews.

### 1. Scope of Review

This implies the matters or different questions that fall within the competence of the judge. Virtually all administrative law scholars agree that unnecessary meddling in administrative activities is disruptive and counterproductive. They also agree that the courts have the obligation to keep administrative behaviour fair, reasonable and accountable. Depending on the legal system, the scope of review is determined by scholars, the courts or texts. For instance, section 706, entitled the "Scope of Review" in the United States Administrative Procedure Act (APA) codifies the court's opinion on the scope of review.

The scope of review is governed by some principles and requirements which the courts rely on. The deference principle upholds the constitutional separation of powers doctrine as guide to the determination of scope. Despite the tendency toward judicial activism, which has brought general broadening of the courts scope of review, deference to administrative authority and expertise by the courts is still the rule rather than the exception. The substantial evidence rule requires the courts to see whether there is any substantial evidence supporting the challenged decision. The fundamental rights requirement implies the expansion of the scope, when fundamental rights are at stake. The "de novo review" requirement means new trial, the court orders a fresh proceeding in an administrative law dispute so that arguments and evidence in the controversy can be weighed again by a new independent tribunal.

Generally, also there is what is commonly known as the "no review clause" which are matters that are exempted from review. Under Section 701(a) (1) (2) of the APA, agency actions are unreviewable if "statutes preclude judicial review" or "agency action is committed to agency discretion by law." However, there have been controversies the world over on the reviewability of "unreviewable" administrative actions.

## 2. The Principles (Doctrines) Governing Administrative Litigations

Warren argues that the legal doctrines have been used to protect the courts from having to hear untimely and unwarranted suits and the administrative agencies from hasty, unnecessary and disruptive excursions in the administrative process. He discusses these principles and concludes that at times they are tough legal obstacles to overcome. These principles are standing to sue, primary jurisdiction, exhaustion of available administrative remedies and the ripeness principle.[46]

The standing to sue means that a genuine dispute exists, with the court being placed in a position to provide judicial remedy (relief) to a

[46] Warren, 416–428.

legally injured party (the aggrieved person has suffered an 'injury in fact'). The standing issue asks the court to answer the question: "Should the petitioner have the right to 'stand' before the court and argue his case?" Primary jurisdiction is allowing the administrative agencies with initial jurisdiction before the intervention of the judge in the resolution of administrative disputes. The exhaustion of administrative remedies is a sister to primary jurisdiction and entails that the courts should stay clear of disputes within the public agencies until the petitioner has completed or totally exhausted all channels of resolution provided for by the agency. Ripeness implies that the case is mature enough to be ready for judicial review, that the petitioner has satisfied all the three preceding principles.

## 3. Obstacles to Obtaining Review

These obstacles can be at the level of the courts (reluctance) as well as their environments. Judges at times are politically inclined, psychologically impacted by power separation and feel they lack technical administrative knowledge. Besides, court interventions can disrupt the normal functioning of the administration, thus challenging the administrative continuity and frustrating the public. Also, the principles (doctrines) governing administrative litigations can prove to be obstacles. The legal, political, economic and cultural environments can also serve as obstacles. Thus, issue of the transferability and applicability of principles and theories of administrative law in foreign lands.

# Part One
# French Administrative Law

In France, there is Droit Administratif General and Droit Administratif Special. The specific or special administrative law (droit administrative spécial), refers to the law of the different public services, public economic law, urban planning law, and territorial development law. The General which is the focus of this work consists essentially of administrative organization and action. From the French tradition, *Droit Administratif* involves essentially, Administrative Organization (centralization, deconcentration and decentralization laws), the principle of legality, Ways of Administrative Action (the public services and administrative police powers) Procedures of Administrative Action (unilateral administrative acts and administrative contracts) and Administrative Justice or litigations. It involves basically administrative organization and action.

# Chapter Two
# Administrative Organization in France

The administrative organization is a confluence of political and administrative dimensions and involves essentially the State and decentralized entities.

## 2.1. The Administrative Organization of the State

The organization of the State can be central or deconcentrated. The central administrative authorities are competent and make decisions applicable to the whole territory. The deconcentrated authorities have limited territorial competence, are at the same time part of the central and local administrations organized hierarchically and placed under the authority of government members.

### I. Central Administrative Authorities

At the central level, there is the sharing of authority between the President of the Republic and the Prime Minister. The distribution of functions depends on whether the political regime is in the period of political cohabitation or not.[47] The real application of policy is done by the ministers in their respective departments.

#### A. Administrative Attributions of the President of the Republic

In line with the constitution, the president of the republic has regulatory and appointive powers in normal circumstances.[48] He is assisted in his duties by the attached services

---

[47] Political cohabitation is when the executive and legislative majorities are distinct, and for political convenience the President appoints the Prime Minister from a different party.

[48] Article 13 of the Constitution of the Fifth French Republic of October 4, 1958.

As regards the regulatory powers, and according to Article 13, the President of the Republic signs ordinances. This is in line with the hypothesis previewed in article 38 which states that: ordinances are taken on the basis of a temporary issue, with the accord of the parliament that authorizes the government to intervene exceptionally and for a limited time in the domain of law. Article 47(3) also authorizes the government to establish the finance bill when the parliament has proven unable to vote the bill within the time limit prescribed by the constitution. Further, he signs decrees deliberated by the Council of Ministers (Consiel de ministres). This can be in line with the constitution, a law or regulatory text.

The power of nomination is enormous as stipulated in article 13(3) of the constitution. In line with article 13(4) this list can be increased by an organic law. These appointive powers considered to be the discretion of government can be used strategically to ensure the implement of government policies especially during the periods of cohabitation. All the decisions taken in the exercise of the regulator and appointive powers must be countersigned by the Prime Minister or the minister concerned.

In the case of exceptional circumstances, the president can, within the framework of article 16 necessary measures. This is in line with *Rubin de Servens* Case (1962), where the Council of State (Conseil D'Etat) ruled that the decisions taken during such periods permit him to intervene in the regulatory and legislative domains. Besides, the decisions taken during these exceptional periods are exclude from countersign.

The reinforcement of the powers of the President by the 1958 constitution has led to the increase of attached services at his disposal. These services help the President in determining political choices, policy orientations to be implemented. They include the Secretary General of the Presidency, the cabinet of the presidency, foreign policy experts and security experts.

### B. Administrative Attributions of the Prime Minister

He has common law attributions which imply that he is competent to exercise all administrative attributions which have not been expressly attributed to any other authority. On the basis of the constitution, the Prime

Minister directs government action.[49] Further, he exercises regulatory powers and assures the execution of laws, on the basis of which he can sign, without the intervention of the President, all decrees except those deliberated at the Council of Ministers. He has appointive powers to civil and military posts, with the exception of those reserved to the President. This power of nomination can be delegated to the ministers and other high authorities.

He has the powers to supervise all administrative actions. However, the extent of these powers depends on his relationship with the President. He has arbitration powers in the case of conflict between ministers and can intervene in any issue that he deems important.

The Prime Minister is assisted in the exercise of his functions by the general secretary of the government (secretaire general du gouvernment–SGG). This is under the authority of the secretary general and comprises of advisors and those in charge of missions. In collaboration with the secretary general at the presidency, it is charged with the coordination of government work. It coordinates all the services attached to the Prime Minister's office. The Prime Minister's cabinet which comprises at his discretion advisors and personalities on special mission, is his *etat–major politique*. In collaboration with the secretary general of the presidency, it is charged with assuring the follow–up of the activities of the various ministerial departments

## C. Ministers as Mangers of Administrative Action

As members of government, the ministers participate in its collegial action and on this basis play political roles. Administratively the ministers ensure the management of their respective departments. As a corollary they have to deploy personnel mindful of service needs and have disciplinary powers when there are malpractices. From this standpoint, the ministers possess hierarchical powers exercised on the personnel under their respective services. Also they have power of appointment to certain posts frequently delegated by the Prime minister. They can issue instructions in the form of circulars or service notes which permits them to interpret and apply the laws and regulations in force.

[49] Article 21 of the Constitution of the Fifth French Republic of October 4, 1958.

In principle, they do not have regulatory powers and cannot therefore create new obligations for the personnel and public in the administrative entities under their control. However, they have a large margin of action in two hypotheses: When the law has expressly conferred to them the competence to take necessary measures for its execution; and when (as interpreted by the judge) they are conferred with the competence to take all necessary measures to ensure the smooth functioning of the administrative services under their authority.[50] They can also be associated in the exercise of regulatory powers by the President of the Republic and Prime Minister. On this title, they can on one hand, propose to them measures to be taken which enables them to participate in their formulation; and on the other the ministers must countersign most of the decrees or ordinances signed by the President of the Republic and all the decrees signed by the Prime Minister.

When the government is formed, the attributions of each minister are fixed by the decree, the distribution which can be different from preceding governments. Also the determination of the services belonging to the authority of each minister depends on the deliberated decrees of the Council of Ministers. Further, some services though under determined principal departments, can be conferred to minister delegates and secretaries of State.

The internal organization of ministerial departments is fixed by decrees and laws and ministerial orders. The ministerial structure essentially comprises of the cabinet and central administration. The Cabinet comprises of the collaborators of the minister, freely chosen by him and assigned functions. The composition of the Cabinet depends on the texts and the minister's discretion. The members of the cabinet have triple functions which are administrative and political. They assist the minister in the exercise of political functions, guide the action of services by indicating the policy orientations of the minister, and coordinate and arbitrate the directorates.[51] The central administration comprises of ministerial directorates placed under the authority of directors who occupy

---

[50] CE *Jamart F*ebruary 7, 1936.

[51] Legrand, Andre and Wiener, Celine. Initiation au Droit Public, Formation Administration Concours. La Documentation Française, 2003.

their post under the direction of the government. This signifies that they are appointed and revoked discretionarily by the Council of Ministers. They constitute the stable element of the services of the minister and remain in place after the departure of the minister. They are divided under bureaus regrouped under sub–directorates.

## II. Deconcentrated Services

The law of March 2, 1982 distinguishes the functions at the level of the department and region under the authority of a Prefect *(préfet)* who exercises power in strict liaison with the external services.[52] The Law of February 6, 1992 on the territorial administration of the republic consecrates the principle of subsidiarity and holds that the essentials for the implementation of public policies will be done at the level of regions.

### A. Prefect of the Department

*Le Préfet de Département* is the most important personality of the deconcentrated administration. But he is surrounded by many departmental chiefs of services placed at the head of external services of the different ministerial departments. The *préfet* has specific powers which he exercises with the assistance of collaborators but with a dependent status.

He is the delegate of the government in the department. The Constitution in its article 72 states that he is responsible for national interests, administrative control and the respect of laws. He is the holder of State authority in the Department, and represents the Prime Minister and each ministerial department in the department, and directs under their authority the civil administrative services of the State. The administrative attributions were above all political but have increased with time. He is the information agent of the central power. On the basis of this political aspect, he informs the government on the political situation of the department. Further, he is the government representative at the local level.[53] As confirmed by many texts, he is therefore the principal beneficiary of the

---

[52] Loi n° 82–213 du 2 mars 1982 relative aux droits et libertés des communes, des départements et des régions.

[53] He represents he entire government not only the Minister of Interion, even if it is this minister that is responsible for the management of the prefectural corps.

delegation measures, in most civil administrative ministerial departments with the exception of those of justice, finance and national education. He has powers of representation of the State in public ceremonies, and he exercises power of action in justice in the name of the State. He entitled with the power of control of decentralized entities. Furthermore, he has administrative and judicial police powers, where he is assisted by the *préfet délégué à la sécurité et à la defense*. Finally, he holds extensive powers in the economic and social domains.

In the exercise of their functions, the prefects are assisted by collaborators. The Cabinet assists essentially in the political role and is charged with all the affairs with political ramifications. The director of cabinets assists in all questions related to public security. The secretary general of the prefecture, the sub–prefect *(sous–prefet)* who also occupies an echelon in the prefectural career, performs three functions. As assistant to the prefect, he is called upon to substitute him when need be especially in the prefectures which are at the same time departments and regions. He ensures the direction and coordination of prefectural administration. Finally, he occupies the office of the sub prefect of the district (arrondissement) of the headquarters of the department. The Directions and Bureaus comprise of the personnel of the Ministry of Interior and consist the services of the prefecture. Since 1982, they are only charged with the attributions of the State within the department. The territorial *sub–prefects* are the delegates of the prefects at the level of the arrondissement.

The status of the prefect has evolved with time since at the beginning it was essentially political. Since the IV Republic there have been efforts to create a prefectural corps, a status which can give them a minimum of career guarantee. But this status is derogatory and does suppress the idea that the prefect is at "the discretion of government."[54] On this title, the prefect is subject to the obligation of loyalty, which entails that that he is obliged to defend in public and in all circumstances the position expressed by the government in place and also to include his political or religious opinions in his dossiers. He benefits neither

[54] Article 25 of the Law of 11 January 1982.

syndicalist nor strike rights and is submitted to the obligation of residence which can be waived only by the authorization of the Minister of Interior.

The prefect is faced with double dependence from the perspectives of nomination and revocation. For a long time, the appointment of prefect was not submitted to any special conditions. Their nomination remains discretionary, however the liberty of the government is limited by the fact that at least four out of five prefects must be chosen amongst sub–prefects or high civil administrators, in principle graduates from the National School of Administration (ENA). In addition, the prefect is discretionarily transferred (principle of mobility). In general, each change in government entails significant prefectural movements. Besides, advancements are made exclusively on the basis of choice and he can be put on reserve at any time. In the case of fault, the prefect is subject to disciplinary sanction including revocation and automatic retirement, with less procedural guarantees in comparison to ordinary civil servants.

## B. The Prefect of the Region

The necessity of the *Préfet de Région* is due to the vastness of certain administrative services beyond the department. After successive reforms, there was the harmonization of regional circumscriptions in 1960 no matter the ministerial departments which led to the creation of the prefect of region in 1964. He is obligatorily the prefect of the department where is found the headquarters of the region. He is therefore the prefect as the others submitted to the same status and does not have hierarchical powers on the colleagues who are at the head of the department.

The attributions are both departmental and regional. He exercises functions which are incumbent on the prefect of the department. At the regional level, he plays an important role in economic matters. He particularly participates in the elaboration of the national plan and follows up its execution at the level of the region. From the administrative viewpoint, he exercises direct authority on all the civil services of the State in the region, with the exception of the activities of some rare ministries that enjoy a certain autonomy: national education, justice and finance.

The auxiliaries of the prefect of the region are the general secretariat of regional affairs and the regional administrative conference.[55] The general secretariat is a some sort of *etat–major* comprising of functionaries of category A competent in administrative and technical domains. They are placed under the authority of the general secretary of regional affairs (SGAR). It is an administration of missions, which is not responsible for management tasks, but is charged with the study of a certain number of dossiers enabling the preparation of dossiers for the decision of the prefect of the region. The regional administrative conference (CAR) comprises of permanent members (the prefects of the departments within the region, the secretary general of the departmental headquarters, and the general treasurer of the region). The other members are convoked when the affairs relevant to their competence are examined. The prefect of the region, who presides the meetings, can invite at his discretion all qualified persons susceptible to provide information or clarifications during sessions. The Conference is a collegial institution charged with giving opinions to the prefect of the region before his attributions are exercised in certain domains. It is obligatorily consulted regarding the individualization of investments with regional interests and the distribution of envelops of investments credits to respective regions. This is same with the preparation of plan contracts and in a general manner on the totality of regional orientations and programmes in matters of economic and social development and territorial planning.

## 2.2. Territorial Entities in France

The constitution states in its article 72 that, in the conditions previewed by the law, the collectivities {territorial} are administered freely by elected councils.[56] The Constitution enumerates the territorial

---

[55] Secretariat générale aux affairs regionale (SGAR) and conference administrative regionale(CAR).

[56] This can be through the principle of representation and even local referendum. The law of February 4, 1995(art. 2142–3 of Code général des collectivités territoriales (CGTC ) adds the possibility of popular initiative Le Code général des collectivités territoriales (CGCT) regroupe, en France, des dispositions législatives et réglementaires relatives au droit des collectivités territoriales. Sa

collectivities or communities of the republic namely the communes, departments, regions, collectivities with special status and overseas territorial collectivities.[57]

In 1982 and 1983, the central government, under President François Mitterrand passed several decentralization laws. The 1983 Laws (Gaston Defferre Laws) dating from 7 January and 22 July defined the responsibilities and finance of the new bodies.[58] This "quiet revolution" was to increase the financial and administrative independence of local governments. The Law of March 2, 1982 introduced three main changes. First, it transferred the executive power of departments from the prefect to the president of the elected council. Second, it granted a legal status to region with executive power and administrative independence from the prefect. Finally, the law removed the administrative supervision of the prefect in accordance with the principle of free administration of local authorities.

The new nomenclature as a result of the constitutional revision of 12 March 2003 augmented the number of territorial collectivities. This reform entails the partial abandonment of the other principles, consecrating the Jacobean ideology of the uniformity of status of territorial collectivities of the same category. The representatives of the State have the charge to protect national interests, administrative control and the respect of the laws."[59] This text therefore highlights three principles that regulate the status of territorial collectivities: election of their organs, their liberal administration and the existence of the control of legality.

---

partie législative a été promulguée en 1996( Loi numéro 96–142 du 21 février 1996)_et la partie réglementaire en 2000 (Décret numéro 2000–318 du 7 avril 2000).

[57] Article 72 of the Constitution of the Fifth French Republic of October 4, 1958.

[58] Loi n° 83–8 du 7 janvier 1983 relative à la répartition de compétences entre les communes, les départements, les régions et l'Etat Loi n° 83–663 du 22 juillet 1983 complétant la loi n° 83–8 du 7 janvier 1983 relative à la répartition de compétences entre les communes, les départements, les régions et l'Etat.

[59] Article 72 of the Constitution of the Fifth French Republic of October 4, 1958.

## I. Decentralized Local Organs

There exist the deliberative and executive organs of the local entities. The first are the local assemblies and the second are the mayors and their assistants, departmental and regional executives.

### A. The election and mandate of local assemblies

In line with article 72 of the constitution, the administration of local collectivities is ensured by elected councils. All the local assemblies are elected by direct universal suffrage. The local decentralized organs are the municipal councilors, general councilors (Conseillers Generaux), and regional councilors. The municipal councilors are elected through direct universal suffrage for duration of six years. The general councilors are elected through a uninominal majority ballot in two rounds for a mandate of six years. The regional organization is original in relation to other levels of local administration because it is somehow bicameral since the regional council is assisted by a second assembly called the economic and social council.

The mandate of the local assemblies can be stopped by dissolution in line with the principle of "No tutelage without text". The motives for dissolution must be clearly stated by the law. In the case of urgency, the municipal council can be suspended for a period of one month by a motivated prefectural order. It can also be dissolved by a degree taken by the council of ministers. The general council and the regional council can be dissolved by the motivated degree taken by the council of ministers when their functioning proves to be impossible, the parliaments must be informed immediately.

### B. Designation and mandate of local executives

The general principles are the same at the three levels of the local administration: the executives are elected by the assembly. The mayors are elected from the municipal council. The mayor and his assistant are elected during the first session following the election of the council. The departmental and regional executives follow the same procedure. The president of the general council is elected within the council during the first session following the partial renewal for a duration of three years. At the same time with the election of the president, the permanent commission of the general council is elected. The regional executive is elected following the same principles.

## II. The Attributions of Territorial Local Collectivities

The executive and deliberative organs have specific and complementary functions. The functions will be examined following the previous logic of levels of the local administrations.

The mayor, the president of the general council and the president of the regional council perform similar functions at their respective levels of jurisdictions. The mayor performs functions as agent of State and council. As agent of the State the mayor performs two categories of functions: those which he exercises under the control of the municipal council and the administrative control of the representative of the department and those he exercises under the authority of the representative of the State in the department. In the exercise of the first, he acts as the organ of the council and is submitted to the tutelage of the prefects, and in the second he is the State agent and the prefect has hierarchical powers over him. The council from this perspective is therefore a circumscription of the administration of the State which is competent in many activities. The mayor therefore is charged with the publication and the execution of laws is an official of judicial police and civil status. As a communal agent, the mayor has proper powers which he exercises and the municipal council can not intervene and other powers under its control. The principal powers are those he holds as an authority of administrative police.[60] To accomplish his functions, the mayor discloses municipal personnel to whom he exercises hierarchical powers and directs. There is assist the personalization of power but he is civilly and penally responsible.

The president of the general council has as mission essentially to prepare meetings of the council: establish the budget bill, prepares preliminary reports before all submissions for the council, he has power to convoke and thus to precede sessions. He executes the decisions adopted, collects revenue and engages expenditure, signs contracts approved by the

---

[60] Articles 2122–21 and 2122–27 of the General Code of Territorial Collectivities (CGCT).

council, represents the department in justice and is assisted by the services of the department. He has some administrative police powers on public goods which he exercises independently from the council. The president of the regional council has similar functions with the exception of police powers.

## III. The control on local collectivities

The constitution in its article 72 it should be reiterated states that, "In the territorial communities of the Republic, the State representative, representing each of the Members of the Government, shall be responsible for national interests, administrative supervision and compliance with the law." This is an attempt to ensure the respect of legality by the collectivities. The tutelage can be on the person or the act.

### A. Tutelage on the person

The laws on decentralization have maintained the traditional rules on the supervision of persons. The mayor and his assistants occupy a particular position among the elected local officials. They are the only ones that can be suspended for a maximum duration of a month by a motivated ministerial order and revoked by the decree of the council of ministers. The existence of this disciplinary power is because of their functional duality as agents of the council and the State. Such procedures are not previewed for the other municipal councilors, elected departmental and regional agents. The municipal and general councilors can be forced to resign by the decision of administrative tribunal when they refuse to accomplish the missions imposed on them by law. This is the same with regional councilors but the decision is taken by the State Council. This can also be the case when they become ineligible during their mandate.

### B. Tutelage on the act

The administrative judge has the powers to annul local acts on the basis of illegality not opportunity. The prefect can inform the decentralized authority of his intention to defer the act to the judge and request that the act be withdrawn, or abrogated. The prefect can request the suspension of the execution of an act that will be accorded by the judge when there are serious doubts on its legality. The decentralization laws have maintained the power of automatic substitution; this is when there is the breakdown of local authorities and in financial matters with the intervention of the regional chambers of accounts.

## 2.3. Reorganization of Communal Administration

The local framework has been seen as un–adapted to new realities. First, France is the country in Europe with the highest number of communes. The challenge is that many communes are too small to enjoy the economies of large scale production and at times there are problems of urban agglomerations which are beyond the confines of a commune. Second, there are some questions that are too small to be treated by the whole commune. As the small communes have resisted disappearance, France has opted for the organization of structures for cooperation between communes. The cooperation can be as regards public establishments, syndicates and projects.

The CGCT fixes certain common rules applicable to all public establishments of inter–communal cooperation (EPCI). They are created on the request from the one or more municipal councils or on the initiative of one or more prefects of the concerned departments after the opinion of the departmental commissioners. The administration is ensured by a deliberative organ comprising of elected delegates by the municipal councils of the member communes, and whose mandate is linked to the councilors who designated them. The commune syndicate is cooperation by services. It is the most elementary form of inter–communal cooperation. It is a public establishment endowed with legal personality and financial autonomy, associating communes to permit or facilitate the creation and management of service or equipment common to the totality of concerned members. Cooperation can be by project, whose objective is not simply to facilitate the solution of problems of each commune, but the realization of communal problems of development. Another public establishment is the city council (communauté urbain) which has a defined territory and not a determined service to manage. Besides, with the multiplicity of services, they are endowed with general not special competence.

The 2003 reforms were spearheaded by President Jacques Chirac to increase the efficiency of local administration by reducing superposition of different layers of local administration, coordination and management costs. It led to transfer of responsibilities and financial resources to local authorities. The 2014 reforms have intention to create ‘metropolises’ and reduce the number of regions.

# Chapter Three
# Administrative Action in France

In France, this comprises the Ways of Administrative Action (the public services and administrative police powers) Procedures of Administrative Action (unilateral administrative acts and administrative contracts) and as corollary Administrative Justice or litigations.

## 3.1. The Provision of Public services

The notion of public service is one of the most important in French administrative law, as well as, one of the most complex. Its history is intertwined with periods of rapid ascension and relative fall, either from the ideological plan or on legal theory. Public service can be seen as an activity or an organism. Simply put an activity constitutes public service when it is ensured or done by a public person to accomplish public interest.[61]

At the origin, the public service was limited to the regalian functions of the State. It gradually spread to those activities that were considered reserved to private initiatives, and it became the 'corner stone' of administrative law, which determined both its domain and finality. Later on, the notion stretched with the appearance of diverse forms of management, despite the fact that its scope of application was contested by liberal economist. Without doubts, it is at the heart of the mission devolved to public power and measures its legitimacy.

## I. The public service as source of legitimacy

It can be dated to the *Blanco judgement* of 8 February 1873, by the Tribunal of Conflict. It established the first apparition of public service, at least, its consecration as a key notion of administrative law and the competence of administrative jurisdiction. Much later, State interventions,

[61] Chapus, Rene, 2001, 579.

including those of local authorities, multiplied in diverse domains, notably, economic. Logically, the judge considered that even if these interventions were not previewed by law, and when their authors did not intend to create a public service, it was indeed, such a service.

This construction was unanimously considered by epoch jurist as the justification of public power and the prerogatives which it disposes. Duguit in particular, saw in the State, 'the cooperation of public services'. Hauriou, more reserved on the extension of service domains, saw in it the means to incite the State 'to obey nothing but public utility' by an 'auto–limitation purpose of its powers. The criterion of public service became socially useful, and a factor of democracy, and seemed to impose itself as a delimitation and legitimation of public action.

On the one hand, this corresponded to the ideology born of the Resistance, inspiring the preamble provision of the 1946 constitution. On the other hand, the original definition of public service as an activity of general interest, exercised by a public person, under the regime of administrative law was challenged. There was the emergence of services managed by public authorities applying the rules of private law (industrial and commercial public services). Besides, services conferred to private individuals submissive to rules of public law. These tendencies rendered the delimitation of frontiers became delicate.

However, the field of public services (and of public sector in the widest sense) depends greatly on political conceptions and thus have experienced grievous setbacks. The advocates of principle of free competition, the deregulation and privatisation movement challenge this essence of public service.[62]

## II. The different categories of public services

Public services are diverse according to the domains of intervention, and not by their forms.

### A. The domains of intervention

This classification is based on the sphere of activity of the public service. There exist a diversity of such activities.

---

[62] Legrand et Wiener, 2003,106.

**The regalian functions** came first and have never been contested, since they are inherent to the notion of sovereignty. These functions are in respect of justice, maintenance of public tranquillity, national defence and even the recovery of taxes. This recovery depends solely on the state machinery and the totality of public services.

**The sanitation and social services** had an analogous development with hospitals and the social welfare and social security services of the State and local authorities. It is in this sector that was born during the first decade of the 20th Century, what was called 'municipal socialism'. In this case, some municipalities put at the disposal of the poor inhabitants social services (public toilets, baths and holiday camps). As such, the State Council ruled their actions as legal, because they satisfied social needs, which private initiatives could not provide.

**Economic domain** was an initially controversial. The reticence in the intervention in this domain was because it was against the principle of freedom of trade and industry. Today, it is greatly accepted that the creation of public service does not constitute an unfair competition with the private sector, so long as it corresponds to the general interest.

**Education and cultural sector** can be public services. The law of the education public service has never been fundamentally contested. The preamble to the constitution has rendered it compulsory.[63] This initiative extends to research. The intervention in the cultural and leisure services, on the other hand, was considered at first as stepping on a domain reserved to private initiative. Today, it is considered a public service, as long as it is dominated by artistic representation of general interest.

## B. The legal classification

It rests on a binary distinction between administrative public services (*services publics administratifs*) (SPA) and those with an industrial or commercial character (*services publics à caractère industrial et commercial*) (SPIC). This distinction has a historical foundation, with SPA appearing first, but today, they do not respond to this clear logic,

---

[63] The free and secular organisation of national education at all levels is the responsibility of the State.

since certain services combine elements of the two categories. The legal regime of public services depends on the category.

## III. Management organs

Whatever their nature, public services can be managed by very different bodies. The modality of functioning can be equally different. The essential variable is their submission to public law or to private law. There is, however, an element of unity in the principles that govern their activities, and which is explained by the obligation to better serve the general interest, wherever they are found. The management can either be a public authority, a public body which emanates from it or a private person.

### A. Direct management by a public authority

It is when an authority (State or local authority) manages a public service, it is said that it is State–controlled. It is included in the system of the national authority and does not have a legal personality. It is accorded movable and immovable properties for the accomplishment of its mission. But it does not have financial autonomy, in the sense that its expenses and income appear in the budget of the authority, except that it chooses to append it in an annex budget. The guardian authority has the advantage of ensuring total control of the service. The inconvenience is that the service has no management autonomy.

### B. Public establishment

It is a moral person of public law under the State or a local authority, carrying out a public service on their behalf. There exist the following categories: Administrative Public Establishments or industrial and commercial {établissements publics administratifs (EPA) ou industriels et commerciaux (EPIC)}.

With respect to control, public establishment option offers several advantages. It provides great flexibility: endowed with moral personality and its own budget. It can easily adapt to the specificity of the service to which it is in charge, as well as the evolution of its needs. That is why this option is sometimes called 'decentralisation by service'. There is a relative autonomy in relation to the national authorities and the possibility for the representatives of service, users and personnel to participate in decision making as members of Board of Directors. The guardian authority does not lose its powers of direction, which it exercises in the form of directives and authorisation through the control of legality.

## C. Delegated management to a private body

Delegation can result from law, like the case of social security or from a contract. The latter mostly consist of service concessions which confides to a private body, the exploitation of this service. The contracts of delegation of a public service are always administrative contracts, and the authority that concludes the agreement, is bound to respect the procedure required to ensure public tender and competition of contenders. It is important to add that the authority disposes for the interest of the delegated service, several prerogatives towards the concessioner. These include fixing applicable tariffs to users, imposition of contract amendments, or still, anticipated contract termination if the service loses its utility, and obtaining regular reports on the activities and the finances of the service. On the other hand, the concessioner is bound to respect the general principles regulating the functioning of public services.

Management by a private body can be paradoxical, even abnormal, in relation to the notion of public service. This is when the nature of an offer is such that it can only be offered by a public body. This phenomenon is sometimes explained by the wish to inculcate private rules and methods and confer a responsibility to the interested quarters, like professional orders. It is important to point out that public authorities are at liberty, except provided otherwise by the law, to choose the form of management that they prefer, at a particular moment.

# IV. The nature and applicable law

On the basis of their nature and the management organ, services are regulated either by public law or by private law, with eventual combination of the two laws. On the one, we have Administrative Public Services (*Services publics administratifs*) (SPA) and Industrial or Commercial Public Services (*services publics industriels or commerciaux*) (SPIC) managed by a public authority. On the other hand those whose functioning is ensured by a private body.

### A. Administrative Public Services (SPA)

They are almost totally governed by administrative law.[64] It is the rules of administrative law that determines their organisation, the regime of acts they take and those of the property they hold. The personnel they employ are either civil servants or contract workers, but, who have the status of state agents. The relationships they have with their users are regulated by administrative law, and it is through this law that their responsibility is appreciated when the activities cause damage. However, there are always exceptions to these rules, when submission to private law is evoked in diverse cases.

### B. Industrial or Commercial Public Services (SPIC)

Here, the regime is mixed. As it is a public service, their status and property depends on administrative law, as well as their managers and accountants. But since their activities are industrial or commercial in nature, it is private law that regulates its personnel, its relationship with users and the responsibility that it incurs if it provokes damage. The contracts it enters are regulated by private law, but the judge has brought an exception to this rule: if the contract has as objective the fulfilment of a public works, or contains exorbitant clauses of common law, it shall be considered as administrative.

### C. Services under the management of private bodies

Logically, they escape in principle, from the rules of administrative law. They are only submissive to the relationship they have with their guardian authority, the unilateral acts that their status authorises them to take. For example, the authorisation to practice the profession of medicine given by the Order or the sanctions it pronounces. This can also be the case of the construction works that it carries out on account of the service, when it is a concessioner. Here again, the judge has added to this list, contracts by which it engages other private persons to execute part of this work.

---

[64] Administrative jurists believe that they are the "veritable public services."

## V. The 'laws' of public service

Except in cases where the existence of public services is rendered obligatory by the constitution (education, justice, police), or by parliament for what particularly concerns local authorities (social welfare, fire fighting), the creation of these services are left with the initiative of public powers. They equally have the power to terminate them, when the justifying circumstances no longer exist, or when implicated with a financial burden much heavy than their utility. As long as services are in activity, and whatever their management mode, they are submissive to functioning principles called the 'laws of Rolland' (lois de Rolland),[65] the name of the public law teacher who systematised them in the 30s. These principles are three in number: continuity, adaptation and equality of treatment of users.

### A. The principle of continuity

It is inherent to the vocation of services: once authorities recognise it as indispensable to the satisfaction of collective interest, it must function without interruption. This obligation is of a variable intensity according to the service, for instance it is strong for those who ensure security.

The obligation of continuity is at the origin of several stipulations of public law. It provides for example, that a government called to step down, has to ensure the fulfilment of current affairs until the constitution of a new government. It also substantiate the theory of 'civil servant by fact' and 'occasional collaborator' of service. In case of exceptional circumstances, all legal acts taken by a public agent acting *ultra vires* or by an individual shall be adopted. When an individual provides his free services to the service, the damage he caused or suffered shall be repaired by the application of more favourable rules of administrative responsibility without fault.

The regulation of the right to strike by civil servants is particularly the effective concretisation of the principle of continuity. This right is recognised by the constitution, in the context of the law that regulates it. This law has effectively intervened to ban strike action by certain category

---

[65] Legrand et Wiener, 2003, 109–111; Chapus, Rene, 2001, 604–609. These laws are named after Louis Rolland.

of agents like the police. It has also provided for 'minimum service' provision.[66]

### B. The principle of adaptation

It can be defined as the obligation of the service to be at all times ready to better satisfy collective interest to which it corresponds. This obligation is greatly influenced by the modalities of evolution of service and the changing circumstances.

Just like the principle of continuity, the principle of adaptation (mutability) applies to all forms of service management. It permits users to attack the refusal to take default measures if the service is no longer functioning satisfactorily.

### C. The principle of equality of users before the public service

Whether it concerns service offers or on the contrary constraints, this principle is directly linked to that of equality of citizens before the law proclaimed in 1789 and reaffirmed by the preamble to the constitution. Its position in the hierarchy of norms is eminent, given that the State Council sees in it, a general principle of law, and the constitutional Council, a principle of constitutional value.[67]

This principle constitutes a guarantee against arbitrariness, in the sense that there is ban in discriminatory treatments. The benefits of service offers are for everyone, without unjustifiable differences. When users find themselves in unequal situations, it is legal to provide different treatments. However, differential treatments are founded on the grounds of social vocation of service, which tends to offer services to those who otherwise could not afford. Examples include education priority zones.

## 3.2. The Administrative Police Powers

Simple in its principle, the notion of administrative police, nevertheless, turns out to be more complex in some of its implications. It

---

[66] He Council of State has qualified continuity as a "fundamental principle" in CE 13 June 1980, *Mme Bonjean.*

[67] C.C 18 September 1986, p 141, 15e Consid., which entails the neutrality of public services.

is not always easy to distinguish between the administrative and the judiciary police, nor between the respective powers of the diverse competent authorities in the matter. These powers are far reaching, for they condition in a wide range, the possibility of collective existence (the guarantee of human rights and of citizens, necessitate public force). But they have the risk of violation to public freedoms: that is why their exercise is regulated time and again by a plethora of protective rules.

## I. The domain of administrative police

This domain covers the activities destined to guarantee the maintenance of public order. This has been guaranteed by laws since time immemorial. Public order comprises three components: public security, public hygiene and public tranquillity. Therefore, it is aimed to prevent the risks of accidents, disorders affecting the quiet enjoyment of the inhabitants, or dangers to public health. But, as usual, certain activities have later appeared to endanger public order, but which do not truly fit in the existing framework. That is why the State Council has enlarged the traditional trilogy, with elements which it called public morality and the respect of the human person.

The activities for the maintenance of public order are of very different nature. Some are of a legal order, like bans or restrictions to ensure public hygiene. Others are of material order like traffic control. But with this latter example, it is important to distinguish between administrative police and judicial police.

The difference is theoretically clear: administrative police prevents violations of public order, whereas the judicial police has as objective to punish. The consequence of this distinction is logical: according to the constitutional principle of separation of powers, the judicial police is of the judicial authority and tribunals. But in practice, the distinction between the two activities is usually delicate. Firstly, they are carried out by the same persons: the police and gendarmes, and sometimes, Mayors act as administrative authorities and police officers or agents of judicial police. Further, it is not often easy to delineate these activities: the administrative police, may sometimes, not only prevent, but also punish the violation of public order, by dispersing a manifestation or expulsing an illegal immigrant. In the inverse, the judicial police prevents crimes, when for instance, it organises the surveillance of persons suspected to commit a crime. Finally, because there exist mixt operations, the same agents, during such operations, act successively in the name of the two polices. For example, when agent controlling road traffic (administrative police), identifies an offender (judicial police).

In this confused state, is born inextricable problems for individuals, when they have to determine the competent jurisdiction to obtain reparation for a damage which resulted from a police operation.

## II. The holders of administrative police powers

There exist different levels of territorial administration. The prefects were invested with these powers in their departments during the revolution. The mayors are exercising in their council areas since the law of 1884, retaken under the General Code for Territorial Collectivity. Otherwise, the State Council admitted in 1919 that the President of the Republic disposes of the same powers at the national level.

The exercise of these different competences does not go without some complexities. Firstly, if the police are municipal in small and medium councils, they are national in towns: the personnel are thus part of the national police, and the powers bestowed on the mayor to ensure public tranquillity are transferred to the prefect. Secondly, some domains are shared between several authorities: concerning road security. Prefects are in charge of national roads, presidents of general councils in charge of departmental roads, and mayors in charge of roads going across their council area. Finally, police powers are logically attributed to prefects for measures beyond council areas, like decisions restricting the consumption of water during droughts.

Further, there is sometimes coexistence, or to the contrary, combined police powers. On the one hand, in fact, the police with special powers have been instituted. A police with special powers normally takes precedence over a police with general powers, but if measures within the competence of the former are not taken, and which appear necessary, the latter takes over the rights.

On the other hand, there could be combination of the powers of the general police. The principle is that a local authority does not have the powers to take more liberal measures than those decided at the national level. But if she has the possibility, and the local circumstances so permit, can enact more rigorous dispositions. For example, the imposition of limitation on vehicle speeds, when they cross the town. Another example concerns a ban imposed on a film authorised at the national level.

## III. Conditions of exercise of administrative police

This police, because of its objective, obey an ambivalent regime. As it is indispensable to social life, the authorities who exercise it, dispose of wide powers. Nevertheless, because the acts through which they are concretised are just like others, susceptible to the violation of public freedoms, the legislator and the judge have put them under strict conditions of regularity.

### A. The prerogatives attached to the police

The administration can pronounce the closure of establishments, ban on sales or movement, even the requisition of premises, for example, to host persons who are victims of a disaster. She is equally right to forcefully enforce the measures taken, for example, the removal of vehicle or seizure of newspaper. Since these measures are not regarded as sanctions, their regularity are appreciated in accordance to existing laws. She therefore escapes from the principle of retroactivity of laws, eliminating or alleging sanctions that are applicable in the penal or disciplinary procedures.

### B. The rights of persons who are the objective of the measures are protected

These measures must naturally conform to general rules of substance and procedure regulating administrative acts, even if, emergency is often invoked by the administration to dispense with. But still, they equally have to obey specific principles, and those that are emitted by the administrative judge are applicable with particular vigilance.

On the one hand, it concerns those decisions that the administration does not have the power to take. On the other hand, more like in other domains of administrative activities, the judge demands that the measures taken be at the same time necessary and proportional to the situation.

Similarly, administrative police is viewed not only as a power, but equally as a responsibility. Prefects and mayors are under an obligation to oversee the application of regulations that themselves or superior authorities enacted. They are equally under an obligation to prevent or stop illegal incidents in the absence of relevant regulations. Failure engages the responsibility of the administration.

## 3.3. Administrative acts

The administration takes different categories of acts, which are subjected to particular legal regimes, dominated by the principle of legality. Some of these acts might have severe consequences on the users, thereby put under strict protective rules. The principal categories of administrative acts are unilateral administrative acts and administrative contracts.

## I. Unilateral administrative acts

The power of the administration is expressed by the right to take unilaterally administrative decisions, modifying the legal order and imposing rights and obligations on the citizens. These acts are of diverse nature and contents. They can be used to enforce the law or by virtue of an autonomous regulatory power, accord authorisations or infringe sanctions, applicable to all categories of persons, or only to determined individuals.

They are of two categories: the first group are those with a general scope, that is to say, regulations. The second group are those of individual decisions, which concerns only defined physical or moral persons, even if their impacts are felt by other people.

## A. Regulations

Just like laws, regulations are applicable to the whole community, like the ban on drugs or to a category of persons, like the Highway Code. The authorities with competence to enact regulations are either enumerated by the constitution or by special laws, that is to say, invested with at least part of this competence by the general rules which govern the organisation of the administration. We have for example, the regulatory powers of the Prime Minister; the regulatory powers of mayors, prefects and Independent Administrative Authorities (AAI) and finally the regulatory powers of ministers.

The administration is in a position to enact regulatory texts. But the regulatory power, like all the powers of the administration, has its finality, the general interest. As this power is full of prerogatives, it constitutes a mission which the administration cannot dispense of, and in certain hypothesis, a duty. The administration is in a position to act within a reasonable time on the textual stipulations, and its responsibility can be engaged in case of prolonged inaction.[68]

The exercise of regulatory power is equally obligatory in the fulfilment of administrative police powers, when public security and health demands. For a long time, the administrative judge regarded that the responsibility of the administration could only be engaged if the inaction of the administration constituted a grievous fault. Nowadays, the judge has reviewed its position, by admitting that a simple fault is sufficient.

## B. Individual decisions

They are those that concretise general rules, by their application to individuals. The word 'individual' all the same, should not be taken to the letter, because it equally includes decisions that concern several persons. For instance, an advancement decision or the list of successful candidates in a public exams: they have a collective character, but nevertheless classified in the individual decision category because the persons concerned are designated by name. At the inverse, a ministerial order determining the competence of the head of a department is considered a regulation, for it makes reference not only to the holder of the position, but also the successors. There equally exist decisions which the judge considers neither as regulations nor individual decisions. For example, a decree pronouncing the dissolution of a municipal council or still a decision classifying a site. These uncertainties damage the clarity of the law, and can have concrete damaging consequences, notably, when need arises to determine the competent judge.

---

[68] See the case of *Dame veuve Renard*, Council of State of 27 November 1964.

## II. Administrative Contracts

Also, the administration can, in the accomplishment of the mission incumbent on it, enter into contracts. Some of these contracts are not different from those entered between individuals, for example, a contract for the supply of office equipment. Such are generally placed under the regime of private law. Otherwise, others are entered in the domains which constitute the essence of administrative activities, for example, a concession for the management of a public service. It stands–in as a consequence of public law, and the regime to the administration has prerogatives which are not of an individual nature.

The increase in missions incumbent on the administration has led to the increasing number of contracts. State and local services constitute today the major part of the clientele of private enterprises. There exist domains where recourse to contracts is impossible, for example, the recruitment of civil servants, but, in reality, they can intervene in the different sectors, for diverse reasons. We can distinguish two categories: administrative contracts submissive to public law, and contracts of private law. The legal regimes are completely different; however, the borders are sometimes imprecise, when

### A. The criteria of administrative contracts

There is no difficulty to qualify a contract, when this is done by the law. This is the case of public works contracts and agreements to occupy a public domain. In other cases, the nature of the contracts is determined by the judge. The method of classification is thus: they have in principle, administrative characteristics, contracts which are entered between two public persons; it is the same for those which have as objective, the fulfilment of a public service or whose performance contains exorbitant clauses of common law.

- ✓ The first criterion results from the quality of the co–contractors

This is the most direct, and results when a contract is concluded between two moral persons of public law (appended in principle with an administrative character). At the inverse, given that two private persons can only enter into private contracts, it is different when one of them can be considered as acting, even indirectly, 'on behalf' of a public person.

✓ The second criterion is on the objective of the contract

It rest on the notion of public service: a contract passed between two moral persons of public law is administrative if it has as objective, the fulfilment of a public service.

✓ The third criterion is on the terms of the contract

If the administration concludes a contract as if it were a private person, for example, a contract for the supply of goods, such a contract is reputed as a private law contract. If on the contrary, exorbitant terms of common law are included (that is to say, its reserved prerogatives, which are not found in agreements between private individuals) the contract is administrative.

## B. The legal regime of contracts

It comprises for the administration, prerogatives and also subjection (submission).

✓ The subjections

On the one hand, there exist strict competent rules of application. The authorities fit to engage the State or local authorities are limitedly enumerated by laws (for the former, we have ministers and prefects and the latter, mayor for the council and the president of the deliberative assembly for the division or region), for authorisation to act. On the other hand, similar strict rules of procedure guide the choice of co–contractors, to prevent favouritism and to properly manage public goods: competition, publicity of operations and the offer of priority to the 'best' are obligatory.

✓ The prerogatives of the administration over its co–contractors

The purpose of the administration is for the general interest, and thus, it can exercise control on the activities of the co–contractor. If it is a public works contract, and it can give the co–contractor 'mission orders' and eventual financial sanctions in case of in–execution. It equally benefits from the power of unilateral termination of the contract, for fault committed during execution, or when it thinks that the execution does not correspond to the needs of the service (the co–contractor, in this case, has the right of indemnity). Finally, the administration can modify the terms of the contract, if circumstances have changed since the conclusion date. In such a situation, the administration must indemnify the co–contractor for the additional imposed charge. But if co–contractor rejects the new contractual conditions, the administration can terminate the contract and confer it to another enterprise.

## III. The rules applicable to administrative acts

Whatever the nature of the act that the administration is about to take, the legal regime to which they are submitted have important common characteristics: Each of these acts must respect superior norms, as well as rules of procedure and the substance they intend to protect, the general interest or as usual, the rights of citizens.

### A. The hierarchy of norms

The notion of law implicate that no rule should contradict an act superior to it. The constitution is at the apex of national norms and in line with control of constitutionality cannot be infringed by a law. A general rule has more status than ones that govern particular cases. For a long time, the obligatory respect of the hierarchy of norms was in line with the principle of legality, since it was from the law alone that the administration had to conform its actions. But today, this appellation is not exact, because new norms of reference have progressively appeared. The constitution, in particular, its preamble; a body of rules that could be qualified as deontological, as proffered by the State Council and referred to as general principles of law, Further and more recently, duly incorporated international conventions. The sources of 'legality' are, therefore, multiple; but the importance of the principle is on the manner in which the judge assures its respect, which remains unchanged.

The principal norms, to which the administration is subjected, are: the constitution, general principles of law, laws, and international conventions. In addition to the abovementioned, there are other sources to which administrative acts must conform to. The first results from the fact that the hierarchy of norms follows that of the authorities in charge of their enactment. The decree of a minister imposes on a ministerial order, which itself imposes on regulations taken by deconcentrated authorities like prefects. The second comprises of judicial decisions. Jurisdictional decisions evidently impose on the administration, which has the powers to abrogate or modify regulations declared illegal. This is to stop the annulled decision and to eventually repair the damage which it caused.

## B. The legal framework of acts

The rules applicable to the enactment of administrative acts, whether from the legislator or the judge are many. On the one hand, the need to protect individual interest above the traditional right of defence, which has led to the enforcement of exigencies, imposes the following administrative procedures. On the other hand, the wish to instil transparency in decision processes and to authorise access to documents it produced and in its keeping. Attention is equally placed on the manner in which the administration takes its decisions.

### 1. The general principles of administrative procedure

✓ The competent authorities

Whatever the decision, it must be taken by the authorities charged to that effect. Incompetence is determined in relation to the objective of the act; the place of effects; and finally the date it was taken.

✓ The process of decision elaboration

It is bound to numerous rules, one on the assurance of the quality of the decision by the production of notices from the competent technical organisation or from the milieu concerned, and another, which makes the process more contradictory than unilateral.

✓ The cooperative character of the procedure

This results from the difficulties that individuals could suffer from the complexity in the circuit of administrative machinery. It gives a service the obligation to re–orientate a document to another service which is competent, in case it was addressed to it by error. This obligation is completed by that made by the competent service to show proof of acknowledgment of receipt.

✓ Decisions must be written, dated and signed by the authors

The decisions have to be written to ensure administrative continuity and the signature provides the authenticity regarding the author of the text.

- ✓ Reasons must be given for individual unfavourable decision

Decisions must indicate the legal reasons and motives which led their author to act as such. In case of problem, aids the judge in his control, who can easily detect errors. It equally limits the administration to take decisions adapted to the existing circumstances.

- ✓ Administrative acts must be brought to the knowledge of users

Regulatory acts are subject to publication, either on the official publications, if it is of a general interest, or in the administrative bulletins, if their field of application is much limited, because of their objective. Individual decisions are personally notified to those concerned.

### 2. The obligation of transparency

The administration has for a long time lived under the sign and protection of secrets. As a depository of the general interest, it was considered that it should be free from individual pressure, and should render no accounts to the citizens on the manner in which it functions. Apart from an express authorisation by the law, no one, except the control organs could access documents which were in its keeping. The situation changed at the end of the 60s, under the influence of two convergent schools of thoughts: On the one hand, the awareness on the risk that the development of the computer system and interconnection of files could engender on individual freedoms. On the other hand, the general worry to democratise public management, by giving it a transparent character. Two laws adopted in 1978 responded to these preoccupations: the law of 6 January 1978 relative to Information System, Files and Freedoms and the law of 17 July 1978 on the Freedom to Access Administrative Documents.

## 3.4 The Administrative Justice in France

Administrative justice in France has evolved from sovereign immunity to rule of law and from administrative hearings to court trails. In France, article 7 of the law of 22 December 1789 held that the local administrations should not be troubled in the exercise of their administrative functions by any judicial power. The law on the judicial organization of 16–24 August 1790 stated that "The judiciary functions are and remain separated from the administrative functions." The legislative assembly in a Decree of the 16 Fructidor An III, cancelled court judgements against the members of the administrative corps and declared that it is prohibited for the courts to rule on administrative acts. It was the King for a long–time that decided on administrative litigations as the hierarchical superior. It is in Year VIII that his decisions were prepared by a judicial council; the *Conseil d'Etat* (CE) which was followed up by the king. In 1872 the C.E became a jurisdictional organ with its proper authority. Article 9 of the law of 27 July 1872 states: The C.E decides with sovereignty on the petitions of administrative disputes.

In simple terms, cases concerning the administration were done essentially through hearings. When an administered contests a decision taken by an administrative authority within the administrative system, this is qualified administrative hearings (*recours administratif*). This can be done first before the person who took the contested decision (*recours gracieux*) and second before the hierarchical superior of the person who took the contested decision (*recours hiérarchique*).

The court trials (*recours contentieux*) are distinct from at least three perspectives: they are submitted to the judge who provides a ruling on the case. The ruling must be based on pre–established legal principles. The hearing must follow strict conditions of time, form and procedure.

The competence of tribunals and the law they apply, are in principle, inseparable. Just like the administration is generally submissive to public law, but that some of its acts are under private law, it can be judged by either jurisdictional orders. It is therefore important to review the jurisdictional organisation and the functioning of administrative justice.

## I. Jurisdictional organisation

There exist in France, two jurisdictional orders: judicial jurisdiction is under the supreme authority of the Court of Cassation *(Cour de Cassation*), which has the power to annul decisions of the lower levels Courts. The administrative jurisdiction headed by the Council of State and comprises of simple administrative courts and with recent reforms, the Administrative Courts of Appeal and Specialized Courts.

## A. Jurisdictional duality

The principle of separation of administrative and judicial authorities is an illustration of the principle of separation of powers. The Constitutional Court has repeatedly judged that it constitutes a fundamental principle and that any petition aimed at annulling a decision taken by a public authority or public body, can only be under the administrative justice system.

From a simple principle, the distinction between the domain of the administrative judge and the judicial judge appears to be a source of complication in reality. For instance, the State Council appeared to be very close to the administration, making it difficult to be confided issues concerning individual interest. On the one hand, economic interventionism has led to the extension of the powers of the administration, but whose exercise is confided to private persons. Since it is considered that her decisions constitute a form of public power exercise, thereby affirming the competence of the judge in internal recourses against such decisions.

The limits between the competences of the two orders are usually vague, and not easy to clearly demarcate. In an attempt to simplify the competences, many complications arise. Since the start of the 19$^{th}$ century, road accidents linked to public works operations were of administrative judge. Imagine a situation where a bulldozer involved in public works operations crashes on a private vehicle; is it a traffic accident, engaging the competence of a judicial judge or a public works accident engaging an administrative judge?

We see then that there is a need to find an arbitrator to regulate eventual 'conflicts' of competence between the different jurisdictional orders. This arbitrator existed since the law of 24 May 1872. It is the Tribunal of conflicts.

## B. Tribunal of Conflicts

It is an equal representation tribunal composed of eight permanent members, half elected from amongst the judges of the final court of Appeal and half from the judges of the State Council.

The risk of having equal pairs is the impossibility to have a majority in the tribunal. It might happen that there is a parity of four against four, requesting a ninth person to separate the two camps. This person is the honorary president of the Tribunal of Conflicts, the Minister f Justice, Keeper of the Seals. He is never on sit, except during formal ceremonies (installation of the tribunal after fresh elections of its members) and when there is the need to separate the parity.

In principle, this tribunal is a special tribunal in that it does not hear cases. It simply rules over conflicts of attribution, that is to say, which jurisdictional order will hear the matter submitted to it. It is in exceptional circumstances that in ruling over conflict of decisions, it actually judges the substance of a case.

## 1. Conflicts of attribution of competence

They are of two types

✓ Positive conflicts attribution

It is a conflict between the administration and the judicial judge, concerning the competence of the latter. It arises when a judicial tribunal has been seized of a matter, and the administrative authority is of the opinion that it is not of judicial competence. This was the situation in the *Blanco case*.

Then, it is naturally the administration which engages a conflicts procedure. The prefect of the department where the adjudging judicial tribunal is found intervenes by addressing to the public prosecutor a 'competence declination' asking the tribunal to declare its incompetence. If the tribunal rejects the declination, meaning it considers itself competent, it shall defer judgement for fifteen days, to give the prefect time to prepare a reasoned 'conflict order'. The keeper of the seals then seizes the Tribunal of Conflict which has two options. It can 'annul' the conflict order, which then permits the judicial judge to continue examining the case. Or 'confirms' it which obliges the petitioner to seize the administrative jurisdiction within two months following the ruling of the tribunal.

✓ Negative conflicts attribution

It opposes the two jurisdictional orders. It is therefore, not the contrary of positive conflicts, which is an opposition between a judicial judge and the administration.

A litigant has successively seized both an administrative tribunal and a judicial tribunal on the same matter, and each declaring its incompetence. Each tribunal pointing that to its opinion, it is of the competence of the other jurisdiction. The litigant now seizes the Tribunal of Conflict to decide on the fact that one of the jurisdictional orders erred. The tribunal annuls one of the decisions and sends back the litigant to the jurisdiction that passed it.

To facilitate things, a decree of 25 July 1960 has instituted what is known as two '*renvoi* proceedings'. The first is obligatory, when one jurisdiction passes a declaration of incompetence, and the jurisdiction of the other order has been seized of the matter, it does not have to pass another declaration of incompetence. It has to immediately seize the tribunal of conflicts to determine the jurisdictional competence. This procedure is applied by all jurisdictional degrees (first instance, appeal). It has, therefore, removed the hypothesis of negative conflict, which is now encountered only in exceptional circumstances.

The second renvoi proceeding is facultative and is applicable by the Final Appeal Court or the Council of State. When an issue raises a serious jurisdictional competence, one of these jurisdictions can seize the Conflicts Tribunal to solve the matter.

## 2. Conflict of decisions

Three times after 1872, failure has been observed in jurisdictional procedure. A litigant seizes a first jurisdiction, the latter did not declare its incompetence, but passed its judgement. The litigant then seizes another order, this time, the administrative jurisdiction, which considered itself competent and in return ruled on the matter. Here there are two contradictory judgements from the two jurisdictional orders, depriving the litigant the possibility to obtain reparation. This constitutes a denial of justice.

To remedy this situation, illustrated by the *Rosay case*, the legislator voted the law of 20 April 1932. This law authorises the litigant in such cases to seize the Tribunal of Conflicts to adjudge on the substance of the case, to resolve the contradiction and to pass a definitive ruling on the matter.

## II. The structure of administrative jurisdiction

The Council of State was created by the constitution of year VIII. It had two essential functions: consultative and jurisdictional. Following two important reforms in 1953 and 1987, administrative tribunals, and then administrative court of appeal were created, thereby strongly influencing the role of the Council of State. Today, the organisation and the functioning of administrative justice are regulated by the Code of Administrative Justice, enacted by an ordinance and decrees of 4$^{th}$ May, 2000.

### A. Organisation of the Council of State

The Council of State comprises around 300 members. Some are recruited after graduation from ENA as junior officials of the Council, and later become petition masters (maître requête). To diversify its personnel, about one quarter of its workers are recruited from amongst civil servants who have at least ten years' experience in the civil service and above thirty years of age.

The petition masters become State councillors, as vacancies appear. At the Council, advancement is in accordance to longevity in service, in the order of the roll. This situation is considered as a guarantee of independence against the public power. One third of the position of councillors can be given to external persons of at least 45 years old. Adding to its members, are twelve councillors in extraordinary service, appointed by reason of their competences, for four years by a decree of Council of Ministers.

The Council of State is presided in theory by the Prime Minister (who takes part only during formal ceremonies), and done by the vice president, appointed by a Council of Ministers amongst the State Councillors in ordinary service. It is comprised of five administrative sections, which have to carry out consultative functions: interior, finance, public works, social and reporting and studies section. Consultations are obligatory for all law and decree projects.

In addition there is the litigation section which carries out the jurisdictional function. Councillors in extraordinary service do not participate in jurisdictional function. When a matter is of particular importance, it is submitted to the general assembly of the Council, which comprises the vice president, the six section presidents and the 28 councillors in ordinary service. In the case of emergency, a more restraint formation, known as the permanent commission seats.

## B. Reforms on competences

Administrative justice has been a victim of its success. For a long time, the Council of State was a common law judge in administrative matters. The result was a floodgate of cases before it. A decree–law of 30th September 1953, then instated a first degree of jurisdiction of administrative tribunals (making a total of 35 in France and overseas). The Council of State therefore becoming an appellate jurisdiction. It did not solve the flooding problem, and a law of 31st December 1987, led to a new reform, creating a new degree of jurisdiction, administrative courts of appeal (we have seven in number), making the Council of State principally a final judge of appeal. Its organisation, therefore, resembles that of judicial justice, except that the Council still possess some attributes of a court of first instance or a judge of appeal.

## C. The attributes of the Council of State

It has always been an appellate jurisdiction. As an appellate judge, its function essentially consists to verify the conformity to law of decisions rendered by lower jurisdictions. It is therefore, not a judge of fact. But, for proper administration of justice, it can act as a judge of fact.

Although the administrative tribunals are courts of first instances in administrative matters, exceptionally, the legislator has allowed the Council of State to continue to be a judge of first instance, for severally reasons. It is before it that are brought recourse in annulment of decrees, regulatory acts of ministers or those of national competitive examination juries. These are of capital importance and are of national application, thereby needing the jurisdiction of a supreme and national order. It also concern litigations from abroad. Its decisions are final and not susceptible to appeal.

Despite the existence of administrative courts of appeal, the Council of State still has some competence of a judge of appeal against certain decisions of the administrative courts for the recourse against municipal or local elections. By reducing the degree of jurisdiction into two for recourse against elections, the legislator did not want to eternalise litigations.

## III. The competence of judicial judge on administrative matters

In principle, only the administrative judge is competent to judge the administration. There are situations, where this rule has exceptions. Apart from the fact that this exception results from the law, notably in matters of responsibility of public authority, there are others for diverse reasons.

### A. Reasons of a constitutional order

The principle of separation of powers holds that the administrative judge does not have the competence to judge the functioning of the judicial public service. For this reason, it is incompetent to appreciate the validity of judgements of judicial jurisdictions, and all other acts it prepares and executes. This is even so, when these acts are accomplished in irregular conditions, and constitutes an eventual service fault. The responsibility of the administration, in such cases, can only be engaged before the judicial jurisdiction.

To this effect, the administrative judge has to declare itself incompetent to engage the responsibility of the administration during judicial police operations, for the search of those culpable of an offence and to refer to the criminal justice system. Also, preparatory and executory acts are not of the competence of administrative judge. Nevertheless, judicial competence does not only arise from acts which result directly from judicial acts.

### B. Exceptions resulting from court rulings

It has been noted that judges exempt from the competence of the administrative judge and the application of administrative law litigations born of the activities of industrial and commercial public service. This is so for the simple reason that the administration manages them in the same conditions like any other private enterprise. This extends to repartition principles in other important domains relating to individual rights.

In addition, all questions relating to the civil status are under the judicial judge. He is also competent or charged with the protection of fundamental liberties and property rights.

### C. Where the solution to a dispute depends on another question

When a matter is brought before a judge, it might happen that the solution depends on another incident which has to be regulated first, before the principal issue. There exist two types of questions of this type: When the issue can be resolved by a judge seized of the principal question, it is said that it is a preliminary question. On the contrary, when it can only be resolved by another judge, it is said that it is prejudicial. In the first case, the judge resolves the preliminary question and the principal question. In the second case, he shall first instead defer judgement, and send the prejudicial question before the competent judge and then await his response to treat the principal matter. Further, legal experts have made a distinction between two types of judicial tribunals. Unlike civil judges, the criminal judge can on the contrary, appreciate the legality of administrative acts to which the solution to the question depends, whether individual or regulatory.

## IV. The general rules of litigation procedure

The procedure before the administrative judge is less formal, as far as the submission of complaints is concerned: It may comprise of a simple letter, and the request for a lawyer is rarely sort. The judge has wide discretion and the procedure is inquisitorial, with the assistance of the claimant. There, however, exits conditions of delay and formulation of request, to which claimants must conform.

### A. Applications to the courts

First, the petitions must comprise the means and conclusions. The petition must indicate what the administration acted irregularly or faulty, and what is expected of the judge. When the claimant fails to invoke the illegal motive, it will not be done so for him, except it is of a public order.

The judge does not insist on the claimant to produce irrefutable proofs to support his claim, because it is difficult to produce such documents from the administration. It is for this reason that the inquisitorial procedure is used, where the judge asks the administration to explain itself, failing which, the request is considered founded.

Second, the recourse must be directed against a decision. As a consecrated formula, the litigation must be directed to a prior decision. In the absence of such, the claimant must provoke a decision by the relevant application before the competent public authority. Silence of the administration for two months can be considered as a decision against which a litigation is possible.

### B. Conditions of admissibility of recourse

These conditions are as regards quality, time limit and procedure of examination.

#### 1. The interest to act

It is very liberally appreciated: it can be material or moral, immediate or foreseeable, individual or collective. All physical or moral persons can contest an act before the judge, even if not directly concerned and the group of those concerned is constantly enlarged by the judge.

#### 2. Recourse prescription period

As a general rule, it is two months from the date of notification of the individual decision or the publication of the regulatory act that the claimant can contest.

#### 3. The procedure of recourse examination

This procedure is written and contradictory: During preliminary examination by the judge, there is an exchange between the claimant and the administration, each knowing the arguments brought by the others. The intentions of the parties are taken down by a judicial officer which serve as the bases of fact and law during the public hearing. Lawyers are only admitted to speak before the Council of State where they are allowed to develop the arguments raised at the preliminary examination. After which the Government commissioner presents with all independence, his conclusions, that is to say, a legal and factual analysis of the case, supported by a proposed solution. The case is then put under deliberations (in camera) and then the decision is written and rendered public.

## C. The effects of the recourse

Petitions do not have a 'suspensive effect', that is to say, it does not stop the execution of the contested decision, even when it is impregnated with huge consequences.

On the other hand, the effects of jurisdictional decisions are important and immediate. They have compulsive nature (autorité de choses jugée), to which the administration must submit. The decisions annulled, whether individual or collective, lost their effects. The indemnities accorded must be paid; and the judge disposes several means to put pressure on the administration. The judge can impose a date limit for enforcement, failing which, each passing day; there are penalties to be paid. Besides, the claimant can seize the court that passed the decision, if the delay of three months has passed without enforcement, due to the bad faith of the administration. The court can pass an injunction, accompanied by forced enforcement. The end result however depends on the type of litigation in question, whether recourse for power abuse of responsibility.

## V. Litigations against abuse of power

This action can be brought against any administration for diverse reasons.

## A. The fields of recourse

It is particularly vast, because it covers the unilateral administrative acts of the highest public authorities, like those of low authorities, as well as regulations and individual decisions. However, three categories of decisions are excluded. We have 'acts of government' which are decisions not under an administrative action and measures of an internal order which only concern the users of a particular institution, without serious consequences. Finally, we have administrative contracts, which are bilateral acts, and therefore, under a special litigation regime.

## B. The means of annulment

The means of annulment can be of external or external of irregularity. The external comprises of the incompetence of the author of the act or non–respect of formalities or procedure. It should be noted that non–respect of formalities does not nullify an illegal decision, if it is not substantial. That is to say, those that have an influence on the writing or the substance of the act. For example, the need for a prior notice or a reasoned report, before the decision is taken.

Internal irregularity comes about as a result of the absence of a legal foundation of the act, or an error of fact committed by its author, or the pursuit of the latter of a goal which is not in conformity to general interest.

### C. Control intensity

The judge does not control at the same degree all administrative acts. To some, he exercises a restraint control on the exactitude of the material facts which motivated the decision. In others, the judge exercises a deeper control, which he generally qualifies as normal control, which includes the qualification of facts. Here, the judge chooses the solution which he thinks is best adapted to the situation at hand.

In case of grievous compromise, the judge has adopted the notion of a manifestly appreciated error, which permits him to sanction the errors he thinks are grievous and evident. This is further manifested, when the judge carries out an advanced control, which focuses on the proportionality of the measures adopted.

### D. The consequences of recourse

The decision of a rejected recourse benefits the authority in relation to the thing judged. The claimant cannot longer engage another recourse on the same facts. In case of an annulment decision, the authority is absolute: the decision disappears from the legal periodicals, and this consequence is in principle retroactive (retrospective), since the decision was attached with illegality from the onset. However, this consequence is grounded with serious difficulties.

## VI. Litigations on responsibility

It is often said that the administration cannot be held responsible, except expressly provided by a law. With time, this immunity appeared abnormal and unjust, and the *Blanco case* expressly provided the reverse principle.

## A. The bases of responsibility

Like in civil law, the existence of a fault having provoked a prejudice obliges an obligation of compensation. Further, however, the administration admits that a prejudice can be compensated without fault.

### 1. Responsibility with fault

The issue is to whom the fault is attributable, to the agent or the body to which he functions. The *Blanco case* held that the responsibility has to be appreciated by taking into consideration the necessity to reconcile the rights of the State with individual rights. The later evolution has been favourable to users, where the administration, by working definition, sees its responsibility engaged either in the place of its agents or concurrent with them.

✓ Fault which can be attributed to the agents

In this category, there are personal and service faults. Personal fault is committed by the agent out of service and without connection to it. It can still be committed through service, but with the intention to harm a third party, with an inadmissible gravity. A service fault is committed by an individual agent in the framework of his service, which does not engage his personal responsibility. This allows for better compensation and unjustifiable attacks against the agents. Further, there can be a combination of fault committed by an agent, engaging his personal and service fault.

✓ Fault exclusively imputable to the administration

They are called services faults. The administration acts through the intermediary of agents, and it is through them that the administration is found at fault, but precise responsibilities are at time difficult to determine. Such anonymous character of fault can be found in the hypothesis where for instance, the mal functioning of rescue unit, or excessive delay in the execution of a jurisdictional decision or the enactment of a text of application of a law and all other omissions and negligence.

### 2. Responsibility without fault

This notion is without doubt, one of the most original and progressive of administrative law. It consists of admitting that a person who has suffered from injury be compensated, without proving the existence of fault. Even if the administration proves the contrary, that it is not at fault: a simple causation link between the damage and the fact in issue, suffices to obtain compensation. The responsibility without fault is recognised under two hypotheses: when the administration engages in risky situations or ventures, and when there is a rupture in the equality before public charges.

## B. Conditions of enforcement of responsibility

There are conditions of substance and those of procedure. The conditions of substance relate principally on the nature of the prejudice suffered. It must be direct ad certain. It must be capable of being evaluated in monetary terms. The conditions of procedure concerns the determination of the authority at fault. The other rules of litigation procedure are the same, except that on recourse prescription period: it is four years.

The compensation accorded by the judge covers in principle, the integral prejudice suffered, but which cannot be above the evaluation done by the claimant. No compensation is payable, when the damage is imputable to a force majeure.

# Part Two
# Administrative Organization in Cameroon

Politically and administratively State structures have to be organized in different ways in order to ensure coherence, authority, coordination, participation and performance. Politically, when the constitution divides competences between many levels like the case in the United States and Germany, there is the federal form of State. On the contrary, if the political competences are concentrated at the central level so that there is only one centre of power impulsion, the State is said to be of the unitary form. Administratively, the technique depends on the distribution of administrative competences between the state levels, central and non–central. Centralization, deconcentration and decentralization are the key words of administrative organization. The imperative of bringing the administration nearer to the people renders the use of deconcentration and decentralization inevitable. Each administrative technique has corresponding administrative authorities, individuals or groups of individuals who have the competence to act in the name of administrative entities. Although the legal approach is adopted it is worth mentioning that the literature of decentralization, deconcentration and devolution is confusing and at times inconsistent. Some authors use the terms interchangeably, and to others devolution and deconcentration are part of administrative decentralization. For the purposes of this study, the French approach is adopted which clearly distinguishes the concepts. The 1996 Cameroonian Constitution states in its article 1(2) that; "The Republic of Cameroon shall be a decentralized unitary State. It shall be one and indivisible, secular, democratic and dedicated to social service." All States with different degree of successes attempt to centralize the management of the public service. Power flows from the summit through the non–central authorities or external services to the bottom. The Decree

N 2008/376 of 12 November 2008 establishes the Administrative Organization of the Republic of Cameroon in line with the aforementioned techniques.

# Chapter Four
# The Administrative Organization of The Cameroonian State

The central government ensures coordination and avoids anarchy through hierarchical controls of the deconcentrated authorities and supervision or tutelage controls of the decentralized authorities. The Cameroonian laws details the organization and functioning regarding each of these techniques

## 4.1 Administrative Centralization: Central Administrative Authorities

The central authorities in Cameroon are mainly the President of the Republic and attached services, the Prime Minister and the attached services and the ministers.

### I. The President of the Republic and Attached Services

The reality of the Cameroonian political regime being presidentialist entails that the President is the pivot of all institutions. He is the head of state, chairman of ruling party, magistracy, armed forces and administration. Law N. 06 of 18 January 1996 to amend the Constitution of 2 June 1972, in its article 8 continuous with the tradition of article 9 of the 1972 Constitution to hold the President of the Republic as the supreme directing person of the administration. He is the supreme head of the administration and exercises this power through regulatory and individual acts. Since the President of the Republic cannot effectively exercise all powers incumbent on him, there is the necessity of delegation of competence.

### A. The Administrative Attributions of the President

As the 1972 constitution (art 9), the 1996 revised constitution (art 8) gives the President enormous powers which he can exercise using regulatory and individual acts.

#### 1. Regulatory Acts

The President is the principal, if not the exclusive holder of regulatory powers. This is the most important power of the President. It is the power to edict general norms, susceptible to be applied throughout the national territory and in all matters except those reserved for the legislature. It is on the exercise of this regulatory (statutory) authority that the President sets up and organizes the administrative services of the State. On this title he sets–up, regulates and directs all administrative services necessary for the fulfilment of his task {Art.8 (9).}

#### 2. Individuals Acts

This is the power of appointment which is usually an individual act. The constitution states clearly that he shall appoint to civil and military posts of the State. All the decrees to organize the government after the constitutional revision confirm that; "The President of the Republic, Head of State, appoints the Prime Minister and, on his proposal, the other members of the government. He puts an end to their functions." As the President cannot effectively exercise all this attributions attempts have been made since 1975 to decongest and coordinate state's services within the presidency and with the creation of the Prime Minister's office.

### B.The Presidency of the Republic

The President is assisted in the administrative functions by services of the presidency. The presidency is composed of many structures. But in general administrative matters, there exist notably the general secretariat, civil cabinet and minister delegates. As far as the administrative functions are concerned, the general secretariat at the presidency is the most important body. It is headed by the Secretary General who exercises three fundamental functions of coordination, collaboration, and judicial adviser:

- He coordinates the activities of the ministerial departments to ensure global coherence of administrative action;
- As the privileged collaborator of the President, he receives directives from the latter and watches the execution of decisions made by him;
- He is legal adviser to the government and ensures the respect of legality.

These are attempts to solve the problem of "coordination and congestion". The Secretary General usually receives delegation of powers and the assistant Secretary Generals delegation of signature.

## II. The Prime Minister Office and its Services

The post of Prime Minister (P.M) in Cameroon has been subject to vicissitudes, created and dissolved to adapt to the political environment of the time. The amendment of the 1972 constitution by law N° 75/1/ of 9 May 1975 created the post of Prime Minister in Cameroon. But the Prime Ministers services were suppressed after the constitutional reform of 1984. However, these services were created again with Law No 9/001 of 23 April 1991 amending articles 5, 7,8,9,26,27 and 34 of the constitution.

The1996 Constitution states the functions of the P.M as follows:

- He shall be responsible for the enforcement of laws
- He shall exercise statutory authority and appoint to civil posts, subject to the prerogatives of the President of the Republic in such areas.
- He shall direct all the government services required for the accomplishment of his duties (art. 12).

The Prime Minister in Cameroon is not like that of a parliamentary regime. The government which is headed by the P.M has to "implement the policy of the Nation as defined by the President of the Republic (art 11). The recent decrees to organize government confirm that; The Prime Minister heads the government's action. The Government is responsible for the implementation of the national policy as defined by the President of the Republic.The post of Prime Minister can be seen as the administrative deconcentration of presidential powers in certain domains.

The Prime Minister is assisted by main collaborators notably the Chief of Cabinet, the Secretary General and Assistant; Technical Advisers, personalities in charge of missions, and attached personalities in the accomplishment of his functions. There are also directorates, divisions, services, and secretariats which carry specific functions in the Prime Minister's Office. In general the attached services are: The Higher Authority of the Public Service; the National Commission on Human Rights and Freedoms; Observatory on the Fight against Corruption, National Programme on Governance; and National Communication Council. Besides, the Service in charge of stabilization Plan and Economic Stimulus was recently attached.

### III. Ministerial Departments

According to Alain Bockel, the Ministerial department is the result of a conjunction of two principles: division of labour and hierarchy. First, the different missions of the State are divided in large sectors of homogenous activities (specialization and responsabilization). Second, the totality of services grouped under the authority of a politico–administrative personality, the Minister. The Ministerial department is therefore a totality of hierarchized and similar missions grouped under the authority of a Minister. The ministerial departments are in a sort of performance contract with the government in their specific spheres.

#### A The Number of Departments

The creation or suppression of ministerial departments depends on the following factors: scope and nature of government activity; preoccupation of administrative efficacy; for example division of large ministries so as to ensure sound management; ephemeral or durable importance given to a problem or an event e.g. Ministry of construction after war, Ministry of Plan and Stabilization; political preoccupations by ensuring equilibrium within governments notably party or regional; consideration of some persons or satisfaction of pressure groups.

The number of ministerial departments is therefore not fixed by law. This accounts for the frequent transformations in their number, nature and designations.

## B Hierarchy and Structure of Departments

An analysis of the organization of government in Cameroon shows differences in the appellation of the heads of departments. The recent decrees to organize government are consistent with its composition including:

- The Prime Minister
- The Vice Prime Ministers, if applicable;
- Ministers of State, if applicable
- The Ministers;
- The Ministers without portfolio;
- The Ministers in charge of Missions;
- The Minister Delegates;
- The Secretaries of State.

This is logically the formal hierarchy of members of government. Ministers without portfolio, Ministers in charge of Missions are under the direct authority of the President to accomplish specific missions. The minister delegates are placed, as the case may be, under the authority of the President of the Republic, the Prime Minister or Ministers for the accomplishment of permanent specific tasks. The Secretaries of State assist ministers in their tasks and may be responsible, under the authority of the latter, with the management of particular sectors. Particular set of texts, and special texts, when need be, determine their proper attributions. It should be noted that Minister Delegates and Secretaries of State assist in selected ministerial departments as need be.

It is sufficient to glance at the administrative framework or organizational chart of the ministerial departments to establish the existence of a number of specialized units which enables the smooth flux of work. If the administrative framework does not show the informal relations, it gives an exact image of division of labour and indicates at first glance; which post exist in the organization; how they are grouped into units and; how the formal authority circulates between them. Generally, in the ministerial departments there exist ministers, general secretariats, private secretariats, departments headed by directors, assisted by sub–directors, general inspectors, chiefs of service, office heads and technical advisers. They also have external deconcentrated services which deal with problems at local levels.

The ministerial structures are headed by important personalities. The Secretary General (S.G) is the authority who directs the General Secretariat. He/She is the main collaborator of the minister, coordinates the activities of the department and ensures the execution of decisions made by the Minister. The fact that the S.G is appointed by presidential decree gives him some security and independence. On the other hand, the private secretary is appointed by the minister. He/She registers and files mails, documents and carries out tasks assigned by the Minister. The General Inspector and the assistants see to it that the administrative goals are achieved. They inspect and verify the smooth functioning of the services. The presence of technical advisers mark the triumph of technocracy for logically, "there is hardly any step the State wishes to take in devising the law or executing the details of a policy in all services without vital dependence at some stage on the advice of scientific expert."[69] All of the above help the Minister in the accomplishment of tasks.

Generally, one witnesses a multiplicity and diversity of specialists in the administration. There have been tendencies towards "minister–technicians" or "minister–functionaries."[70] There also exist many specialists like engineers, accountants, jurists, medical doctors, and economists who participate in the administration. These personnel serve as perturbations of the general hierarchy. In such a situation, Jameux holds that "... a relation of power is a relation between actors by which one of them exercises ... but not necessarily in all points of view more influence than others."[71] The employment of specialists makes control by the general administrators more difficult because they have neither the knowledge nor the power to do so.

---

[69] Finer, 780

[70] Bayart, Jean F. L'Etat au Cameroun (Paris : Presses de la Fondation des Sciences Politiques, 1984), 223–224

[71] Jameux, Claude, « Organisation du pouvoir, pouvoir de l'organisation » (in Economie et société–Science de Gestion, 1984) ,154

## C The Functions of the Minister

The Minister has two main functions: the political and the administrative. Politically, the Minister is a member of government. He/She serves as the representative of the State in all activities of the department. He/ She participates in ministerial councils and inter–ministerial meetings. In Cameroon, the government plays a subordinate role. The Ministerial Council is a customary forum whose consultation is optional and has no effect on the validity of the presidential acts.

Administratively she is the head of the services of the department. She has to manage the services and personnel under his/her authority. There is controversy whether the minister can exercise regulatory powers or even have possibility of implementing personal politics. The constitution reserves statutory powers to the President of the Republic and to some extent to the Prime Minister. But as all chiefs of service, the judge holds that the ministers can take necessary measures to ensure the smooth functioning of services placed under their control (see C.E. 7 February 1986, *Jamart).* Ministers issue circulars and directives of regulatory character.

As regards personal politics, the 1996 constitution states that the government implement the policy of the nation defined by the President. But the same constitution states that "The President of the Republic may delegate some of his powers to the Prime Minister, other members of government and other senior administrative officials of the state, within the framework of their respective duties" (article 10 (2). This permits the minister to not only exercise regularly powers (C.E.4 Nov. 1976 *Dame Si Moussa)* but also to conceive personal politics. More so, by the proposals they make, Ministers can give personal orientation to political measures to be adopted by the President. But these powers remain residual and exceptional. The multiplicity and diversity of structures at the central level pose the problem of coordination.

## IV. Coordination at the Central Level

The coordination of structures and personnel is done both at the helm of the State as well as by some pivotal ministerial departments.

## A Coordination at the Summit

In a parliamentary regime, it is the prerogative of the Head of Government, not the Head of State. In a presidential regime it is the competence of the President. In a mixed regime (France) the competence is shared between the President of the Republic and the Prime Minister, with the intervention of the Secretary General of the State. In the United States the Executive office of the President puts at the disposal of the President, specialized and competent advisers. This office coordinates the activities of different departments and assures the liaison between the executive and the legislative.

In Cameroon, the Prime Minister is charged with the coordination of governmental work. The P.M is a liaison between the departments and presides inter–ministerial meetings.[72] The Secretary General of the presidency coordinates the actions of the services attached to the presidency. To ensure celerity, efficacy and coherence, the Secretary General, Prime Minister and the Ministers must collaborate. Agreement within the executive is also made possible by the existence of ministerial councils, cabinet councils, restricted councils, occasional inter–ministerial committees and inter–ministerial working sessions.[73]

Laubadere defines consultative administration as the institution of organs by the active administration, intended to furnish it with opinions which it is free to follow or not.[74] At the top, ministerial councils and inter–ministerial meetings serve as consultation forums. The ministers serve as gatekeepers and should aggregate the interests of the various departments.

## B Ministry of Public Service and Administrative Reforms

The recent decrees to organize government are consistent on the fact that it is charged with the elaboration, implementation and evaluation of government policies in matters of public service and administrative reforms. Most public servants have files in the archives of this ministerial

---

[72] Article 6, Instruction Générale No 006 du27 Novembre 1992 relative à l'Organisation du Travail Gouvernemental

[73] Ibid, Article 9–13

[74] In Tsessue, 4

department. The integration, advancement and retirement decisions are issued by this ministerial department. It is responsible for the management of public servants with the–exception of those of national security, armed forces, magistrates and personnel of prisons administration; the preparation of legislative and regulatory measures relative to the status of the personnel; coordinating action of personnel training. It is further responsible for inflicting disciplinary actions against civil servants and State employees following the conditions determined by regulatory texts; the studies relative to the evaluation of human resources needs, in liaison with the ministerial department responsible for planning.[75] In addition to personnel management, the financial resources of the State have to be coordinated.

## C Ministry in charge of Finance

Traditionally, this department is responsible for the coordination of financial activities as the distributor of credits and controller of their use. According to recent decrees to organize government, it is "responsible for the elaboration of government policies in economic, financial, budgetary, fiscal and monetary matters." To accomplish this function, the Minister in addition to the prerogatives in the preparation of the budget, possesses two important powers: to countersign all texts with financial incidence on the state and is represented in all the ministerial departments by finance controllers. These controllers are charged with controlling the regularity of decisions of commitment of credits. The visa of the controller is compulsory for the engagement of expenditure. The refusal to grant this visa is tantamount to a veto on the expenditure. The Minister of Finance, therefore, has the means to ensure administrative coordination through the very important role played in the provision and realization of state resources and expenditures.

When authority is concentrated in the hands of the central government, there is centralization. Politically speaking, centralization can lead to national unity. But the administrative machinery is heavy and the process of decision making slow. Even when taken, the decisions are not

[75] Décret N° 94/160 du 16 Aout 1994 portant réorganisation du Ministère de la Fonction Publique et de la Réforme Administrative., Décret N° 2005/086 of 28 March 2005 to organize the Ministry of Public Service and Administrative Reforms

adapted to local facilities because of work overload. There is therefore the need to take the administration nearer to the people through techniques of deconcentration and decentralisation.

### 4.2 Administrative Deconcentration: External Services of the Central Administration.

In this system, authority is given to local representatives of the central government to take decisions of local interest in the name of the central government which supervises their action. The non–central (local) authorities are no longer simple agents of execution like in the case of integral centralization. They are given a certain margin of initiative notably the power to make certain decisions without consulting the central power. The deconcentrated authorities in Cameroon include governors (region) senior divisional officers (division) and sub–divisional officers (sub–division).

Decree No 2008/376 of 12 November 2008 establishes the administrative organization of the Republic of Cameroon; Decree No 2008/377 of 12 November 2008[76] fixes the attributions of the heads of administrative circumscriptions and determines the organization and functioning of their services (Art. 1). It states clearly in its article 2 that the Governor, Senior Divisional Officer (*préfet*) and Sub–divisional Officer (*Sous–préfet*) are the heads of administrative circumscriptions. The Governor and Senior Divisional Officer represent the President of the Republic, Government and each of the Ministers. The Sub–Divisional Officer represents the Government and each of the Ministers (Art.3). All the three authorities appointed by presidential decree are placed under the hierarchical authority of the Minister in charge of Territorial Administration.

---

[76] This Decree abrogates all previous contrary provisions, notably Decree N° 78/485 of 9 November 1978 fixing the Attributions of Heads of Administrative Circumscriptions and of the bodies and persons charged to assist in the exercise of their functions.

## I. Governor of the Region

The Governors who resides in the Region have specific attributions whose accomplishment is done with the assistance of the services attached to the office.

### A Attributions of the Governor

The Governor plays political, administrative and judicial functions. The attributions of the Governor are discussed in articles 4 to 15 of the Decree No 2008/377 of 12 November 2008. Appointed by presidential decree, the Governor is the highest personality of the Region, is holder of the authority of the State in the Region. On this basis, in line with article 4(1), the Governor:

- *Represents the State in all acts of civil life and in justice;*
- *Sees to it that laws, regulations and decisions of government are enforced;*
- *Ensures the implementation of the economic and social development plans and programmes;*
- *Ensures the maintenance of public order, in application of the rules and regulations in force;*
- *Takes necessary measures to preserve social peace and the smooth functioning of State deconcentrated services in the Region;*
- *Assures, if need be, the effectiveness of the continuity of public services in the administration and bodies under his control;*
- *Assures relations with consular posts.*

Further, the Governor executes in a general manner all missions conferred by the central authorities {Art. 4(2)}. Besides, the Governor ensures, under the authority of the competent Ministers, the general supervision, coordination and control of the activities of State deconcentrated civil services in the Region, with the exception of those of the Ministry of Justice (Art 5). He manages civil servants and state employees within their areas of jurisdiction with the exception of those of the Ministries of Justice, Armed Forces and National Security (Art.6). This activity includes evaluation, advancement, recruitment, dismissal, award of leave, permissions, establishment of irregular absences, disciplinary powers of the personnel within sphere of competence as the case may be.

The Governor has at his disposal the police, gendarmerie and army, within the framework of regulations laying down the conditions of employment of such forces, and any powers that can be granted by the laws and regulations, as well as by the government (Art. 10). He exercises regulatory powers through orders (arrêté) and decisions. He exercises supervisory powers (tutelage) of the state on the Region and regional public establishments, in conformity with the legislations and regulations in force. Besides, the Governor supervises and controls the management of credits allocated to his services, administrative authorities as well as state deconcentrated services in the Region. He submits periodic reports of the coordination or stewardship through hierarchy to the President of the Republic.

## B Services of the Governor's Office

Article 16 to 34 of the Decree No 2008/377 of 12 November 2008, enumerates and details the services of the Governor. Article 16 states that for the accomplishment of his missions, the Governor disposes: the Private Secretariat, Cabinet, an Inspection of Regional Services and the General Secretariat.

The Private Secretariat is placed under the authority of a Private Secretary who is appointed by the decision of the Governor and charged with: the registration, treatment, classification, diffusion and follow–up of confidential couriers/mails; issues reserved to the Governor; and the maintenance and functioning of communication channels.

The Cabinet is under the authority of the Chief of Cabinet and is responsible for: special affairs; audiences and protocol; honorific distinctions and compensations, organizations of missions and tours; personal security of the Governor; problems of security, public order and relations with military authorities, police and gendarmerie forces; and issues related to arms and munitions. It comprises of: the Communication Service; Protocol Service and the Security Service.

The General Inspection of Regional Services is placed under the authority of a General Inspector charged with: internal control and evaluation of the functioning of administrative authorities; organization and supervision of evaluation and control missions, information of

Governor and central authorities of the functioning and performance of services; organization of seminars and refresher courses on modernization and amelioration of services and implementation of strategies to fight against corruption. In their missions of control and evaluation, the General Inspector and the Inspectors of Regional Services have access to the documents of controlled services.

The General Secretariat of the Governor's Office is headed by a high personality called the Secretary General appointed by a presidential decree. He ensures under the authority of the Governor, of which he is the main collaborator, the instruction of affairs and execution of decisions taken. He receives the necessary delegation of signature. On this title, the Secretary General: coordinates the activities of the Governor services; defines and codifies internal procedures; ensures permanent training and refresher courses of personnel; and celerity in the treatment of documents. The General Secretariat comprises of: Divisions of Administrative and Legal Affairs; Police and Administrative Organization; Economic, Social and Cultural Affairs; and that of Regional Development. In addition it has Services of Reception, Courier and Liaison; Documentation, Archives and Translation; and that of Financial and logistic Affairs.

## II. The Senior Divisional Officer of the Division

The Senior Divisional Officer (SDO) resides in the headquarters of the division and is placed under the direct authority of the Governor. Appointed by presidential decree, the Senior Divisional Officer is the highest personality of the division, is holder of the authority of the State in the division. He has specific attributions whose accomplishment is done with the assistance of the services attached to the office.

### A. Attributions of the Senior Divisional Officer

The attributions of the S.D.O are similar to those of the Governor, but performed at the divisional level. These are stated in articles 35 to 43 of the Decree No 2008/377 of 12 November 2008. In general terms, the SDO, on behalf of the government, is charged with the permanent and general mission of information and coordination in security, economic, social and cultural matters at the divisional level. On this basis and in accordance with article 36 of Decree No 2008/377 the SDO:

- *Represents the State in all acts of civil life and in justice;*
- *Ensures the maintenance of public order, enforcement of the rules and regulations in force; and the implementation of development plans and programmes;*
- *Take necessary arbitration to preserve social peace and the smooth functioning of State deconcentrated services in the division;*
- *Ensures if need be, the effectiveness of the continuity of public services in the administration and bodies under his control.*

In addition, the SDO fulfils all attributions or missions which are conferred by competent authorities. Besides, the SDO ensures, under the authority of the competent Ministers and the Governor, the general supervision, animation, coordination and control of the activities of state deconcentrated civil services in the Division, with the exception of those under the competence of the Ministry of Justice (Art 37). He manages civil servants and state employees within his area of jurisdiction with the exception of those falling under the Ministers of Justice, Armed Forces and National Security. His first assistant ensures interim as full right in the case of absence.

## B Services of the Senior Divisional Office

Article 44 to 50 of the Decree No 2008/377 of 12 November 2008 enumerates and details the services of the SDO. Article 44 states that for the accomplishment of his missions, the Office comprises of the Private Secretariat and services of General Affairs; Administrative, Legal and Political Affairs; Economic and Financial Affairs; Social and Cultural Affairs; and Local Development. The DO plays essentially the same roles at the level of the sub–division.

From the forgoing, one can conclude that the difference between functions performed by deconcentrated authorities and even the setup of their respective circumscriptions is that of degree not of nature. They play fundamentally the same functions depending on the level of the administrative circumscription.

# Chapter Five
# Administrative Decentralisation in Cameroon

Decentralization is a technique of administrative organization where there is the process of devolving political, administrative and fiscal powers (autonomy) from the central to autonomous non–central governments under the supervision of the former. It is a system of organization where the State transfers its attributions to institutions (territorial or not) legally distinct from itself and benefiting under the supervision of the State, a certain autonomy in management. There exist two forms or variants of decentralization: territorial (geographical, horizontal) and technical (vertical, functional or by service) decentralization.

In a decentralized State, the functions of public administration are exercised by State authorities and multiplicities of public law bodies notably the 'self–governing' local government. With decentralisation, there are two moral persons, the State and the decentralized body. In order to ensure control and coordination between the administrative entities, there exist hierarchical and supervisory (tutelage) controls. The decentralized body is not submitted to direct hierarchical authority or control but simply to supervisory control.

## 5.1 Territorial Decentralization: Local Government

Territorial decentralization is the transfer of power from the central to the non–central entities which enjoy high level of autonomy within an administrative jurisdiction or part of the territory. The organization of Councils was fundamentally regulated by Law N° 74–23 of 5 December 1974 on the Council Organization with a multitude of subsequent amendments. This law was challenged by economic crises, rampant poverty, State's omnipresence and globalization tendencies which signalled the need for democratization and good governance, especially through the decentralization processes. Nevertheless, as Cheka argues, the process of decentralization in a given context unavoidably depends on the degree of favourableness of the legal environment and the dynamism of the stakeholders.[77] The constitutional provisions have been reinforced by three decentralization laws promulgated on 22 July 2004, and the 2009 law on local fiscal system which have presumably provided a favourable legal environment. These are steps in the right direction, but in some cases the implementation or texts of application are still awaited. Besides, the effectiveness of the decentralization is still bedevilled by political, economic and administrative challenges.

## I. The Legal Environment of Decentralization

Significant efforts have been made since 1996 to create a conducive legal environment, though not completed with the enactment of legal instruments and the creation of more favourable extra–legal environment. The analyses of these laws will determine to what extent they help to enhance the organic, administrative, political and financial autonomy of the decentralized territorial entities.

### A Constitutional Provisions on Decentralization

The decentralization process has constitutional blessings as Law No. 96/06 of 18 January revising the 1972 constitution clearly stipulates in Part X, article 55 that,

> 1) Decentralized local entities of the Republic shall be Regions and Councils;
>
> 2) Decentralized local authorities shall be public law moral persons. They shall enjoy administrative and financial autonomy in the management of local interests. They shall be freely administered by boards elected in accordance with conditions laid by law.

[77] Cheka, Cosmas, "The State of the Process of Decentralization in Cameroon" *Africa Development,* Vol. XXXII, Number 2, Council for the Development of Social Science Research in Africa (CODESRIA), (2000), 181–196.

The duty of regional and local authorities shall be to promote the economic, social, health, cultural and sports development of the said entities.

3) The state shall exercise supervisory powers over regional and local authorities under the conditions laid down by law;
4) The State shall ensure harmonious development of all regional and local entities on the basis of national solidarity, regional potentials and inter–regional balance.

Unlike the Councils, the 1996 Constitution gives some details regarding the status and legal regime of Regions. This is clarified and completed by the 2004 law on the rules applicable to Regions. According to article 56 of the 1996 Constitution, the State shall transfer to Regions jurisdictions in areas necessary for their economic, social, health educational cultural and social development. Article 57 adds that the organs of the Region shall be the Regional Council and the President of the Regional Council. The Regional Council shall be the deliberative organ with regional councillors voted for a term of five (5) years comprising divisional delegates elected by indirect universal suffrage and representatives of traditional rulers elected by their peers and shall be headed by an indigene of the Region. The members of parliament of the Region shall sit in the Regional Council in an advisory capacity. The President of the Regional Council shall be the executive organ of the Region. In this capacity, shall be the interlocutor of the State representative. He shall be assisted by the Regional Bureau which is elected at the same time with the President among the members of the Council. The Council and Bureau shall reflect the various sociological components of the Region.

Besides, a delegate appointed by the President of the Republic shall represent the State in the Region. In this capacity, he shall be responsible for national interests, administrative control, ensuring compliance with laws and regulations and maintaining law and order. He shall under the authority of the Government supervise and coordinate civil state services in the Region (Article 58).

The Regional Council, President of the Council and Regional Bureau may be suspended by the President of the Republic when they carry out activities contrary to the constitution; undermine the security of the State or public law and order; or endanger the State's territorial integrity. In such circumstances, they can be dissolved or dismissed by the President of the Republic after consultation with the Constitutional Council (Articles 59–60). It adds in article 62 that the law may take into consideration the specificities of certain Regions with regard to their organization and functioning. The Constitution concludes that provinces shall become regions; however the effective implementation of this is still awaited.

With these stipulations by the highest law of the land, the decentralized entities and their authorities are protected. First, as the constitution is at the apex of the national legal hierarchy, no other law, decree or any other rule should violate its provisions on the autonomy of these entities else it becomes unconstitutional. Second, any administrative decisions or actions that violate these provisions are unconstitutional, thus illegal and void.

In addition, to the legal framework provided for by the constitution, decentralization is regulated by the following laws:

- Law No 2004/17 of July 22, 2004 on the Orientation of Decentralization
- Law No 2004/18 of July 22, 2004 to lay down Rules applicable to Councils
- Law No 2004/19 of July 22, 2004 to lay down Rules applicable to Regions
- Law No 2009/011 of July 10, 2009 on the Financial Regime of Decentralized Territorial Entities.

## B The Orientation of Decentralization

Law No 2004/17 on the orientation of decentralization lays down the general rules applicable to decentralization. It states in article 2 that decentralization consists of devolution or transfer by the state of special powers and appropriate resources to the decentralized entities. It adds that decentralization constitutes the driving force for the promotion of development, democracy and good governance at the local level. Articles

3 and 4 of this law reiterate the constitutional provisions regarding the decentralized entities.

The devolution of powers to decentralized entities is accompanied by the transfer by State of necessary resources and necessary means. Power is shared between the regional and local authorities on the bases or principles of subsidiarity, progressiveness and complementarity (Art. 9). The entities can set up or join various groupings to achieve their missions. Moreover, the State exercises supervisory powers over decentralized entities. The State has to ensure harmonious development of entities and substitute the liability of authorities. Any person or body can propose to the local authorities any measure aimed at fostering development or improving functioning of the entity. Any inhabitant can request communication or obtain copies of reports on budget, accounts or statutory orders (Art. 13). No decentralized authority shall deliberate outside its statutory meetings, or on maters outside its jurisdiction or which undermine State security, law and order, national unity and territorial integrity. Such acts will simply be nullified by the minister in charge of decentralized entities.

## 1. Devolution of Powers

The State has to transfer to decentralized local entities under conditions laid down by the law, the powers necessary for their economic, social, health, educational, cultural and sports development (art. 15–1). These devolved powers shall not be exclusive, for they are exercised concurrently by the State and authorities under terms and conditions provided by the law. These authorities are free to maintain operations and cooperation ties between themselves and with other entities including the State.

There are human and material implications of devolution of powers. The decentralized authorities have to freely recruit and manage the staff needed for the accomplishment of their missions, according to the laws and regulations in force. However, State public agents can be transferred or seconded upon request by local authorities (art. 19). Resources required by decentralized entities to exercise their powers shall be devolved upon them through either the system of tax transfers or ceded revenue (endowments), or both methods. A Common Decentralization

Fund for the partial financing of the decentralization process is instituted in which each year the finance law shall fix on the recommendation of government the portion of government revenue to be allocated to this fund (art. 23). Where the shortage of funds can jeopardize the execution of public services, the State can intervene through special allocations. Judges of the Audit Bench audit all accounts kept by public accountants.

## 2. Organization and Functioning of entities

Decentralized entities have an elected deliberative organ which is elected by an executive from among the members. They have their own budgets, resources, patrimony, public and private property and staff. They have their own services and when necessary, receive assistance from deconentrated government services (arts.29–31).

The Council or Board deliberates on the management of the property and on real estate transactions made by the authority concerned. Leases, informal agreements and any other conventions to the renting or acquisition of building or real estate of buildings or real estate rights are concluded in accordance with standard procedures (arts. 36–37). Members of the executive and revenue collector may in any form either directly or indirectly bid for and be awarded contracts. Local public services managed under council supervision operate according to the ordinary law provisions applicable to State public services of similar nature. The President of the Regional Council or Mayor represents them in court.

## 3. Supervision and monitoring entities

Formerly, decree No 77–91 of 25 March 1997 determined the supervisory powers over Councils, Council Unions, and establishments. It gave the right to administrative authorities (centralized or deconcentrated) to see to it that municipal councils function effectively and according to the law. These supervisory powers or controls over councils (*Pourvoir de tutelle sur les communes)* were exercised by the Minister of Territorial Administration and Decentralization (which has been split into two: Territorial Administration; Decentralization and Local Development). The Minister of Territorial Administration exercises the supervisory powers and under his control the Governors and Senior Divisional Officers. At times, the President of the Republic and the Prime Minister can also intervene. The administrative supervision (tutelage) can be on persons as well as decisions (acts).

Law No 2004/17 states that the State shall ensure the supervision of regional and local authorities in accordance with the provisions of this law. Under the authority of the President of the Republic, the Minister in charge of the decentralized entities and the representative of the State at the regional (governor) and local (SDO) levels shall ensure supervision (art 66). The acts or decisions issued by decentralized authorities are forwarded to the representative of the State who issues a receipt forthwith.

A National Decentralization Board is set up, and its organization and functioning shall be laid down by the decree of the President of the Republic. It is responsible for the monitoring and evaluation of the implementation of decentralization. In addition, a Local Services Inter–Ministerial Committee has also been set up awaiting the decree of implementation (arts. 78–79).

## C Rules Applicable to Councils

Law No 2004–18 lays down the rules applicable to Councils in accordance with the provisions of the law on the orientation of decentralization. The Council set up by presidential decree is the basic decentralized local entity (arts. 1–2). Following the format of the law, discussions are made on the management of resources, transfer of powers, council organs, and special regime applicable to urban agglomerations and cooperation.

### 1. Management of council property

This regards the management and use of private property of the State, public property and national land. The state may transfer to the Councils all or part of its movable and immovable private property, or enter into agreement with the said Councils on the use of such property (art 9). Regarding public coastlands and waterways, the Council seeks the authorization of the Regional Council after deliberations for local projects. Projects and operations on national land are executed in accordance with the land tenure laws.

## 2. Powers devolved upon councils

These powers are economic, social and educational. The economic development powers include the role played by Councils in economic actions; environmental and natural resource management; and planning, rural development, urban development and housing (arts. 15–18). The health and social development powers include those rules devolved to Councils relating to the health of the population and social welfare (art. 19). The educational, sports and cultural development powers include education, literacy, technical and vocational training; youth, sports and leisure, culture and the development of national languages (arts. 20–22).

## 3. Council Organs

Part IV article 23 of the law states that the Council organs are: the municipal council and the communal executive.

### a The Municipal council

The Council comprises of councillors elected in accordance with the terms and conditions laid down by the law. The municipal Council is the deliberative organ and settles council matters by deliberation. It holds its meetings in the council hall. It is chaired by the Mayor or where he is unavoidably absent, by the Deputy Mayor in order of precedent. It meets in ordinary session once every quarter, for a period not exceeding seven (7) days. An extraordinary session can be convened by the Mayor and in some cases by the representative of the state.

The Council may be suspended by reasoned order of the Minister in charge of decentralized entities where it: acts unconstitutionally, undermines state security, threaten country's territorial integrity or cannot sustainably perform its normal duties. The President of the Republic may dissolve the Council by decree under the above circumstances and where there is persistent breakdown or inability to restore normalcy after a period of two (2) months.

### b Council executive

The executive organ of the Council comprises of the Mayor and Deputy Mayors. The Mayor heads the Council and is assisted by the

Deputy Mayors in order of their election (art. 58). The office of the Mayor is incompatible with that of; member of government, member of parliament, administrative authority, diplomatic authority, president of court, manager of public corporation or establishment, secretary general of ministry, director in central administration, president of regional council, law enforcement officer, council staff and finance official (art. 66).

### i. Duties of the Mayor

Mayors represent the Council in all civil matters and before the law courts. To that end, the mayor under the supervision of the Council is responsible for:

- ✓ Preserving, maintaining and administering council property and asset and safeguarding them;
- ✓ Managing council revenue and supervising council services and accounts;
- ✓ Issuing building or demolition permits and land tenure authorizations;
- ✓ Preparing and submitting the budget, authorizing expenditure and prescribing revenue collection;
- ✓ Directing council projects;
- ✓ Ensuring the implementation of development programmes financed by the council;
- ✓ Taking measures concerning the municipal road network;
- ✓ Inviting tenders, concluding leases and awarding contract;
- ✓ Executing deeds for the sale, exchange, sharing, acceptance of donations or legacies…;
- ✓ Ensuring environmental protection and accordingly taking measures to prevent or eliminate pollution and nuisances, protecting public parks and helping to embellish the council;
- ✓ Filling council vacancies and, in general implementing decisions of the council (art. 71).

Further, the Mayor is the authorizing officer or vote holder for the Council budget. He shall recruit, suspend or dismiss workers governed by labour laws and collective agreements, assign and manage staff placed under his authority (art. 74). The Mayor and his deputies are civil status registrars (art. 77).

### ii. Assistance to council executive

The Council Executive shall be assisted by a Secretary General who is the main coordinator of council administrative services and enjoys delegation of signature for the smooth functioning of the services. The Minister in charge of decentralized entities can by order appoint and dismiss Secretary Generals of councils (art.80). Under the control of the representative of the State, the Mayor is responsible for the municipal police and the implementation of orders relating thereto. The creation of a council police service is authorized by the decision of the council which defines its duties, logistics and functioning. The purpose of the council police is to ensure public order, safety, peace, security and sanitation (arts. 86–87).

### c. Suspension and termination of duties

In case of infringement of the laws and regulations in force, or serious misconduct, Mayors and Deputy Mayors may be suspended by the order of the Minister in charge of decentralized entities, for a maximum period of three months, after hearing them or requesting them to furnish written explanations on the acts for which they are accused. After such period they shall either be rehabilitated or dismissed, the latter is done by presidential decree (art. 94). The specific reasons can be embezzlement, serious misconduct, non–performance of duties, no longer fulfils conditions, appointment to an incompatible post and resignation.

## 4. Special Regime applicable to Urban Centres

Since 1987 the number of City Councils have increased to fourteen namely Bamenda, Nkongsamba, Yaounde, Douala, Bafoussam, Bertoua, Ebolowa, Maroua, Garoua, Ngaoundere, Limbe, Kumba, Kribi and Edea. Part V (arts.109–119) of the law applicable to councils details the rules governing these special councils. The presidential decree raises these urban conglomerates to City Councils because of their specific nature. A City Council is a moral person of public law enjoying legal personality and financial autonomy. A City Council comprises of an agglomeration of at least two councils: the councils which constitute the community are called "sub–divisional councils". The name of the City Council is preceded by the words "……. City Council" (art. 109). Article 110 enumerates a plethora of powers devolved to the Urban Communities which are similar to those of Councils.

## a City Council (Communautés Urbaines)

The City Council functions, *mutatis mutandis*, in accordance with the regulations governing councils as provided by this law (2004/18) and the law on the orientation of decentralization. The City Council (*Communautés Urbaines)* comprises: the City Council and the Government Delegate to the City Council. The City Council is made up of sub–divisional council mayors and representatives chosen within sub–divisional councils. The council of the city discusses all the matters which fall under its jurisdiction.

A Government Delegate appointed by decree of the President of the Republic fully exercises the duties and powers of a Mayor at the head of a City Council. He is assisted by persons appointed by order of the President of the Republic. He convenes and chairs city council meetings, and with his assistants constitute the City Council Executive (art. 115). In the discharge of his duties, the Government Delegate is responsible for:

- Preparing and implementing the decisions of the City Board
- Preparing and implementing the budget of the City Council
- Organizing and managing city services
- Managing resources and property of the city
- Overseeing city projects
- Representing the city at official ceremonies (art. 116)

## b The Sub–divisional councils

The provisions of the laws on the orientation of decentralization and rules applicable to Councils are applicable *mutatis mutandis* to sub–divisional councils. Mayors of sub–divisional councils are *ex officio* members of the City Council. In addition, the sub–divisional council designates five (5) councillors to represent it in the City Council (art. 121).

The setting up of a City Council entails the transfer by sub–divisional councils of powers and resources to the said City Council, in accordance with the provisions of this law in force. The creation of any inter–council service is subject to the prior approval of the sub–divisional councils concerned (arts. 129–130).

### 5. Inter–council Cooperation and Solidarity

Decentralized cooperation is realized under an agreement whereby two (2) or more councils decide to merge their various resources with a view to achieving common objectives. It may be done between Cameroonian and foreign councils, under conditions laid down by the laws and regulations in force. The cooperation agreement, which is authorized beforehand by the decision of the Councils, is forwarded by the representative of the State for prior approval by the Minister in charge of decentralized entities (arts. 131–132).

The Council Union is the coming together of councils of the same division or region, by at least two–thirds ($^2/_3$) majority of the decision of each Council with the view of realizing inter–council operations. It shall be set up by an agreement signed by the Mayors of the councils concerned it shall be an inter–council public establishment, endowed with legal personality as well as administrative and financial autonomy (arts. 133–134). The organs of the Council Union shall comprise: a Union Board and a Union Chairperson. The former comprises of the mayors assisted by two (2) councillors each, and the latter is elected among the members. The Union budget is prepared, adopted, executed and audited in accordance with the provisions of the agreement creating the Union.

## D. Rules applicable to Regions

The law defines the sharing of powers between the state and regions in the areas of competence so transferred. Law No 2004/19 lays down rules applicable to Regions, in accordance with the provisions of the law on the orientation of decentralization. The Region is a regional entity comprising of several divisions. The chief town of each province that is transformed to a region, becomes the chief town of the Region. (arts. 1–3). In accordance to the laws in force, a Region may: carry out activities to supplement those of the State; and propose to councils under its jurisdiction all measures to foster the coordination of local development and investment action (art. 7). The rules on the management of regional property, powers devolved upon regions, governance and inter–regional cooperation and solidarity are similar to those of councils. It is essential, however, to elaborate on the regional organs and financial provisions.

## 1. Regional Organs

Regions shall comprise of: the Regional Council and the President of the Regional Council.

### a. Regional Council

The Regional Council is the deliberative organ of the Region. It comprises regional councillors elected for a five–year term. It shall comprise of: divisional delegates elected by indirect universal suffrage and representatives of traditional rulers elected by their peers. Members of parliament of the region shall attend proceedings of the Regional Council in an advisory capacity (art. 26). The Regional Council settles regional matters by deliberations. It decides on matters provided for by the decentralization laws.

The Regional Council meets in ordinary session once every quarter when convened by its president and can also meet in extraordinary session with specific agenda. It shall comprise of four committees each headed by a committee member.

### b. President of the Regional Council

The President of the Regional Council shall be the chief executive of the region. He shall be assisted by a regional bureau elected at the same time with him from among the councillors. The Regional Bureau shall reflect the sociological composition of the region (art. 60). The Regional Council shall elect during its first session, a president assisted by a bureau comprising a senior vice–president, a vice–president, two questors and 2 secretaries. As the chief executive, the president shall:

- ✓ Be spokesman before the representative of the State;
- ✓ Represent the Region in all civil matters and before the law courts;
- ✓ Prepare and implement the regional council deliberations;

- ✓ Authorize the revenue and expenditure of the region…
- ✓ Manage the region's property and monitor such management…. (art. 65).

### 2. Financial provisions for regions

The resources necessary for the region to exercise its authority shall be devolved on it either through the transfer of taxes, subsidies or through both procedures. The draft budget shall be prepared and presented to the council by the President of the Regional Council. The budget and special revenue and expenditure authorizations shall be adopted by the Regional Council.

## E. Financial Regime of Decentralized Territorial Entities

Law No 2009/011 of July 10, 2009 governs the financial regime of decentralized entities fixing the conditions for the elaboration, presentation, execution and control of execution of budgets of territorial entities. It applies to regions, councils, city councils, communal public establishments and other territorial entities created by law (art 1). In its article 2 the law makes it clear that, "the territorial entities are moral persons of public law. They enjoy legal personality, administrative and financial autonomy in the management of regional and local interests. They manage freely their revenue and expenditures, within the framework of budgets voted by deliberative organs." The budget is defined and seen as an instrument for the accomplishment of local programs and objectives, in line with the economic and financial objectives of the State. Various provisions are made on the content of the budgets, the composition of the revenues and expenditures and the budgetary principles especially annuality, unity, equilibrium and specialization. At this introductory stage, it is germane to discuss the preparation, execution and control of budgets of the decentralized entities.

### 1. Elaboration of the budget

The budget is prepared by the chief executive and voted by the deliberative body latest the 15th of November of each year (arts. 38, 41). The budget of the territorial entities is approved by the order of the competent supervisory authority within 15 days after it is formally deposited. This approbation confers it executory character. The special authorizations of revenue and expenditures are voted and approved in the same way as the budget.

## 2. The execution of the budget

The President of the Regional Council, the Government Delegate, the Mayor or the President of the Council Union are authorizing officers or vote holders of their respective budgets (art 54). The operations on the execution of the budget are incumbent on the authorizing officers and accountants under the conditions defined by particular texts on the regulation of accounts of territorial entities. The recovery of revenue and payment of local expenses are done by the accountants of territorial entities called "municipal revenue collectors" or "regional revenue collectors." In their absence, the functions of collection are of right exercised by the nearest treasurer accountant. The functions of the authorizing officer and those of the accountant are and remain separate as concerns both the execution of revenue and expenditures. But, both exercise their functions in close collaboration.

## 3. Control of the budget

The control is first done by the deliberative organ during the examination of the budget or the administrative account, it exercises control on the budget execution as well as the attached programs and projects. It can also constitute *ad hoc* commissions on subjects regarding financial management and reports are submitted for its appreciation. It can inform the supervisory authority or any other competent authority about any irregularities (arts. 104–105). Second, there is administrative control of regularity and performance management requirement on entities that have received subventions, guarantee or caution can be done by specialized services of the State (art. 106). Third, the legal control of the accounts of territorial entities is done by competent accountants. Finally, independent audits can be done at the request of the supervisory authority, the deliberative or the executive organ.

This law No 2009/011 also creates the National Committee on Local Finances charged notably with the optimal mobilization of revenue of territorial entities and the good management of the local finances (art. 109). It should also be noted that this law is supplemented by Law No 2009/019 of December 15, 2009 on Local Fiscal System which lays down the taxes, levies and royalties collected by the decentralized structures.

## II. Challenges to Territorial decentralization

In spite of the decentralization wave, many local governments especially in developing countries are facing problems, dangers or crises. Attempted solutions have fallen short to provide veritable decentralization. In Cameroon, there have been the organization of seminars, creation of structures, motivation of local stakeholders and above all the improvement of the legal environment. Despite these efforts, local governments have been and are still facing challenges that have made them to fall short of veritable decentralization.

### A. Causes of Local Governments Crises

There are some fundamental problems that explain the situation of local governments especially in Cameroon. The council system in general is in crisis because of excessive centralization and supervision, financial crises, mismanagement, penury of qualified staff and the democratic challenge

#### 1. Excessive Centralization

In Cameroon, due to rural exodus, excessive and uncontrolled urbanization, the rural areas are scarcely populated and poor. The urban areas even with the concentration of facilities cannot cope with the social problems. The local government is obliged to deal with increasing problems of unemployment, criminality and social unrest without a proportionate increase in resources. Worse still, the central government and local authorities tend to concentrate in the urban areas (especially capitals) neglecting the others which accentuates the urbanization and rural problems.

Most African countries, especially those of the French tradition are characterized by centralization and unification tendencies, giving priority to the ideology of national integration. There are always attempts to concentrate power at the center, the argument being that this is to ensure socio–economic development of the State, thus the need of central planning. Arguably, decentralization will weaken central power and there will be dispersion of efforts.

In order to ensure the almightiness of the State, there is a unique center of decision, the central authorities have used various techniques to ensure administrative supervision which critics qualify as excessive (appointment of municipal authorities). As such, the communal system has been facing incapacity due to excessive supervision that is paralyzing at the organic level and demobilizing at the functional level.[78]

## 2. Financial Problems

Worldwide, the charges of local governments are increasing, but their resources are not increasing proportionally. This can be due to fiscal incivility, mismanagement, the insufficiency of financial means, financial and economic crises, which challenge the autonomy of local governments. Due to financial weaknesses, many States are not only ensuring simple parentage, they are over–intervening in the management of local governments. This financial subordination greatly compromises their freedom and independence.

## 3. Mismanagement Problems

The problem is that in many cases the available resources are not well used. There is penury of qualified staff, yet a plethora of unqualified workers that absorb the greatest share of communal budgets. In addition, the authorities are corrupt, adopt inappropriate policies and even make poor estimates. All these have made the situation of local governments fragile, no doubt they have been victims of political, administrative and economic temptations and manipulations.

## 4. The Democratic Challenge

The democratization of African countries with the coming of multi–party politics especially since the 1990s is good news for local democracy. In an atmosphere of competition, the decentralized authorities will do their best in the management of resources in order to ensure re–

---

[78] Momo, Bernard, «Réflexions sur le système communal Camerounaise: Contribution à l'étude de la Décentralisation Territoriale au Cameroun» *Juridis Info* No 24, Octobre–Décembre, (1995), 81–92.

election. In some multiparty councils, there are real debates and disagreements which are good for democracy. But the danger is that government may discriminate against the opposition–dominated councils. Also when the local residents believe that there has been electoral fraud, there is more incivility and civil disobedience. The risk is that incumbents can use various manipulations in order to ensure control.

## B. Attempted Solutions to the Crises

With the all–round crises of local governments in developing areas some solutions have been attempted with doubtful effectiveness. This can be explained by lack of seriousness, inapplicability of some solutions, the adverse effects inherent in some and lack of financial backing. In Cameroon, in addition to reforms concerning the enactment of legal texts tilted towards awarding the necessary autonomy (political, administrative and financial) to local governments, there have been combination of local governments, financial improvements, training, evaluation and enhancement.

### 1. Combination of Local Governments

In Cameroon, this has led to the creation of Council Unions and City Councils. The latter entities which are special status councils have been subject to debates. They are found in a hybrid situation (deconcentration/decentralization) for despite the fact that government delegates are appointed, they remain moral persons of public law (deliberative organ elected, financial autonomy) and are part of the decentralization process as seen in the 1996 Constitution and 2004/18 law on rules governing Councils. In general terms, to enjoy the economies of large–scale production, there have been attempts to bring together or encourage inter–communal cooperation. This has been done in areas with particular economic, demographic, social or political importance. Arguably, with the creation of super–councils coordination between sub–councils is easier. But these combinations at times are done for political reasons not for efficiency. Besides, as the saying goes, "0+0=0", so the unions can simply be seen as addition of miseries. Further, the appointment of local authorities endangers local democracy for they can avoid the sanctions of the electorate or the inhabitants

## 2. Financial Improvements

Many countries have attempted to create institutions that can provide financial and other assistance to councils. In Cameroon, to ensure inter–communal cooperation there has been the creation of a Special Fund of Equipment and Inter–council Intervention (FEICOM).[79] It is created by article 91 of Law No 74–23 and organized by Decree No 77–85 of 22 March 1977. It is a public establishment endowed with legal personality and financial autonomy. Law No 95/23 of 5 August 1995 states that the principal objectives are to: provide mutual help to councils as regards treasury advances, financing communal and inter–communal works, recover fiscal revenue of councils and finance the training of communal personnel. Its resources come mainly from discounts, state subventions and contributions from patents, licensees and cattle tax. But resources of this institution are generally mismanaged. It is usually dominated by political men, although this can be an advantage for these men can provide legitimacy and lobby for resources, but the risk is that technical aspects can be sacrificed. It can also argue that councils the principal beneficiaries are not usually represented in its management.

Further, a Decree signed by the President of the Republic on 15 September 2015 attributes salaries to local government authorities as follows: Government delegates (400,000FCFA), deputy government delegates (200,000FCFA), mayors (250,000FCFA) and deputy mayors (150,000FCFA) per month. This is expected to serve as motivation to these authorities and diminish the mismanagement of the local government funds.

## 3. Personnel Training

To ensure that qualified and competent personnel are provided to the local governments, many countries have created opportunities and institutions for their training. In Cameroon, according to Decree No 77–494 of 7 December 1977 the Center for Training of Municipal Administrators (CEFAM)[80] is a public establishment endowed with legal personality and financial autonomy. It is charged with ensuring the

---

[79] Le Fond Spécial d'Equipment et d'Intervention Intercommunale(FEICOM).

[80] Centre de Formation pour l'Administration Communale(CEFAM).

training, re–training or refreshing of the administrative and technical personnel of the councils, council unions and other council establishments. But the non–existence of a communal public service, makes it that the products of this Center are not sent to the councils which need them. The Mayors have neither the means nor the obligation to recruit personnel trained at the Center. A rational recruitment system could be adopted to limit anarchical recruitment of personnel based on clientelist considerations.

## 4. Evaluation and enhancement

In line with the decrees to organize the government, the Ministry of Territorial Administration and Decentralization is charged with the elaboration, implementation and evaluation of government policies in matters of territorial administration, civil protection and decentralization." Specifically, regarding decentralization, this ministry is charged with; the elaboration and follow–up of the implementation of regulations relative to the organization and functioning of decentralized territorial entities; the exercise of State supervision of decentralized territorial entities under the authority of the President of the Republic. It assures the supervision of the Special Fund for Equipment and Inter–communal Intervention, public bodies responsible for the implementation of decentralization, and Center for Training of Municipal Administration (CEFAM).

Furthermore, many structures have been created to enhance the decentralization process in Cameroon notably–National Decentralization Board, Inter–Ministerial Committee for Local Government Services and National Committee for Local Government Finances. In addition, some programmes have been established to prepare decentralized authorities for decentralization. These include inter alia Support Programme for Decentralized Urban Development Capacities (PACDDU) the National Programme for Participatory Development (NPPD) and Community Development Support Programme (CDSP).

Faced with decentralization and increased responsibilities, most local governments in developing countries must adopt new roles. These new roles were either previously exercised by the national governments or arise anew out of necessity in the face of daunting tasks. Also, local governments with increasing responsibilities and diminishing resources are obliged to do more with less. Centralized administrations have failed to stimulate development. Experiences from the more advanced countries show that local governments are where most of the state functions are performed. They play critical roles in developmental efforts from all perspectives. Being in contact with the grassroots, local governments are better able to serve the population. Today, with the globalization tendencies States are forced to delegate powers to sub–national governments, each expected to work with multiplicities of actors. Centralization is no longer fashionable in a world that is more competitive, fragmented, liberalized and business–oriented. But for the local governments to play their development roles effectively, they must be democratic and autonomous.

## 5.2 Technical decentralization: Specialized Institutions

Technical decentralization is a technique of administrative organization which entails the transfer of powers to specialized institutions or bodies without geographical basis. In an introductory work, it is difficult to exhaustively discuss on technical decentralization because of the diversity of legal regimes and the multiplicity or better still proliferation of specialized institutions governed by individualized laws.

The concept of specialized public person is different from territorial collectivity (council, region) in that: while the territorial collectivities have an activity of the general administration limited to geographical circumscription, the specialized persons have an activity limited to particular tasks concerning a determined category of the administered. The specialized administrative entities are of different types, with different reasons for creation, organization and legal regime but are all submitted to state supervision.

## I. Types of technically decentralized entities

Three combined criteria can be used to distinguish specialized institutions: First, the object of service, whether the activity is fulfilled by a private person or uniquely by public power. Second, whether the source of resources is from private persons or taxes and subventions. Third, the modalities of organization and functioning, whether they are similar to those of private ordinary enterprises or employ methods that only the public sector can utilize.[81] The public establishments are the main specialized institutions, and the establishments with public utility are fewer.

### A. Public Establishments

With the multiplication and diversification of public establishments, it is difficult to give a precise definition. Generally, they are moral persons of public law and have as mission the management of public service. It is only a public person that can create a public establishment. These establishments are expected to have proper patrimony, a budget and individualized accounts which entail financial autonomy. There are fundamentally two types of public establishments: First, administrative public establishments; they are public bodies usually created and dissolved by parliament. Second, industrial and commercial public establishments; with the economic and political challenges, the modern State intervenes in the industrial and commercial sectors formerly reserved for the private sector e.g. public enterprises.

### B. Establishment with public utility

These are moral persons of private law or associations pursuing goals which are particularly important for the community and as such having some public prerogatives and obligations. This is when private enterprises are allowed to perform functions that had previously been monopolized by government for public good; contracting out the provision or management of public services or facilities to commercial enterprises; transferring responsibility for providing services from the public to the private sector through the divestiture of state–owned enterprises.[82]

## II. Rules of Creation

Public establishments are subjected to the principle of specialty. In effect, they possess what is known as competence of attribution. This

---

[81] Legrand, Andre and Wiener, Celine, Initiation au Droit Public (France: Formation administration, concours, la documentation franciase, 2003), 90.

[82] http: // www.ciesin.org/decentralization/English/General/Different_forms.html accessed 12/06/2016.

entails that they can only act on what is expressly and explicitly authorized by the law. This is in contrast with the territorial collectivities which have competences of common law; they can do everything that is not expressly forbidden by the law in force.[83]

The justifications for the existence of specialized institutions are many and varied: defense of individual in their common interest e.g. professional orders (pharmacist, doctors, architects, lawyers, etc); consecrate the existence of an institution, endow it with a certain autonomy within the public sector e.g. Universities; exploit the flexibility and goal oriented nature of private law rules and methods e.g. joint ventures.

## III. Legal Regime of Specialized Institutions

It depends on the type of specialized institutions. The rule is that when there is an administrative character for the public establishment, the public law regime is applicable. On the contrary, when it has a commercial and industrial character, the private law regime is applicable. Public establishments generally submit to public law and administrative jurisdictions. However, those exercising industrial and commercial activities can exploit the rules of private law in their relationship with their employees, third persons and clients.

With the proliferation of public establishments of different types, it is difficult to precise their judicial regimes, but institutions exercising administrative activities are more largely submitted to the rules of public law than those exercising industrial and commercial activities. But then some public establishments have "double faces", they are hybrids having the ingredients of both. The regime is mixed though in different proportions. As regards private persons, those who normally belong to private law in their execution of public services partly use public law for their activities.

## IV. The Rules of Organization and Functioning

The specialized institutions are legal and moral persons, that is, they are subjects of law that are not individuals. They have a patrimony,

---

[83] Ibid.

can sue or be sued and have extra patrimonial attributes – a name, texts etc. They are therefore endowed with certain autonomy though in different degrees: possess a proper patrimony; have an autonomous budget with resources and expenses, and organic autonomy: Executive organ (Director, President, Rector), deliberative organ (Senate, Council). But they are not totally independent; there is State intervention or supervisory controls.

Technical decentralization is attenuated by State supervision in different degrees depending on the type of specialized institution. The central power appoints or controls the appointments of the administrative authorities of these institutions. The competences of these authorities are usually submitted to preliminary authorization of the central power. The establishment and execution of their budgets is submitted to the state controllers. In some specialized institutions, government intervention is so profound that one may talk of deconcentration not decentralization.

## Conclusion of Part two

In fact, neither the system of centralization, that of deconcentration nor that of decentralization should be used exclusively. They are means of achieving general interest, they should be dimensions and none should be exaggerated. In normal circumstances, they should be balanced. But at times, there is disequilibrium in favor of centralization (France/Cameroon) or decentralization (Britain, Swiss)). In administrative organization, each technique has its merits and demerits. Further, the administrative techniques are distinct but complementary.

The Cameroonian authorities have made enormous legal and extra–legal efforts to improve on decentralization. Yet despite the attempted solutions many challenges remain which serve as blockages to achieving veritable decentralization. The creation of a favourable legal environment for administrative set–ups is an indispensable condition for effective public administration. Efforts have been made in this direction, but the laws themselves have limitations coupled with implementation problems. Beyond the rules of administrative organization, the next concern is the rules governing administrative resources.

# Part Three
# Administrative Action in Cameroon

State resources are the means to ensure the accomplishment of goals through administrative action. The State has three fundamental functions: the legislative, executive and judiciary functions. It should be re–iterated that the administration is the State's means of doing things. It is from the administrative functions that administrative action stems and these functions constitute the *raison d'être* of the administration. The administration, to ensure the implementation of policies, provides public services, maintains public law and order and at times awards contracts. In its capacity as public power with the objective of satisfying general interest, the administration is accorded prerogatives exorbitant to common law (private law) or the prerogatives of public power. The administrative actions are multiform, as it uses public laws and at times private law rules and intervenes in many domains or areas with the use of different measures. In its actions, the administration uses various ways and follows specific procedures.

# Chapter Six
# Ways of Administrative Action

In general terms, the administration ensures general interest through the provision of various public services by the public bodies under the regime of administrative law. But for the public services to function smoothly the administrators have to ensure that there is public law and order through the use of police powers. While the public service focuses on the provision of services, the administrative police is preoccupied with activities of regulation.

## 6.1 The Provision of Public Services

The public service has been considered by jurists as the key of the vault and as the justification of public power and the prerogative it disposes. With the intervention of the State in the social and economic domains, and the interpenetration between public and private laws, there has been a lot of controversy as to what is the "public service". Léon Duguit [84] saw the State as a simple "cooperation of public services" and Maurice Hauriou thought that the State should obey nothing than the public utility which should serve as auto–limitation of its power.[85] The public service should therefore be seen as the delimitation and the legitimization of the administrative actions. The original definition of the public service as an activity of general interest by a public body under the regime of administrative law is challenged by the tendencies of deregulation and privatization. It is necessary to understand the scope, principles, management of the public services and situation of the users.

---

[84] Léon Duguit (1859–1928) was a leading French scholar of administrative law. He authored notably *L'État, le droit objectif et la loi positive 1901, Les transformations du droit public 1913.*

[85] He was a French jurist who greatly shaped french adminitrative law: *Précis de droit administratif et de droit public général* (1892), *Principes de droit public* (1910) *Précis élémentaire de droit administratif* (1925).

## I. Scope of the public service

The public service is both an activity and a structure. It is diverse as regards the criteria, life, domain in which it intervenes and the forms it takes.

### A. The Criteria of public service

Classically, for there to be a public service, three conditions are necessary. These conditions have been challenged in theory and practice. But they still serve as guidelines for the definition and recognition of public services.

#### 1. The Finalist element

All public service activities must have the objective of general interest. The existence of the public administration is fundamentally due to the existence of public interest, the interest of the commonwealth which should be higher than the private or individual interests. Theoretically, that the administration exists for this, there is no dispute for it is the notion of general interest that provides the legal foundation of the public service. But then general interest is an abstract, changing and contingent concept. Also, general interest is not the monopoly of the public administration, nowadays the private sector intervenes more and more in the provision of such services and there are also tendencies for the privatization of the public administration. Besides, general interest is more a political concept where there is the search for legitimacy than a purely legal one.

#### 2. Organic element

The entity charged with the execution of public service should be a public body. In fact, the public services should be executed by the State and other public bodies particularly the deconcentrated and decentralized entities. It is logical that public bodies created for that sake should execute the public services. However, some private persons have been invested with the powers to accomplish public services, however, controlled by administrative authorities directly or not. The public bodies have also been engaged in the implementation of some services which are essentially private in nature.

### 3. Legal element

The body charged with the management of a public service must function under a special regime of public law (rights, prerogatives and obligations of public power). This entails the application of administrative law which is derogatory to common law. In the now famous *Blanco Case* (1873), the court ruled that "the liability incumbent on the State is neither general nor absolute… It has special rules which vary depending on service needs." This condition is not obligatory, for there are some public services (e.g. industrial and commercial) which use legal procedures dominated by private law. In addition to unilateral administrative acts, the public services are accomplished through contracts, however with the application of public law.

Combining the above criteria or elements, in spite of the exceptions, in general terms, the public service can be defined as an activity assured directly or indirectly by the administration with the target to satisfy the general interest and submitted at least partially to the public law regime

## B. Creation, Extension and Suppression of Public Services

At the national level from 1960, the creation and suppression of public services was the competence of the statutory power, which must be approved by the parliament (art. 23 (3) of the constitution of 4th march 1960). Nevertheless, the constitutions of 1st September 1961 (art. 12(2), that of 2nd June 1972 (art. 9(2), and the 1996 revised constitution in its article 8(9) give the statutory power an exclusive competence in the matters of creation and suppression of administrative services. It states that the President of the Republic "shall set up and organize the administrative services of the State." Following the rule of parallelism of form and competence, the authority that creates is competent to suppress. The dissolution of public services occur when the circumstances that justified their creation no longer exist or when the financial burden is too great compared to their utility.

However, the initiative of the legislative still remains if it touches the fundamental guarantees accorded for the exercise of public liberties or if it entails the creation of a new category of public establishment in an already existing category (scientific, administrative, industrial or commercial). It is in this light that Law N°. 87–20 of 17 December 1987 created the Cameroon Radio Television (CRTV), and Law N°. 87–011 of 15 July 1987 authorized the President of the Republic to dissolve the National Fund for Rural Development (FONADER)

### C. The domains of intervention

Formerly, they started with the regalia functions with the intervention of the State in the social and economic sectors; they have extended to the other domains. The functions have evolved and are determined by the State itself in function of its political, economic and social conceptions.

#### 1. The regalia functions

These functions appeared first and have never been contested as they seem to be inherent to the notion of sovereignty of the State. The regalia functions correspond to the liberal state (Gendarme/police State) which was simply responsible for the maintenance of public order and tranquillity through soldiering, judging and policing. It has to ensure diplomatic relations and national defence. It has to collect taxes on which the functioning of the State depends and the totality of public services. It simply had to provide a favourable environment for the exercise of economic activities by private individuals.

#### 2. Economic functions

But with the rampant crises and the challenges of development, the State became interventionist, regulating the functioning of the economy. The State became among others a planner, banker, farmer, manufacturer and transporter. The State has to provide or ensure the provision of infrastructures, energy, transportation and telecommunications that enhance development. The growth of the public services is legal even if there is the risk of perturbation of free competition and the market laws. It helps the State in the accomplishment of economic, monetary and fiscal policies.

### 3. Social functions

The State intervenes in the social welfare, sanitary, education and cultural sectors. The Cameroonian state manages many hospitals and health centres where services are subsidized from the national resources. There exist state universities, professional schools and vocational, high, secondary and primary schools. This is in line with the constitutional provision in the preamble that "The state shall guarantee the child's right to education. Primary education shall be compulsory. The organization and supervision of education at all levels shall be the duty of the State."

## D. The Legal classification

These public services can be distinguished on the bases of the object, means of financing and the modalities of organization and functioning. From this standpoint, there is a binary distinction between the administrative public services and the public services with industrial and commercial character.

### 1. Administrative public services

They constitute theoretically the most "natural", "veritable" "par excellence' category of public services that is why they are termed "public services so to speak." They include services such as schools, hospitals and the police. They are created by public bodies with the intention to satisfy general interests and belong to administrative law. Their financing is from fiscal resources and state subventions. Consequently they apply the rules of public management and accounts with no direct search for profits. With the difficulties of definition, the administrative services are usually conceived in the negative as the services which are not industrial or commercial.

### 2. Public services of industrial and commercial character

These services are more recent and emerged with State interventionism. They are created to accomplish general interest (energy, water, transport), but intervene in the same domains as the private enterprises and in analogical conditions. In order to distinguish them from the administrative public services and the private enterprises, they must fulfill three cumulative criteria: First their objective must be to produce or sell goods or even provide services but for collective interest. Second, as regards the modalities of financing, the resources come essentially not from the public budget, but from the payment of services by the users who benefit from them. Lastly, regarding the organization and functioning of the services, they are similar to those of private enterprise and not administrative. They search for financial equilibrium in their exploitation and have private economic relations with their customers (subscription, insurance). The workers are placed under the status of private law, accounts follow the rules applicable to business enterprises and the service activities are governed by private law. But since they provide public services, they are submitted to a mixed regime of public and private laws.

## II. Ways of Managing the Public Services

There are three main modalities used to manage the public services.

### A. Direct Management (*Le système de la régie*)

In principle, the management by the administration (State and its entities) is the normal way of managing the public services. If an activity belongs to the public service, it is natural that the administration directly manages it. The management is done by the structures of the entity which does not possess legal personality. The movable and immovable goods are allocated to the entity to accomplish its mission, but generally it does not benefit financial autonomy as its revenues and expenditures feature in the budget of the entity even if they have annex budgets. This system has the advantage that the entity has total mastery of the service, but the inconvenience is certainly sluggishness, essentially due to the fact that the service does not have autonomy in management. That is why many entities often choose the more flexible formula of public establishments.

### B. System of public establishment

The public establishment is a moral person of public law attached to the State or local entity which substitutes it in the provision of public services. Public establishments can be administrative, industrial or commercial in character and can be termed offices, agencies, companies, even enterprises created to ensure the management of these public services. This is when it is necessary to individualize a service by the creation of a distinct corporate body or moral person so as to assure the individual freedoms. It can also be when attempts are made to respect the interests of a particular group (e.g. Chamber of Commerce, Chamber of Agriculture).

In relation to direct management, the public establishment option first offers more flexibility: it is endowed with legal personality and has its proper budget. It can be easily adapted to the specificity of service and the evolution of needs. That is why this formula is at times termed "decentralization by services." Second, it possesses relative autonomy in relation to the power in place and there is the possibility to enable the users and personnel representatives participate in decisions during board meetings. The public entity retains control but this is less compulsive for it is supervisory not hierarchical subordination. However, the problems of coordination and conflict may arise. The establishments may not also be given enough means to satisfactorily execute the services.

## C. System of Assignment

The delegation of management of service to an individual or private body can be as a result of law or contract. In comparison with the preceding modalities, the public service concession (assignment) is original from two points of view. It implies the use of contractual technique, and it supposes that the execution of the public service is conferred to a particular (individual).

The contract of delegation of a public service is always an administrative contract. The authority representing the public entity who concludes the contract must follow the specified procedure. This authority disposes because of service interests many prerogatives including fixing the price to be paid by users, unilateral modification, regular reports of activities and financial accounts of services and anticipated end of the contract. The co–contractor is obliged to follow the general principles governing the functioning of public services. Nonetheless, these private persons can be awarded certain prerogatives of public power: benefits a situation of monopoly, right to expropriate etc. But the private person does not become a public servant. He remains an entrepreneur and recruits employees following the procedures of private law.

The management by a private organism may seem paradoxical, say abnormal in relation to the notion even of public service. If the nature of the provision of public service is such that they have to be accomplished by the public entity, the delegation of this power to the private sector may seem dangerous. This phenomenon is explained at times by ethical reasons: the wish to support structures that are born of private initiative that attempt to fulfil general interests; or to confer responsibility to interested entities like professional orders. In addition, there are also prosaic motivations, in particular the will to subtract an activity from the rules of public account management. This can also be to avoid abuses, inefficacy of control exercised by the supervisory authority, "de–memberment" of the administration and the creation of ghost agencies which serve simply as instruments of the public entities. In such a situation, the public service can be more efficiency oriented, but there is the risk of the private person exploiting the public. Consequently, this system does not really fit the exigencies of the public services.

The public authorities are free, except with contrary textual stipulations, to choose the form or combination of management that seem to them preferable at a given time. This will depend on the efficacy and legal criteria but also considerations of political, economic and social opportunity.

## III. The Public Service Laws (Principles)

The activities of the public service no matter their way of management are subjected to certain principles. These principles are the essence of the public service, and when they are altered, the public service ceases to be what it ought to be. Inspired by the French, these principles invented by Louis Rolland, the public law lecturer who systematized these rules, thus sometimes called "*Lois de Rolland*" are the principles of adaptability or mutability, continuity and equality. These are the rules which govern the functioning of all the public services.

### A. The Principle of Continuity

It is the fundamental principle of the public services. It is inherent to the vocation of public service; when the public powers have recognized that an activity is indispensable in the satisfaction of collective needs, it must function continuously. The satisfaction of general interest implies that the public services should function regularly without any interruption. The intensity of this obligation varies from service to service, those working on security and hospital services for example must ensure regularity and permanence.

The obligation of continuity is at the origin of many dispositions of public law. First, the administration has the obligation to ensure this regular functioning, if not it engages its responsibility. Second, when the government is dissolved or in case of vacancy, it must continue with the management of current affairs until a new government is formed. Third, it justifies the theory of "public servant by deeds" or apparent public servant and of "occasional collaborators" of service when due to exceptional circumstances, the legal actions of a public agent acting outside the sphere of competence or even a private person are validated. Fourth, it entails that there cannot be forced execution against the administration, thus administrative goods are unassailable and imprescriptible. Fifth, this explains why the right to strike is usually restricted or forbidden from the public servants (see C.E.7 August 1909 *Winkell*, C.E. 7 July 1950 *Dehaene*). In the latter case, the government commissioner Gazier comments that it "is necessary to avoid a situation of eclipse"

## B. The Principle of Adaptation

It signifies that the regime of public services must adapt or be mutable when necessary to the evolution of collective needs and the exigencies of general interest. There should be no legal obstacles (resulting from acquired rights or contract, engagements) to the mutations to be realized. It is the obligation on services to always be in an acceptable state to satisfy collective interest. This obligation implies that the service modalities evolve in function and rhythm of changing circumstances. This may be circumstances of fact as the increase in population that justifies a parallel increase in service or the appearance of new technologies.

For the administration, this rule implies the obligation to take into account the legal, economic and technical modifications that intervened since the creation and the necessary transformations to be done in administrative acts and contracts. To the individuals, it signifies that they do not possess acquired rights when the public powers judge it necessary to modify for public interest (CS/CA 28 April 1983 *Ngon a Rikong*). The users can however attack the refusal of the administration to take measures to ensure that services are functioning in a satisfactory manner in changed circumstances.

### C. The Principle of Equality

This implies the equality of duties (charges) imposed on the citizens and the equality of access to the public service. If there is any inequality, it must be justified by the considerations of general interest or must correspond to the objective difference of the situation. The preamble to the 1996 constitution states that "all persons have equal rights and obligations. The State shall provide all its citizens with the conditions necessary for their development…..Every person shall have the right and obligation to work." It also entails the principle of neutrality which holds that public service should function objectively regardless of political, economic and social belongings.

This principle constitutes a guarantee against arbitrariness, because it forbids discriminatory treatment. The service benefits should be recognized to all persons without the introduction of unjustified benefits. However, if the users are not found in analogical situations (diversity), it is licit to apply differential treatment. Thus the legality of some preferential treatments such as regional balance and the provision of welfare services to the indigent.

## IV. Legal Situation of the User (Public) of an Administrative Public Service

Much has been said about the situation of the customers of industrial and commercial services, but users of the administrative services have been neglected. Roger Bonnard defines user as an administered who receives directly and personally the services[86] e.g. a patient being cured in a hospital, a student using educational services. The users' legal nature and the content of their situation are successively analysed.

---

[86] Précis de Droit Administratif, Paris: Librairie générale de droit et de jurisprudence, 1943 Précis de droit public, Paris : Sirey, 1944.

### A. Users' Legal Nature

Normally, the users of administrative public services are placed under legal and statutory situation. This implies that their status is determined in a general and impersonal manner. Exceptionally, the users can be seen to have formed an adhesion contract with the administration. The administration fixes the terms and the individuals adhere or join. No matter the nature, the user remains under the situation or regime of public law.

### B. Content of Users' Situation

This entails the rights, obligations, and sanctions of being in a situation of a user. The user does not possess any right to the creation, maintenance or suppression of the service. But she disposes the right of access if he fulfils the necessary conditions, and possesses the right to obtain the services furnished by the administration. The user is obliged to obey the rules and regulations of the service. She must follow the service notices and instructions of the authorities. The non–respect of the principles of utilization and the violation of their obligations can lead to administrative and penal sanctions.

In recent times, this "providential state" has been weakened by the globalization forces characterized by liberalization and privatization. On the other hand, due to the globalization challenges, the present neo–liberal state needs the public administration especially for those who cannot stand competition. From the economic perspective, according to Grover Starling, the justification of government action is twofold: promoting efficiency where the market has failed and fostering more desirable distribution of goods, services and rewards among members of the society. When private actions lead to external costs (spill overs) the government must intervene to regulate. More so, the government must ensure the provision of public goods like education, health, roads, research and development. All these necessitate the existence of public services and public order.

## 6.2 The Administrative Police Powers

The administrative police is a public service activity which uses juridical and material instruments aimed at maintaining public order and preventing disorder in order to ensure smooth functioning of the society. Simple in principle, the concept of administrative police is complex in certain of its implications. These powers are extensive because they condition essentially the possibilities of collective existence. This is because the guarantee of rights and freedoms necessitates the existence of public force. However, the exercise of these powers carries the germs of violation of rights and freedoms, that is why they are regulated by many protective rules. There are always issues regarding the competent authorities, the real objective of the police powers, and the relationships that should exist between these powers and the human rights and freedoms or liberties. However, technically, the expression administrative police signify a specific activity of administrative authorities with target to maintain public order and with a specific legal regime.

## I. Administrative Authorities vested with Police Powers

It is not usually easy to delimit the respective powers of the diverse competent authorities who intervene at various levels and in various domains. Depending on the jurisdiction of the authorities, there exist general and special police powers.

### A. Criteria for distinction of the types of police power

In general terms, the general police powers entail competence in all matters and all over the whole territory. The extent of the powers diminishes as one moves from the central to the non–central entities. Special powers generally entail those in specific and determined areas of activity, even if for the whole territory. These two types of powers can be distinguished using three criteria.

#### 1. Geographic Criterion

The general police powers apply for the whole territory (extended), while the special is considered as local or limited. This conception is relative because the municipal police (local) is also general, and the ministers whose activities extend to the whole territory are usually seen as special.

### 2. Organic Criterion

Here, the two categories of powers are distinguished in function of their holders. But there are some authorities who are endowed with both general and special police powers.

### 3. Material Criterion

This is the most applicable. The general police is defined by its domain and content: it applies to all the administered and all activities (e.g. municipal police). On the other hand, the special police either affect a particular category of persons or a determined area of activity.

## B. Cameroonian Authorities holders of the powers

At the national level, the President of the Republic as chief of the executive has general police powers. The deconcentrated administrative authorities as the heads of the administrative circumscriptions have attributions of administrative police. The decentralized administrative authorities (mayor, government delegate, municipal administrator) are responsible for general and special police measures within their respective council jurisdictions.

The regulation of the special police powers determines the competent authority to use the police powers thus created, e.g. the Ministers are special police powers in their respective domains.

## C. Coexistence of police authorities

As they are diverse and exercised by multiple authorities, the exercise of different police competencies can at times be confusing and complex. First the authorities are expected to cooperate and collaborate (general/special, central/local) in the maintenance of public order. Second, there are certain domains that are shared by many authorities, thus the problem of determining who does what. Thus there are possibilities of confusion and even conflict between the authorities. Third, there is the issue of an administrative authority cumulating various types of police powers.

## II. Target of Administrative Police Powers: Maintenance of Public Order.

Police power implies simply the powers of the administrative authorities to regulate the activities of the administered; that is maintaining public order or preventing public disorder. The maintenance of public order is the obligatory target of administrative police, but this notion (public order) is difficult to define for it has a flexible, contingent and relative character. Yet the decisions of the police authorities are legal if and only if they aim to maintain public order (C.E.2, July 1970 *Louba*). If all authors believe that public order is simply part of general interest this concept remains contingent and relative. The concept of the maintenance of public order itself has evolved, and there is the issue of distinction of the spheres of administrative and judiciary police.

### A. The Evolution of Police Powers

The authorities have to prevent public disorder, but if in spite of efforts there is disorder, they have to maintain order and put an end to disorder. There exist the classical and modern conceptions of public order.

#### 1. Classical Conception

During the 19$^{th}$ century, public order was defined in a negative manner–absence of material trouble. It had nothing to do with morality or well–being. The aim was simply to maintain things as they were. This traditional conception of public order corresponds to a bourgeoisie trilogy–security, tranquillity and cleanliness. If the administrator acts not in response to a threat of one or many of these factors, there is diversion of powers and non–respect (vice) of form.

#### 2. Modern Conception

This conception is more extensive. In addition to the classical components, it implies the satisfaction of collective needs, the protection of individual rights and freedoms, harmonious arrangements of social life and the blossoming of the human being. This entails adherence to public morality, absence of brutal and savage activities and the compulsory respect of human beings. The target is no longer only the absence of disorder but the creation of individual and collective well–being, from economic and social perspectives. The conception of public order depends both on the place and the time.

The activities of the maintenance of public order are by nature different. Some are of juridical order which entails enacting rules and regulations that serve as sources of obligations and prohibitions to the public. Others are of the material order which emphasize on the concrete activities, real measures taken to maintain public order, and from this perspective administrative and judicial police can be distinguished.

### B. Administrative and Judicial Police Powers

The difference between the two is theoretically clear: the administrative police tend to prevent violations of public order and the judicial has as target repression. This distinction is logical: following the constitutional principle of separation of powers, the judicial police powers belong to the courts. As regards contention, the administrative judge is competent for litigations that result from administrative police, but the judiciary judge is competent for those of judicial police. In practice, the distinction of the two activities is delicate: First, they are done by the same persons, administrative and judicial authorities and the police officers and gendarmes. Second, it is not always easy to delimit these activities; as the administrative police at times do not only prevent but also repress violations to public order. At times, it also happens that the judicial police prevent infractions. Finally, because there exist polyvalent operations, an authority during an operation, can act successively in the name of the two police.

## III. Particularities of the Regime of Administrative Police Acts

The originality of the legal means of administrative police authorities is that the regulations or individual measures have to be completed at the level of execution by material acts. The administrative police powers are obligatorily unilateral, generally preventive, seemingly discretionary and the administration is submitted to special conditions.

### A. The obligatory unilateral character of administrative police acts

Decisions taken in matters of administrative police are essentially preventive. A manifestation that can disturb public order is forbidden a priori. The authority has to assess in advance what are the risks to public order. The preventive character is not only an element of definition but also a criterion, since it can be used to distinguish administrative police acts from those of the judicial police powers which are essentially repressive.

But administrative police are not exclusively preventive. Some acts are really sanctions. For example, the seizure of an individual's driving license by the senior divisional officer can be seen as a sanction (C.E.4th March 1960 *Levy).* The prohibition of the presentation of certain films in his council area by the mayor can be seen as sanction (C.E. 10th December 1959 *Sté des Films Lutétia*). Even if these are sanctions, they remain attempts to avoid public disorder.

### B. The seemingly discretionary character of administrative police acts.

Some authors believe that the police authorities have the choice of time, choice of measure to take and finally the liberty whether to act or abstain (facultative nature). But at times inaction can lead to the engagement of the responsibility of the administration on the basis of service fault. If the authority commits a fault by not acting, he has the obligation to act.

## IV. Conditions for the Exercise of Administrative Police

The police power, due to its object, is under an ambivalent regime: because it is indispensable to social life, the authorities who exercise it have extensive powers; but because the decisions they take are more than others, susceptible to violate human rights and freedoms, they are put under strict controls of regularity.

## A. Prerogatives of the Administration in matters of Administrative Police

The prerogatives endowed the authorities of police powers are particularly wide and deprive the governed from the means of defence normally available to them. Administrative sanctions are derogations to powers normally awarded to the administrative authorities (e.g closure of establishments, prohibition of sale or circulation,). More so, the police acts have the right to automatic execution (privilege d'exécution d'office). Further, the two procedures used to protect the governed against abuses are excluded as far as administrative police is concerned. Administrative deferment, (référé administrative) and suspension of execution are not applied in matters which concern public order (C.E. 8th October 1971, S.A. "*Librairie François MASPERO).* In addition, the administrators have the powers of forced execution of measures taken, for example the impoundment of vehicles, seizure of newspapers, and destruction of buildings. Finally, the principle of retrospectiveness of sanctions, fundamental in penal or disciplinary procedures, is not commonplace with the police powers. Thus regularity is appreciated in line with the day that the decision or measure was taken to change the previous one and not when the effects were produced.

## B. Protective Measures against Administrative Police

The measures of administrative police must naturally conform to the general rules of content and procedure that govern the administrative acts, even though urgency can be used by the administrators to avoid them. Since the police authorities have extensive powers, they have to be subjected to specific principles and additional vigilance.

On the one hand, the police powers do not have the right to take decisions in some circumstances. Submitting an activity to preliminary authorization or declaration outside the circumstances previewed by the law as well as prescribing authoritatively the means by which a person must end the trouble to public order is forbidden. On the other hand, more than in the other domains of administrative intervention, the judge always request that measures taken should be necessary and proportionate to the situation. The contentious control is therefore exercised in a more and particularly profound manner, the appreciation of contested decisions include for that reason elements of opportunity. Finally, administrative police is analysed not only as power, but also as a duty or obligation. The Senior Divisional Officers and Mayors are obliged to ensure the application of regulations enacted by themselves or their hierarchical superiors. If they fail to do so, and damages result, the responsibility of the administration is engaged. Thus, in their actions, the administrative police powers must follow specific procedures.

# Chapter Seven
# Procedures of Administrative Action

The normal procedure of administrative action is through unilateral acts. Exceptionally, it can be as a result of an agreement with another contractual party. There are therefore two types of administrative acts: the unilateral and the bilateral (contract).

## 7.1. Unilateral Administrative Acts

In order to comprehend the concept of unilateral administrative acts it is germane to discuss the criteria of identification, conditions of legality, effects and disappearance.

### I. The Criteria of Identification

We have to analyse the general definition and the one offered by the Cameroon judge, and its relationship to public law.

#### A. Definition of administrative act in the general theory of administrative law

With inspiration from renowned French authors, this definition is based on three fundamental criteria: The organic criterion defines the administrative act as that which is accomplished by an administrative organ. The administrative organ is distinguished from other administrative State organs (legislative, judiciary) and the private bodies. The material criterion takes into consideration the character, object and finality of the act. The administrative act determines the individual situation while the legislative is general and impersonal (relative). The functional criterion takes into consideration the applicable law. It holds that the administrative act belongs to administrative law and within the competence of the administrative judge.

## B. The criterion of the unilateral act held by the Cameroon judge

In CFJ/AP 20th March 1968 arrêt *Ngongang Njake Martin C/ Etat du Cameroun*, the judge gave the following definition "The administrative act is a legal unilateral act taken by an administrative authority in the exercise of administrative power and creating rights and obligations to the private persons. From this definition the unilateral act has the following features:

### 1. The unilateral administrative act is a legal act

The unilateral administrative act is a normative act (that is one which edicts norms). In addition to the will of the author to modify a given situation, there is the process of law making.

### 2. It emanates from the administrative authority

It comes from the administrative authority in the exercise of administrative power. It is this aspect of the definition which consecrates the organic criterion. It excludes other persons from making administrative acts. It is not from private or non–administrative persons. This position is confirmed by legal scholars and judges in Cameroon.

#### a. The case of private persons

In Cameroon, as underlines Henri Jacquot, "the acts of private persons even if invested with the prerogatives of public power are not considered as administrative acts and their disputes are not part of the competence of the administrative judge". In the arrêt CFJ/CAY of 27th January *1970 Obame Eteme Joseph C/ Republique Féderale du Cameroun,* the Cameroonian judge rejected the request soliciting the condemnation of the Senior Divisional Officer on personal capacity. The exclusion of private bodies or persons from issuing administrative acts was adopted in *Bernard Auteroche C/ Ordre National des Médécins* (CFJ/LAY, 27th January 1968), confirmed in *1977 Feumi Jacques C/ Conseil de l'Ordre des Avocats* and equally confirmed in *1991 Tieko Felix C/ Conseil National des Pharmaciens etc.*

As we have seen, the management of public services is at times conferred to private persons or bodies. It is on the basis of this reasoning that the French administrative judge accepts that administrative acts can emanate from the private (C.T 31 July 1942 *Monpeurt,* C.E. 13 January 1961 *Magnier).*

### b. The case of non–administrative public persons

These include acts of legislative, judiciary and some executive acts. The acts of legislative power, the laws regularly adopted by the parliament are considered legislative acts. The administrative judge has constantly excluded these acts from administrative acts–CFJ/AP 28 January 1970 *Société des Grands Travaux de l'Est C/ Etat Fédérale du Cameroun oriental;* CFJ/CAY 8 December 1970 *Claude Haule c/Etat Fédérale du Cameroun Oriental.*

As regards the acts of judiciary power, a distinction must be made between acts relative to the organization of justice and those concerning the functioning of the "judiciary machine". The first, for example acts creating or suppressing courts are unilateral administrative acts. The second relative to the functioning of courts and other judiciary units are not unilateral administrative acts but judicial acts (see CFJ/AP 16 March 1967 *Tagny Mathieu c/ Etat du Cameroun. CFJ/CAY 28 August 1972 Aoua Hadja C/ Republique Fédérale du Cameroun).*

The acts of administrative authorities, when intervening in legislative and international relations matters are certainly acts from the executive power but are in the domain of governing than administering. They form part of what is called "government acts" and unlike the administrative acts enjoy legal immunity. The Cameroonian laws on the matter have stated precisely that no court should judge government acts. This is confirmed by the courts in CS/CA of 24 April 1980 *Essougou Benoît c/ Etat du Cameroun,* 29 May 1980 *Monkam T. David c/ Etat du Cameroun.*

### 3. The Unilateral administrative act creates rights and obligations for particulars

The measures of internal order such as circulars and service notices which do not create rights and obligations for particulars should not constitute administrative acts. These arguments are relative, for some circulars complete or even modify the provisions of a law or regulation, therefore producing legal effects. Unilateral administrative acts are classified according to their content (regulatory or individual acts) or according to the authority who made them (decree, orders etc).

Thus the conception of administrative act as opined by the Cameroonian judge largely follows the organic criterion. It is very restrictive, for it excludes the acts of private persons and non–administrative public persons from being unilateral administrative acts. From this standpoint, the concern is on the relationship between the acts and public law.

## C. Unilateral act and public law

Is the unilateral administrative act a distinctive factor of public law? According to André de Laubadère the unilateral administrative act is characteristic of public law, private law lies on the act of agreement and he notes that there is nothing in private law which can be compared to executory administrative decisions.[87] Jean Waline affirms that the executory decision is a unique procedure to public law. Surely we take decisions but we cannot unilaterally by our own will, create obligations for third persons. Georges Vedel [88] holds that among the prerogatives of public power, the most characteristic is without doubt the privilege of the administration to take executory decisions, that is to unilaterally make acts which create rights and obligations to third persons without their consent and which are susceptible to be executed by force. More in this line, Jean Rivero holds that in administrative law contrary to what obtains in private law, the administration can modify the legal situation by its own will without the consent of the concerned. It is a prerogative which characterizes public power. Through the procedure of unilateral act, the

---

[87] André de Laubadère (24 septembre 1910, Paris – 1981) est un juriste français, spécialiste du droit administratif. Has authored *La distinction des contrats administratifs et des contrats de droit commun. La formation des contrats administratifs* (1956) *Traité théorique et pratique des contrats administratifs* (1959) *Cours de grands services publics et entreprises nationales: rédigé d'après les notes et avec l'autorisation de M. André de Laubadère. 1959–1960* (1960) *Traité élémentaire de droit administratif: Les grands services publics administratifs, Volume 3* (1978), *Traité de droit administratif* (1980).

[88] Georges Vedel (5 July 1910 – 21 February 2002) was a French public law professor from Auch, France.

administration fixes new rules and modifies existing ones, thus creating rights and imposing obligations on the governed without their prior approval.

It should be noted that unilateral acts are not a monopoly of the public power. They also exist in private groups where there is the expression of power. In the family, there exist parental powers. In the enterprise the manager can issue general and individual norms unilaterally which affect the employees without their consent.

## II. General Conditions of Legality of Unilateral Administrative Acts

All administrative acts are susceptible to be attacked before the administrative judge. The elements of regularity are those norms which when violated the judge can cancel the administrative decision on the basis of what we qualify as conditions for appeals against abuse of powers. These elements are – the author, the content, the form, the procedure, the finality and motives.

### A. The Rules of Competence

These rules are important because an administrative act must be done by the competent authority. Competence is the aptitude to accomplish certain acts which usually regulate human conduct. The issue is the determinants of the competence of an author.

#### 1. Criteria of Competence

Three criteria permit the appreciation of the zone of competence of an administrative authority. Competence "*rationae materiae*" signifies that the administrative authority must only intervene in matters attributed. These matters are usually defined by the constitutions, decrees; laws etc (see administrative organization). Competence "*rationae temporis*" implies that an administrative authority can only exercise competence from the date invested with such powers and at times during determined periods. Competence "*rationae loci*", from the territorial point of view, fixes the geographical limits within which the authorities have to act. There exist, therefore, central and non–central authorities. The competent authorities have to act personally, but in the case of public service exigencies, power can be delegated.

### 2. Delegation of competence

To ensure the continuity of the public service, delegation permits an authority to charge another to act on his name. Delegation of competence is of two types: Delegation of powers and delegation of signature. The first is the transfer of competence from one authority to another. Such a delegation is usually defined by text. The authority to whom power is delegated is wholly responsible for the decision he takes. The second is the transfer of the material task of signing administrative acts to another authority usually nominally designated. The signatory is not responsible at all for the decisions signed. The responsibility rests on the competent authority. When competent, the issue becomes the expression of competence by the administrative authority.

### 3. Expressions of competence

It can be through restricted power (*pouvoir lie*) or discretionary power. Restricted power is when the administrative authority has no possibility of choice. He must accomplish a determined act. Refusal can lead to annulment and engagement of the responsibility of the administration if damages are caused. When a user fulfils the necessary conditions, the administrator is bound to act e.g. a student who fulfils the necessary conditions for entry into the University and compiles documents must be admitted.

Discretionary power is the case where the authority has the liberty to act or not and how to do so. It is normal even necessary that the law gives the administration the possibility of choice, because general interest cannot be easily achieved if the administration is found in a robot situation (programmed behaviour or action). It is the liberty to appreciate the opportunity and see what is good for society. This discretionary power is not arbitrary power. This is so because the discretionary power is simply the power to choose decisions and this does not mean a holiday to the principle of legality (administration remains submitted to law). The violation of any of the rules of competence leads to the cancellation of the administrative act for vice of incompetence.

## B. Rules of procedure

Procedure deals with the modalities of fabrication of legal acts. It is the operations that are called the "*facere*". These are simply the formalities accomplished during the elaboration of the act. The rules of procedure concern the "*négotium*" that is the normative operation. As regards the place of accomplishment of the act, there are some which need effective presence and some which do not. The delays during which the administrators should accomplish the act are usually indicative but some are however imperative (e.g. case of ordinances for specific period, after that time government is incompetent). Legal judgement imposes some delays. Useful delay is the minimum period of time awarded a concerned to receive and react to an administrative act. This is usually in the case of defence right. The concerned should be given enough time (see C.E. 20 Jan.1956 *Negre*). Reasonable delay is the maximum delay within which the administration must edict an act. The non–respect of this delay is a fault that can engage the responsibility of the administration (C.E. 11 December 1964 *Cavim*). The rules of procedure are based on two essential techniques.

### 1. Consultative procedure

This is the case where in the elaboration of an administrative act a body is charged to give its opinion. The consultation is said to be "facultative" when the opinion does not bind the administrative authority and remains without influence on the legality of the decision (*avis facultative*). Consultation is "obligatory" when the authority is obliged to solicit the opinion, but he is not bound to follow it (avis obligatoire). In arrêt CFJ/CAY 8 December 1970 *Sitamze Urbain c/ Etat du Cameroun* the consultation of the disciplinary council before sanctioning was seen as obligatory. More so, in the making of some acts, public inquiries and investigations are necessary (e.g. expropriation).

### 2. Contradictory procedure

In taking certain decisions, the administrative authorities are obliged to permit the concerned to present their points of views and eventually their objections. This is usually in the case of sanctions, where the aggrieved has the right to self–defence. The respect of this defence right is a general principle of law, and its violation leads to the cancellation of the act. The Cameroon administration judge is firm on the respect of this principle. Examples: CFJ/AP 16 March 1967 *Makoube Albert C/ Etat du Cameroun.* CS/CA 24 April 1980 *Nana David c/ Etat du Cameroun.* It should be noted that any violations to the rules of procedure are sanctioned on the bases of procedural impropriety.

### C. Rules of Form

Form concerns the written, the "instrumentum" the "factum" that is the product of the operations (procedure). Here one can think of the general presentation of the act, visas, and motivation.

#### 1. General presentation of the act

The administrative acts are usually written. Exceptionally they can be purely verbal (see C.S./CA 19 December 1975 *Tonkam Pierre C/ Etat du Cameroun.* The mention of the place of the act is necessary in some circumstances but not in others (C.E. 22 December 1911 *Legrand*). The mention of the date is not a condition for the formal regulation of the act. Its absence does not entail by itself the nullity of the act (C.E. 30 June 1952 *Balenciaga*). The act usually has a title and a denomination –decree, ordinance, order, circular, general instruction. The signature is the patronymic of the instrumentum of the act and which aims at establishing the origin and certifying the content. By signing, the author confirms the content and assumes responsibility. The signature therefore should be a condition of formal regularity of the legal act. Also within the act there exist:–

#### 2. Visas

These are references made to the essential acts which are anterior to the concerned text. Three remarks have to be made. First, the visa is not an element of the regularity of an act. The Cameroon administrative judge has constantly held that the absence of the visa does not entail the annulment of the act (CS/AP 1972 *Evina Ada Christophe,* CS/CA 1980 *Nana David c/ Etat du Cameroun*, CS/CA 1980 *Monkam. T. David c/ Etat du Cameroun.* Second, the visa does not qualify the act (see *Affaire "Frampar*). Third; the facultative character of the visa does not exclude the necessity of all acts to have a legal base.

### 3. Motivation

The motive is a fundamental element of the act. It is the antecedent, what precedes and provokes it. It constitutes the raison–d'être of the act. The motives are the fundamental conditions which authorize or impose action, they are objective facts anterior and exterior to the act and which make it possible. The principle is, there is no obligation to motivate without text: In supervisory matters, the acts of the administrative authority to limit the prerogatives and autonomy of the local authorities must be motivated. Decisions inflicting disciplinary sanctions must be motivated (article 95 of Decree N°. 94/199 of 7 October 1994 of the New Statute of the State Public Service).

The above rules compose internal and external legality. Some of the conditions are indicative (facultative) and others are imperative (obligatory). It is only in the latter case that violation can lead to annulment of acts.

## III. The Effects of Administrative Acts

The administrative acts are authoritative decisions (*autorité de chose décidée*). Their effects start when they enter into force and only end when they disappear.

### A. Entry into Force

The administrative act enters into force from its emission, from when it is signed. It can only be opposed or produce consequences vis–à–vis the governed when made known through publicity: Publication for the acts of general nature (e.g. regulations) and notification to the concerned in the case of individual acts (e.g. appointment, advancement, sanctions).

### B. Execution of Administrative Acts

This is where the prerogatives of the public power really come in. The administrative decisions have the privilege of automatic execution (executory character– *L'autorité de chose decidée*). This can be done on the basis of two rules:

### 1. Provisional Execution

This is sometimes called preliminary privilege (i.e. *privilège du préalable*). It stipulates that the governed have no right to judge the legality of administrative acts. These acts are imposed on them and they have to execute and submit to the prescribed order. Provisional execution is seen as the "fundamental rule of public law" (C.E. 2 July 1982, *Huglo et autres*). When the individual doubts the regularity it can be contested through administrative and legal appeals. In order to avoid the paralysis of administrative action, the appeals before the competent jurisdictions do not suspend the execution of the attacked decision.

This rule however has three exceptions:– The dispositions of the General Tax Code suspending the execution of administrative norms (suspension of payment and sale – article 289). Next, the suspension of execution, provided in the law fixing the procedure before the Supreme Court in administrative matters. But this suspension is only accorded when the execution of the act can cause irreparable prejudice and when the attacked decision does not concern public order, security and tranquillity (see administrative police). Finally, the resistance of the governed (passive or violent) to the decision. However, when obstructed by the resistance of the governed, the administration disposes normal and exceptional means to impose its decision. Examples of normal means are penal sanctions (fines), administrative sanctions/seizure of driving licence, and closure of an establishment. The exceptional means is "forced execution".

### 2. Forced Execution

By this way, the administration constraints the individuals to act. This means is used when all else have failed to ensure the obedience of the law. In principle, the use of forced execution is prohibited. In T.C. 2 December 1902 *Société Immobilière de Saint Just*– the judge Romieu concluded that, forced execution is forbidden to the administration before the intervention of the judge. Romieu continues that it is a fundamental principle of public law that the administration should not by itself use public force to assure the execution of acts. It must first address to the judiciary authority, which establishes the disobedience, punish the infraction and permit the employment of material means of coercion. This should be done normally through penal sanction conferred to the repressive jurisdiction (see also C.E. 19 April 1907 *Dame de Sureman*). This rule protects the individuals against the abuses of automatic execution which can favour arbitrariness and cover illegalities (C.E. 27 February 1903, *Olivier et Zimmermann*).

However, the principle that forced execution is illicit admits two types of exceptions. Textual exceptions, when there is a legislative stipulation clearly authorising the administration to employ public force without a preliminary intervention of the judge. In addition to the textual provisions and as upheld by the judge, forced execution is licit in two cases. When there is urgency. This is usually the case of public necessity or when it is necessary to prevent an imminent danger (T.C. 21 July 1949, *Sieur de Berthier*). Romieu holds that the administration has to act immediately and employ force without delay or procedure when circumstances permit it. When a house is on fire the administrator should not ask from the judge the authorisation to send firemen (*pompiers*) there. Forced execution is also accepted when administrative execution is the only possiblity and penal sanctions to the infractions do not exist.

## C. Disappearance of Administrative Acts.

For one reason or the other, the effects of the act can be put to an end. The public powers have to take into account the preservation of acquired rights, general interest, and maintenance of public order and smooth functioning of the public services. The law uses different terminologies and rules depending on the nature of the act and circumstances.

### 1. Abrogation (Non retrospective effect)

Abrogation puts an end to the future effects of the act. It depends whether it is a statutory or an individual act. The abrogation of statutory acts are pronounced by the same author (of the decision) using the same procedure, and in the same form, (principle of parallelism of competence, form and procedure). This can be a guarantee to the governed. The abrogation of individual acts as a general rule is not permitted if it has created rights. It is only possible when rights have not been created. The abrogation of individual acts is called revocation.

### 2. Retreat (Retrospective withdrawal).

It is an annulment *ab initio* of an act. It is submitted to more severe rules. It is valid from the time of signature but can be opposed only after publication or notification. The rules vary depending on whether the act is regular or not. The retreat of regular acts as a general rule is forbidden. But can be possible in the following cases: At the request of the beneficiary; if the act has not created rights and if it is imposed on the administration either by the law or judge.

As regards the retreat of irregular acts, the principles applicable in such situations are contained in an important Arrêt *Dame Cachet* (C.E. 3 Nov. 1922).The administration can retreat its act in the two months which follow notification or publication; It can retreat it if there is already a case before the judge in view of its annulment; Only the beneficiaries are notified, but third persons have the right to appeal.

The unilateral administrative acts are essentially a distinctive factor of public law, though the private persons intervene. The administrators have to follow the laws governing them if not they are not valid. However, there is the influence of conjuncture on the legal regime of acts. The rules of law are usually made for normal periods. When there are exceptional circumstances, these rules are no longer adapted to the prevailing situation and the administrative authorities have to act mindful of the situation. There is therefore conflict between the preoccupation of effectiveness and that of the respect of the law. Another procedure of administrative action which should also be submitted to the law, but done with partners is administrative contracts.

## 7.2. Administrative Contracts

The unilateral act remains today the normal procedure of administrative action, but the contract occupies an important place. The administrative authorities use the instrument of contracts in: the buying of furniture, engagement of personnel, the association of the private persons in the realization of general interest, and the relations between the public persons themselves (state, councils, public enterprises etc). There are two regimes of administrative contracts – those which are identical to that of particulars, that is submitted to private law and consequently belong to the judicial judge; and those of public law that is administrative contracts *stricto sensu* fall within the competence of the administrative judge. After the generalities of administrative contracts, their formation, execution and termination are systematically discussed.

# I. Generalities on Administrative contracts

The general principles of administrative contracts focus on the types and the criteria of determining the contracts.

## A. Types of Administrative Contracts

There exist a great variety of administrative contracts; public service concessions, assignments; the public markets; hire contract; loan contract; invitation to tender etc. Decree N° 79/35 of February 1979 on Regulations Governing Public Sector Contracts, defines an administrative contract as "a written agreement concluded under the conditions laid down by this decree by which a person who is governed either by public or private law, enters into an agreement with the State, a local authority or a public establishment to carry out any work on its behalf or under its supervision or to supply it with goods or services, in return for a sum of money." This definition covers the types of contracts stipulated above which begs the question on what really makes a contract administrative.

## B. Criteria to Determine Administrative Contracts

A criterion is not valid if it cannot be used to say whether or not a contract is administrative. There are fundamentally three criteria that serve as determinants of public contracts:

### 1. Public Person as co–contractor

For the contract to be administrative, the judge holds that one of the parties should be a public person. So an administrative contract should be between public persons themselves or between a public and a private person. In France, at one time, the administrative character was refused to contracts concluded between two private persons no matter the nature of their clauses and even if attached to the execution of a public service mission (T.C. 3 March 1968, SOC, *Interlait*). However and exceptionally, the judge admits that a contract signed between two private persons can be administrative (see T.C. 8 July 1963 *Société Enterprise Peyrot*, C.E. 2 June 1961, *Leduc*, C.E. 18 June 1976, *dame Culard*).

### 2. Target as public service execution

The target (object) of a contract is the operation to be realized. It is necessary that the contractual party be conferred the execution of the public service (C.E. 20 April 1956, *époux Bertin*).The contract must constitute one of the modalities of the execution of the public service: public works (C.E. 20 April 1956 *Consorts Grimouard*) hire of personnel (CS–CA 30 April 1981, *Guiffo Jean–Philippe*). According to the conclusions of Chardeau in C.E. 4 June 1954 *Affortit et Vingtain* "all agents, no matter the clauses of their contracts, who have as mission to ensure the functioning of an administrative public service, and those who collaborate in the target pursued by this service are part of public law."

### 3. The presence of exorbitant clauses to common law

The administrative judge in arrêt *Stein (*C.E. 20 October 1950) defines this clause as "clause with object to confer to parties rights and put to their charge obligations foreign in their nature to those which are susceptible to be freely agreed upon by anyone within the framework of civil and commercial laws". These abnormal and un–egalitarian clauses awards prerogatives to the administration vis–à–vis its contractual partners in the form of power of automatic action, discretionary resiliation, exorbitant control (C.E. 30 Jan 1980–*Ville de Paris*).Or awards these prerogatives to the co–contractor vis–à–vis third persons in the form of right to impose taxes or privilege of exclusivity (monopoly). The question which comes to the mind is whether the different criteria are in hierarchy, are alternatives or form a system. The criterion used depends on the contract itself, thus the criteria have alternative character.

There is controversy among publicists on the distinctiveness of administrative contracts. According to Léon Duguit "there is no real difference between civil and administrative contracts" because "the intrinsic elements of a contract usually have the same characteristics and same effects." On the contrary Jeze holds that "the effects of the administrative contract are not the same as those of the civil contract". However, the problematic of the public administration is to do or make others do, decide or negotiate

## II. The Formation of Administrative Contracts

The administrative contract is a normative act. It is elaborated during a normative operation (negotium) and the agreements are expressed on a written document (instrumentum). The process that leads to the conclusion of a contract is of concern.

## A. Choice of the Contractual Partner

The choice is based on the correct execution of the contract, that is the contractor who given the resources can best execute the contract. There are three classical ways to award administrative contracts.

### 1. Contracts awarded to the tenderer who makes the lowest offer (*adjudication*).

This is not foreseen in Cameroon. Here after bids or tenders have been invited, the contract is awarded to the tenderer who makes the lowest offer. The cheapest order is not necessarily the best in quality.

### 2. Contracts awarded by invitation to tender (*appel d'offres*)

An invitation to treat can either be public or restricted. A public invitation supposes an open call for bids. Restricted invitations are addressed to a limited number of candidates chosen by the administration for economic or technical reasons. Here, the administration in making its choice is not only guided by the best price but also other factors (arts. 33–50 of Decree 86/903 of 18 July 1986 Regulating Public Markets).

### 3. Contracts awarded by mutual agreement (*marché de gré à gré*)

The administration has to invite tenders, but it can choose co–contractor even out of the competitors. Here the administrator has a free will to choose (arts. 51–53 of Decree 86/903 Regulating Public Markets).

## B. Elaboration of contract terms

The administrative contracts are not elaborated jointly by the parties. The contractual clauses or norms are elaborated unilaterally by the administration and the co–contractor has either to accept or refuse the conditions posed. The contract terms is joint to the document of charges considered as a constitutive element of the contract. Thus the administration does not only award contracts but fixes the rules, thus the equality of partners is an illusion in case of administrative contracts.

### 1. Different types of charges documents (*cahiers des charges*)

The clauses of public contracts are contained in the charges documents. These are written documents which determine the general conditions of markets and general obligations of the parties. They precise the conditions to which the contracts are awarded and executed. The contractual clauses are usually borrowed from this document (technique of adhesion contract).

### 2. Characteristics of charges Documents

- They have a unilateral character (done by administration)
- They are preliminary thus anterior to the market or contract.
- Usually of regulatory character (general and impersonal in nature).

## C. Conclusion of the contract

As any contract, the administrative contract is made by the exchange of wills between parties. The next issue is the authorities competent to represent or engage the administration and the validity of contractual norms.

### 1. Determination of competent Authorities

The administrators at the central, deconcentrated and decentralized levels are statutorily habilitated to award contracts. If the contract is awarded by an incompetent authority, it is not valid but if the contractual partner acts in good faith, he can obtain some indemnity through engaging the responsibility of the administration. The conclusion of the contract can be done directly or indirectly.

### 2. Validity of contractual terms

This is verified at two stages, before (authorization) and after (approbation) to the conclusion of the contract: First, authorization which is anterior to the conclusion of the contract. It is usually asked for by the competent authority so as to enable the signature of the contract. Certain contracts of the Council must be authorized by the supervisory power. For the General Manager of the public enterprise to award a contract, the authorization of the Administrative board is compulsory. Second, approbation is posterior to the conclusion of the contracts awarded by the authorities.

## III. The Execution of Administrative Contracts

A contract implies reciprocal rights and obligations. The administration as all contractors has the right to the execution of the stipulated obligations. These principles of common law, however, have to be adapted to the exigencies of the public service. The administration therefore has certain prerogatives, and as a counterpart, the co–contractors have certain rights. (See clause exorbitant to common law).

### 1. The prerogatives of the administration

In administrative law in general, and administrative contracts in particular, the principle of equality is an illusion. Article 1134 of the civil code which states that the agreements legally formed serve as law for those who have done so, does not really hold as far as the administration is concerned. The administration has some privileges which are a challenge to this notably powers of modification, direction, sanction and termination.

#### a. Power of unilateral modification

The administration has the right to unilaterally modify the terms of the contract (see C.E. 1/2/1829 *Moreau*, 14/10/1902, C.E. *Richard Olmer*, 21/3/1910 *Campagnie Générale Française de Tramways*. The unilateral modification in itself is not a fault, but if it causes prejudice to the co–contractor, he has the right to indemnity (CS–CA 1/2/1965 *Tameghi Boniface Amsecom c/Etat du Cameroun.*

This power of unilateral modification is neither general nor absolute. Surely this principle is based on good functioning, mutability or adaptation of the public service, but is subject to some limitations. The modifications should not upset the economy or change the object of the contract. They must be only on the clauses concerning the organization and functioning of the public service and should not concern clauses relative to the financial advantages of the contractor, if so; he has the right to indemnity. The private law principle of the intangibility of contract terms is therefore not consecrated in administrative law.

### b. Right of Direction and Control

The administrative authorities have the power to direct and control the execution of the contract. It is not necessary that this be expressly stated in the contract. This right is particularly remarkable in matters of public works where the entrepreneur has to execute the service orders by the administration, the "master of the work".

### c. Power of sanction

This power of sanction is exercised when there has been a fault in the execution (late, not well done, poor execution etc) of the contract. The administration can do this as a full right and unilaterally without the preliminary establishment of the fault by the judge. The judge can control the adaptation of the sanction to the gravity of the fault, but usually refuses to cancel sanctions taken irregularly, and prefer to condemn the administration to pay for damages.

There are many ways that the administration can exercise its power of sanctions including sanctions of pecuniary character (payment of damages, penalties); some are coercive where the administration substitutes the contractor to execute the contract, and others are resolutive, that is put an end to the contract without any indemnity. (Resiliation–sanction).

### d. Power of unilateral termination

The power of termination is of public order, which can be exercised even if not stipulated in the contract. The administrator therefore has the right to terminate the contract at any time if for public good or interest of the service. The contractors on their part are not totally armless they have some rights.

### 2. Rights accorded the co–contractors

Contractors have to be paid for the execution of the contract. This can be done in the form of advances, payments in the account or payment on final settlement. In normal circumstances, the administration has no power of unilateral modification of the price. Added to the normal payments, the contractor can also claim indemnities if unforeseen changes affect the financial equilibrium or financial equation of the contract. In this case, 3 theories are envisaged which will be treated below.

### a. Theory of administrative action *(La théorie du fait du prince)*

This is when due to measures taken by the administration (administrative hazards) the execution of the contract becomes more difficult for the contractor. This is the case when the administration has used its power of unilateral modification. In this case, the contractor has the right to the total indemnification of the supplementary charges imposed. But for this to happen, three conditions have to be fulfilled: The decision generating the disequilibrium must emanate from the administration (charge of taxes or salary scale etc). The measures should not be general or impersonal; it should affect the contractor in a particular way. These measures must lead to the aggravation of the financial charges of the contractor.

### b. Theory of unforeseen (la théorie de l'imprévision)

This is based on the economic hazards and depends on when there is the upsetting of the financial equilibrium not imputable on the administration (C.E. 30/3/1916 *Gaz de Bordeau)*. But for the contractor to receive the indemnity some conditions must be fulfilled:–The abnormal circumstances should be external and independent of the will of the parties. The situation must be unforeseen. The financial equilibrium must have been upset. The execution of the contract must remain possible. If not the parties have to sign a different contract or call for the judge to terminate the contract (C.E. 9/12/1931 *Tramways de Cherbourg*).

### c. Theory of unforeseen subjection (*La théorie des subjections imprévues*)

This theory is a variation of the preceding, but the hazard here is specifically technical. After execution or due to some unforeseen, the contract has to end.

## IV. Termination of Administrative contracts (extinction).

Normally, the contract should end, by the execution of the obligation of each party, by the expiration of the period of which it was concluded or by the will of the parties. In administrative law a more important place is given to unilateral annulment than private law.

### A. Annulment by the Administration

This can intervene in two cases, because of fault or without fault. In the case of fault by the co–contractor, annulment or cancellation is a sanction. Eventually with the intervention of the judge the contractor can be compensated. As regards annulment without fault, the administrator even with the absence of the clause that permits that, has the prerogative to cancel the contract even if the contractor has committed no fault. In so doing however, he engages the responsibility of the administration "without fault." The legislature also has full right to cancel contracts but this remains exceptional.

### B. Annulment by the judge

This can be in two situations. At the request of the contractor due to the fault of the administration, or at the request of any of the parties due to a change in circumstances entailing a durable economic disequilibrium.

### Conclusion to part three

In its actions, the administration uses various ways and follows specific procedures The State has enormous privileges to ensure the satisfaction of general interest. In order to adapt to modern exigencies, ensure the protection of human rights and with the preoccupations of efficacy and efficiency, the Cameroonian administration has frequently adopted and applied the private law rules. In administrative action therefore, there is the interpenetration of public and private laws. However, public law provides the main foundation of public administration and is based on inequality; as consecrates the superiority of the State to other parties. The administration is different from private persons, it has to act in line with specific laws else its acts be cancelled, and at times it has to pay damages.

# Part Four
# Control to Administrative Action in Cameroon

As a fundamental law of democracy, all power must be controlled. The administration has large powers and its action or inaction can have considerable impact on the society and on the interests and the rights of the citizens. Besides, the rules by which the administration is submitted remain dead letters, if independent jurisdictions do not ensure that they are respected. The challenge is balancing the human rights and freedoms with the State authority; it is striking an equitable and practical balance between the rights of the individual citizens and those of the collective citizenry (society). This is done essentially by what public jurists qualify as administrative law (which should be different from private law) on the basis of which litigations are made. In fact, the specific administrative law is of no essence if violations of the law are not punished. Generally, litigations about administrative action fall in the domain of administrative justice (*contentieux administrative*).

# Chapter Eight
# Specific Administrative Law

In contemporary world, the administrative law challenge is balancing societal and individual rights even if the approaches differ.[89] There are a series of definitions most of which describe rather than define it confirming its eclectic nature. The definition and scope of administrative law differ from the Anglo–Saxon and French perspectives. In the United States, classically, the *Black's Law Dictionary* defines administrative law as the 'body of law created by administrative agencies to implement their powers and duties in the form of rules, regulations, orders and decisions." *Daniel Oran's Law Dictionary* sees it as "Laws about duties and proper running of an administrative agency that are handed to agencies by legislatures and courts. Rules and regulations set out by administrative agencies." Renowned American administrative law scholars have their own points of view. Kenneth Culp Davis defines it as "the laws concerning the powers and procedures of administrative agencies, including especially the laws governing judicial review of administrative action."[90] Warren after a synthesis of various definitions observes that broadly speaking administrative law deals with "how power is transferred from legislative bodies to administrative agencies, how administrative agencies use power and how the actions taken by the administrative agencies are reviewed by the courts."[91] Jacobini *et al* thus defines Administrative law as a branch of Public law which consists of those norms establishing and

---

[89] René Chapus, *Droit Administratif* (Paris, Montchrestien, 1992), 128–129. States that administrative law fulfills a double function rendering administrative action more effective and protecting the rights of the administered.

[90] Davis, Kenneth C. *Administrative law Treatise*. (USA: San Diego, 1979), Chapter 1.

[91] Warren, Kenneth F. *Administrative Law in the Political System* (United States of America: Westview, 2004), 23.

governing public agencies and officials, the rules that such agencies themselves make, and the court rulings that circumscribe agencies and their rules. Much of the process is set forth in basic national and State procedural laws, usually known as the Administrative Procedure Acts (APA).[92] In the United States, therefore, administrative law typically involves the growth of administrative power, authority delegation, political control of the agencies, acquisition and disclosure of information, protection of administrators, procedural due process, formal adjudications, procedural shortcuts, rulemaking/order–making, agency hearings and obtaining judicial review.

From the French tradition, *Droit Administratif* is the branch of public law which deals with the legal requirements on the organization, powers and duties of administrative authorities, their relationships with the administered and the remedies available to those wrongly affected by administrative action. It involves essentially, Administrative Organization (centralization, deconcentration and decentralization laws), the principle of legality, ways of Administrative Action (the Public Services and Administrative police powers) procedures of Administrative Action (unilateral administrative acts and administrative contracts), and Administrative Justice or litigations. For the purposes of this study the French orientation is adopted since the Cameroonian administrative law is inspired essentially by the French. As such since the other aspects have been treated in the other chapters, administrative law is specific, and is strictly and simply seen as law of the administration, its necessity, sources, legality and how administrative power is limited, controlled and judged.

## 8.1 Sources of Administrative Law

Legally, sources are the various techniques of law creation, the totality of normative rules applicable to an academic discipline. Generally, administrative law has been nourished by a hierarchy of norms from international treaties and accords, the constitution, laws, regulations to administrative acts.

---

[92] Jacobini, H.H., Melone, Albert and Kalvelage, Carl. *Research Essentials of Administrative Law*. (USA: Palisade Publishers, 1983), 3.

## I. International treaties and accords

After their negotiation and ratification, treaties are enforceable on the administration, and have a supra–constitutional value. This implies that the treaty has the highest value in the hierarchy of norms. In addition, an individual can invoke a treaty to support a petition before the judge. This principle is automatic in countries (Cameroon, France, and Germany) which have consecrated the thesis of legal monism. This rule has been confirmed in France in many cases, for instance in C.E. 30 Mai 1952 *Kirkwood.* In Cameroon in a court ruling of the CFJ–CAY of 8 June *1971 Compagnie commerciale immobilière africaine des chargeurs réunis C / Etat du Cameroun Oriental* it was established that international conventions constitute sources of internal law and their violation can be invoked to support an appeal before the administrative judge.

In line with the principle of legal monism, the Cameroonian 1996 Constitution states in its article 45 that; "Duly approved or ratified treaties or international agreements, following their publication, override national laws, provided the other party implements the said treaty or agreement." This entails that, provided the other partner(s) abide to the terms of the treaty (principle of reciprocity), when regularly ratified and approved have the authority superior to that of national laws. It is logical that the international legal order by the states should have higher value than their respective laws. But then, international law in general and treaties in particular have their weaknesses.

## II. The Constitution

Robertson P. defines the constitution as a set of rights, powers and procedures regulating the relationships among public authorities and between the public authorities and the citizens. Thus it provides a formal balance, defines and limits the power of government. On the one hand, determines the powers of the various state organs or personalities and fixes the relationships between these organs (power maps–separation of powers). On the other, it states the human rights and freedoms that need to be protected. The constitutions of Cameroon have not only been the fundamental norms of the State but also the supreme administrative charters of the country. That the constitution should be imposed on the administration is clear, the main problems are whether the preamble of the constitution should be awarded constitutional value.

### A. Constitutional provisions

The constitution describes "power maps", provides the powers, and shows the functions of the powers, the relationship between the powers and the limits of the power. It is seen as the State, administrative and policy document *par excellence*. This is because it determines the power network of the society as well as the functions. It indicates generally how policies are made. In many African countries, there is divergence between theory and practice, and constitutions are incomplete or positively misleading.

The constitution is supposed to provide the "birth certificate" of the State as it is created. It is enacted in circumstances of "fresh start", after profound disruption of some kind (independence, revolution, war). Constitutions are not "once for all documents." They are expected to be amended or revised to respond to changing times. Flexible constitutions are easily revised (just like any law), but the revision of rigid constitutions is more difficult as it follows solemn procedures.

Besides, constitutions differ in the extent to which they concentrate or disperse power: First, the separation or fusion of powers at the centre of the State between the government organs. Second, the allocation of State powers between the centre and the periphery. In addition, constitutions may provide loose frame of government (USA), be State codes (France), revolutionary manifestos (USSR), ancient source of power (Jewish) or political ideals (third world).

The Cameroonian 1996 constitution shows how power is separated between the various State organs, the executive, legislative and the judiciary. It determines the respective domains of the law and regulations, describes State organization from the central to decentralized units and the various jurisdictions.

### B. The constitution and its preamble

The preamble usually declares the political philosophy of the regime, fixes objectives and announces the rights and freedoms of the citizens. The question is whether the preamble has the same legal value as the body of the constitution. The problem has been tackled by specialists and judges.

Georges Dupius has best summarized the controversy by proposing three responses. First, the minimal thesis holds that the preamble simply announces the philosophical doctrine; consequently it has no legal authority and should not bind the judge. Second, the median thesis defended by Georges Burdeau, who holds that it is necessary to distinguish between the rules that are sufficiently precise thus immediately applicable from those that are simply precepts of political philosophy. The first are rules of positive law while the second are deprived of obligatory force. Finally, the maximal thesis holds that the declarations of the preamble are constitutional norms like the articles of the constitution, there is no difference.

Without neglecting possible criticisms, judges largely adopt the maximal interpretation. Two main arguments are put forward to defend this standpoint. The historical arguments are that the authors of the first declarations and preambles believed that they had to be respected obligatorily by the governments. Besides, the rational arguments are that the preamble as the rest of the constitution is found in the same document, written by the same author at the same time, there is no national reason why they should not have the same legal value.

It is in this light that the French judge in C.E: May 1954 *Barel* held that the exclusion of some candidates from the National School of Administration ( ENA) on the basis of their political opinions was a violation of the 1789 Declaration of Rights and the preamble of the 1946 constitution which consecrates the principle of equality of citizens in the access to public posts without any distinction of origin, opinions and beliefs. In the case of Cameroon, article 65 of the 1966 constitution clearly states that "The preamble shall be part and parcel of this constitution" .

## III. Legislative/Executive Sources

These include laws from the strict point of view, regulations, ordinances and referendary laws.

### A. Laws stricto sensu

These are bills tabled either by the President of the Republic or by members of the parliament which concern matters reserved for the legislative power and are promulgated by the President of the Republic (art. 26 of the 1996 constitution). More so, the constitution foresees other hypotheses for the intervention of the parliament for instance, the conditions for the election of the President of the Republic are laid down by law.

### B. Regulations.

The constitution states clearly that "Matters not reserved to the legislative shall come under the jurisdiction of the authority empowered to issue rules and regulations" (art. 27). It is on the basis of this regulatory powers that the President of the Republic has the right to "set up and organize administrative services of the State". The strict definition of the parliamentary domain (art.26) demonstrates the rationalisation of the parliament. The domain of the legislature is the exception and the regulatory domain the rule.

### C. Ordinances

Even in subjects reserved to the legislative power, parliament may empower the President of the Republic to legislate by way of ordinances for a limited period and for given purposes (art. 28). Such ordinances enter into force on the day of their publication. They are tabled before the bureau of the National Assembly and the Senate for purposes of ratification within the time limit laid down by the enabling law. They remain in force as long as the parliament does not refuse to ratify them and have same legal value as the law.

## IV. Case Law

In the Anglo–Saxon legal systems, following the rule of precedent (*stare decisis*) the court ruling is a fundamental source of law. On the contrary, with the Romano–Germanic systems, the judges in principle are not expected to make law. In general terms, following the principle of separation powers, judges do not make law, they apply it. But the judges formulate themselves the rules that help them judge. Being specialists in law, their interpretations and orientations especially when the laws are obscure, contradictory, possess loopholes or do not preview situations, inevitably affect the administration as the administered. It should be noted that Article 4 of the French Civil Code forbids the judge to refuse judgement on the basis of absence or obscurity of the law. In their judgement of cases, they also attempt to fill the loopholes of the written law. In the absence of texts, the judge must render justice else will be accused of denial of justice. So the judge can explain existing rules or create new ones. It is therefore widely accepted that the judge exercises an inevitable normative role. The intervention of the judges will be analysed from two perspectives.

## A. Establishment of general rules

In the domain of definition of concepts the administrative judge has been very instrumental. Notions like administrative acts, public service, illicit enrichment, State land, and validation have been clarified by the administrative judge. These notions contribute enormously in the enrichment of administrative law.

More so, as concerns regimes of the legal procedure, administrative action, responsibility of the public power, execution of administrative contracts etc the judge has established rules of good administration which should be applied in the absence of texts forbidding them. These general judge–made rules have a legal value equal to that of regulations. However, they can be modified by regulations on condition that individual rights and freedoms are not violated.

## B. Establishments of general principles of law

In addition to the general principles expressed in the constitution, the judge admits other non–written principles as part of positive law. The existence of such customary rules can be established by a simple analysis of the decisions of the administrative judge, or the submissions of government commissioners to Attorney Generals (Procureurs generaux).

There are many of such principles. Some of them which protect the rights of the citizens include: the principle that all administrative decisions can be attacked for abuse of powers C.E 17 Feb. 1950 *Dame Lamotte*; the principle of the respect of defence right CE May 1944 *Dame*

*Veuve Trompier – Gravier*, CFJ 8 December 1970 *Sitamze Urbain*; the principle of equality of citizens before the public service and justice. The others concern the organization of the public service especially the principle of the continuity of the public service.

The value of the principles in reference to laws is not clear for if the judge can use the principle to render un–operational the law, the legislature can contradict the principles. According to Rene Chapus, these principles have value inferior to the law, but superior to regulations. This entails that they are infra–legislative and supra–decree. More convincing is Georges Morange's opinion that the value of the principle depends on its author. For instance, in countries with constitutional case–law (Germany, USA, France) the principles have constitutional value.

## V. Administrative Acts

These can be done unilaterally or by contract with other parties.

### A. Unilateral Acts

These acts or decisons emanate wholly from the administration. Within the hierarchy and diversity of administrative authorities, the norms are bound to have different values.

#### 1. Types of Acts

In descending order of importance the president, ministers, secretary general and directors take decisions and the appellation depends on the authority. The authors of these administrative decisions are usually précised: presidential decree, ministerial order (arrêtes), prefectoral order, and municipal order. In Cameroon, the president can also issue orders, so presidential order can be taken to apply a presidential decree. Decisions from the deliberations of collegial authorities (e.g. Municipal Council, Administrative Councils) also have an impact on the administration.

#### 2. Hierarchy of Administrative Acts

It is established according to the following rules:

- Regulatory acts (decisions) are superior to individual ones. This is so because the regulatory acts determine general and impersonal situations, while the individual acts concern determined persons;

- While in force, the administrative authority must respect his own or personal decisions;
- An act of the superior authority predominates that of the inferior;
- The inferior authorities must respect the acts issued by the superior authorities;
- On equality, the more solemn act is placed above the less solemn.

### B. Contractual acts

When the administration is partner to a private contract, it is just like an individual and the contractual acts bound the partners in a similar way (principle of equality between contractual partners). This is in line with article 1134 of the Civil Code which states that an agreement between parties is law to them. In spite of the right to modify unilaterally and the total power to annul unilaterally that possesses the administration in the domain of administrative contracts, it is expected to execute the terms of the contract. In a nutshell, the principle of legality comprises of rules external and internal to the administration. The rules governing are hierarchical and those with a lower value have to be in line with those that are higher.

## 8.2 Respect of Hierarchy of Acts

The sources of administrative law are placed in hierarchical order and lower norms are expected to conform to higher ones. The controversy surrounding the place of treaties in relation to national laws has been discussed. The issue now is the control of constitutionality and whether laws can serve as shields to administrative acts.

### I. Control of constitutionality

As the constitution is placed at the apex of the hierarchy of norms, all other rules and decisions have to be in line with it. The control of constitutionality entails that any law or administrative decision which is contrary to the constitution should be declared null and void. The competent organ varies between countries and can be political, judicial or mixed. In the United States, the constitution did not specifically assign the judicial branch the power of judicial review. Chief Justice John Marshal accorded this power to the judiciary in the famous case of *Marbury Vs Madison* (1803) when he argued that the courts should have the right to overrule the acts of the other branches of government as unconstitutional. In effect, this makes the courts the chief interpreters and defenders (or destroyers) of the Constitution

In Cameroon, the competent organ which is mixed, named the Constitutional Council has jurisdiction in matters pertaining to the Constitution. It rules on the constitutionality of laws. It gives final rulings on the constitutionality of laws, treaties and international agreements (Articles 46–47 of 1996 Constitution).

## II. Laws as shield to administrative acts?

The Constitution is at the summit of the hierarchy of norms and some laws may happen to be unconstitutional. The problem is posed in these terms, between the constitutional norm and the act of the administrative authority is interposed a law or any other rule of a higher order whose stipulations are contrary to the Constitution. Yet in Cameroon, in line with the principle of separation of powers, the judge is not competent to control the constitutionality of laws. In other words, the administrative act is in conformity with the law, but not the stipulations of the Constitution. When the law is not in conformity with the constitutional norms, should the administrative acts which are in conformity to the laws be seen as legal? In other words, if administrative acts are not in line with the constitution, can the laws provide shields for them?

The attitude of the judge is based on two divergent hypotheses. First, the constitution is considered as being supreme, thus controlling the direct conformity of administrative action to the constitution which entails neglecting and indirectly annulling the law. This position is qualified the "theory of transparent shield."[93] Second, it is assumed that with the principle of separation of powers, the judge cannot control constitutionality or cancel a law on the basis that it is contrary to the constitution. If the judge feels that he/she does not have the competence to annul the law, the conformity of the administrative action will be controlled directly by the law. In this situation the law forms a 'smoke

[93] This theory was advocated by Frank Moderne.

screen' and this position is qualified the theory of "legislative shield" or "the theory of shield law".

There are two pertinent examples in the legal history of Cameroon that can be cited. Law N° 64/:F/16 of 26 June 1964 forbidding all pursuits against the State and other public entities in view of obtaining indemnification by the victims of terrorism or victims of its repression. Also, law N° 79/17 of 30 June 1979 declaring the incompetence of the judge as regards petitions on the designation of traditional chiefs (contrary to article 32 of the 1972 Constitution). In line with the principle of 'pararellism of competence and procedure' it is the authority invested with the power of designation that is competent. However, this 1979 law has been subjected to a lot of controversy. First, this law was promulgated after the May 1979 *Kouang Guillaume C/ the Cameroon State* case where the judge declared that the decision of designation is a simple administrative act thus susceptible to be attacked in court. This motivation and line of reasoning entailing the adoption of the theory of transparent shield continued in CS/CA 29 October 1979 *Essomba Marc Antoine;* CS/CA 29 May 1980 *Monkam Tientcheu David cases*. The judges might have been inspired by the 1950 French case of CE *Ministère de l'Agriculture C/ Dame Lamotte* where it was declared a petition against power abuse is a general principle of law open even without any text against all administrative acts.

The intervention of the legislature became more vigorous in 1980. By Law N° 80–31 of 27 November 1981 as the ordinary law and administrative judges were forbidden to intervene in all issues relating to the designation of traditional chiefs. This entailed the rejection of transparent shield in favour of legislative shield as confirmed in three main cases ruled by the plenary assembly of the Supreme Court (*Kouang Guillaume C/ Etat du Cameroun; Etat du Cameroun c/ Enfants du Chef Banka; and Collectivité Deido c/ Etat du Cameroon*). It should be noted that the *Kouang Guillaume* case came as an appeal before the full bench of the Supreme Court in 1981 which declared itself incompetent. In spite of the controversy, the fact remains that when shield laws exist, they serve as a temperament to the principle of legality.

## 8.3 The Principle of Legality

At one time, there was no relation between the administration and the law; the administration (State) was placed above and outside the law. The modern State (State of law) is a moral and legal person, and can sue and be sued in court. The law provides power for the State and also limits this power. The existence of democratic institutions like the constitutional council, court of impeachment and Supreme Court helps to limit the arbitrary exercise of power. The simple fact that the administration is submitted to and in its decisions must follow some rules provides some sense of security.

In general terms, the principle of legality simply means the submission of the administration to the law. The State of law evokes a strict legal regulation of social relations and implies the submission of all even the State and its head to the law. A legal State is one that respects the "rule of law", it does not violate rules; it modifies them if and only if the procedures prescribed by the texts in force are followed. Certain organs must be foreseen to control the legality of the acts of State organs, and in case of violation, sanction their illegality. The ultimate goal of the principle of legality is to establish a "State of law" But there are some issues regarding the scope or extent of this principle and whether the multiplicity of limits does not challenge its essence.

## I. From legality to Juridicity?

Administrative law scholars distinguish between the classical and modern conceptions of legality. From the classical view (Le principe de légalité) it means all that is in conformity with the law. Applied to the administration, it means the administration must act in conformity with the law. The classical conception of this principle has been attacked from a double perspective. The jurists and liberal publicists of the 19th Century Europe conceived law *stricto sensu.* Law was seen as exclusively determined norms passed by the parliament using the legislative procedure. Besides, as confirmed by Kamto, the legal state demonstrates the supremacy of the legislative on the administration.[94] It gives the

[94] Kamto Maurice, *L'urgence De la pensée: Reflexions sur une precondition dévéloppement en Afrique.* (Yaounde: Editions Mandara, 1991, 1993), 100.

impression that the administration as a whole must respect the laws and should not abrogate or modify them. With the rationalization of parliaments nowadays the restriction of law to the legislative domain can be deceitful and even dangerous.

The Modern View (Le principe de juridicité) is more extensive conception for law here is taken in its widest sense (all sources of administrative law). Thierry Michalon holds that the legal State is one that does not violate rules in general (juridicity).[95] This principle establishes relations between the Administration on one hand, and law as a whole on the other. According to Kamdem, the substance of the relationship is triple. First minimal exigency: according to which the administration should not violate the law. It implies the compatibility of administrative action and the law. This exigency is usually imposed on the administration. Second, the median exigency: that the administration should not act without the authorization of the law. It signifies that the administrative organs should be covered by law. This exigency is sometimes imposed on the administration. And thirdly, the maximal exigency: that the administrative action must be stipulated in a pre–existing norm. It implies conformity of administrative acts to the law. This exigency is rarely required.[96] But then, the evolution from legality to juridicity is simply terminology and semantics, since law can be seen from the strict and broad senses.

What matters is that the State creates law uses it to maintain public order and satisfy general interest. The State itself created by law has to act within the limits set by law and respect individual freedoms. Administrative law is therefore a double–edged sword which aims at conciliating power and liberty. Both the State and the citizens are protected but are liable for their wrongs (both have rights and obligations). All administrative actions notably administrative police powers, unilateral administrative acts and administrative contracts are concerned by the principle of legality.

In order for the state of law to succeed two conditions must be fulfilled: First, a coherent legal framework with a hierarchy of norms. Second, an instituted and independent justice, crowned with indispensable

---

[95] Michalon Thierry,, 51.

[96] Kamdem, Institutions Administratives (class notes).

authority for the accomplishment of its mission as guardian of laws. Constitutional government must in part be a judicial government. An independent and impartial judiciary free from pressure is indispensable to guarantee the state of law. To ensure their independence, (as obtains in the United States) judges have either to be appointed by the president for life in so far as they remain of "good behaviour" or should be elected by the members of the judiciary mindful of their seniority and competence. As an important third power controlling the constitutionality of laws and the legality of administrative action, it is important that those who make up the judiciary should be free from coercion, intimidation or pressure from government and societal groups[97] If the guarantee of independence to the judges is for paramount importance, it is equally necessary for judges to be "respected and appreciated by society.[98]" Ehrlich was right when he said that "there is no guarantee of justice except the personality of the judge".[99] The judges must be men of integrity beyond all suspicions and greatly respected as defenders of law.

## II. The State of Law– A contradiction?

The principle of legality has been criticized as having temperaments and limits, notably discretionary administrative powers, shield laws, exceptional circumstances and government acts.[100] This question above is posed in an article written by Charles Eisenmann and further developed by Walter Leisner. They argue that if the state of law is not a contradiction, then it has contradictory effects. These doubts about the state of law phenomenon are from different perspectives. Consequently all the challenges should be avoided so as to have a real State of law. Arguably, in a modern state, the principle of legality is subjected to some limits, risks, dangers or problems: – First, in an attempt to have a normative paradise of perfection (normative perfectionism) there is the danger of adoring the rules. It can be absolute and totalitarian, what is not for it is against it. As such there is the risk and confusion between

---

[97] Muna Bernard, *Cameroon and the Challenges of the 21st Century* (Yaounde: Tama Books, 1993), 67.

[98] Muna, 110.

[99] MacIver, 266.

[100] These limits have been treated in other sections of the book.

the end and the means. The law which is simply a means can finally be seen as an end. This is in line with Robert Merton's process of goals displacement. Second, the laws can have high level of abstraction and thus the need for frequent need of interpretation. Besides, with the dynamism of the society, there is the need to frequently revise laws with the risks of manipulation. Further, the providential State is dynamic and interventionist and cannot easily accommodate itself to strict norms. The society evolves and at times need rapid intervention not previewed by the laws.

Third, the State of law is simply the respect of law, but these laws can be arbitrary and unjust. The administration can manipulate the law and use the state of law merely as an instrument for campaign. What the citizens would have not accepted in normal circumstances, they do so in normative form. Thus the normative technique can be opium of liberty. Fourth, it can give too much prerogatives to the executive to the detriment of the legislative and judiciary powers. Theorists have argued that concentration of powers is risky to democracy and protection of human rights. The trinity of powers has to be separate and distinct so as to ensure "checks and balances". In such a situation, there will be restriction of powers, prevention and repression of abuses. With the separation of powers constitutionally endowed, there is guarantee that law and liberty will be respected. The three branches of government must control and constraint each other. "From the very nature of things", says Montesquieu "power should check power" if not legality will be meaningless. Finally, the theory of exceptional circumstances which is constitutionally endowed and leads to enormous increase of administrative powers is a fundamental challenge to the principle of legality.

## 8.4. Theory of Exceptional Circumstances and Increase of Powers

The rules of law are usually made for normal periods. When there are exceptional circumstances, these rules are no longer adapted to the prevailing situation and the administrative authorities have to act to guarantee public order. [101] There is, therefore, conflict between the preoccupation of effectiveness and that of the respect of the law.

In constitutional law, exceptional circumstances mean the emergence of urgent and unforeseen circumstances which render indispensable for the safeguard of the State and the concentration of powers. Public liberties are not neglected, but the exigency of efficacy and public order is emphasized. Such situations are foreseen by legal texts in Cameroon and raises issues of legality of exception.

## I. The Hypotheses of Exceptional Situations

There are two hypotheses of exceptional situations in Cameroon, state of emergency and state of siege.

### A. State of emergency (*L'état d'urgence*)

Article 9 (1) of the 1996 constitution states the "The President of the Republic may where circumstances so warrant, declare by decree a state of emergency which shall confer upon him such special powers as may be provided for by law". The legal regime has been fixed by Decree N° 72–13 of 26 August 1972 relating to the State of Emergency. Three things can lead to the declaration of state of emergency: events presenting by their nature and their gravity the character of public calamity, repeated trouble threatening public order and state security and foreign aggression.

In such a situation, the administration has enormous powers on people and goods. People are obstructed from enjoying their fundamental liberties as – freedom of movement (e.g. Laissez–passer" needed), prohibition of all meetings and publications which can lead to disorder, house arrests etc. The administration can also authorize the officers of the judicial police, civil or military agents to search people's residences. They permanently participate in the maintenance of public order.

### B. State of siege (*L'état d'exception*)

Article 9 (2) of the 1996 constitution states that "in the event of a serious threat to the nation's territorial integrity or to its existence, its

[101] Owona Joseph, « L'Institutionnalisation de la Légalité d'Exception dans le Droit Public Camerounaise. » *Revue Camerounaise de Droit,* No 6, Juillet–Décembre (1974) , 116 , terms it « administrative law of exception. »

independence or institutions, the President of the Republic may declare a state of siege by decree and take any measures as he may deem necessary. He shall inform the nation of his decision by message".

This article 9 (2) can be compared with article 16 of the French 1958 constitution. But they have two essential differences. The French constitution institutes a more complicated procedure (official consultation of the P.M., presidents of the parliament, the constitutional council, and information of the nation by message). The procedure in Cameroon is more expeditious, that is only the information of the nation by message. Moreover, in France there is more guarantee of legal control.

Comparing articles 9 (1) and 9 (2), the state of emergency is limited to six months renewable, while the state of siege is not limited. The president has more powers with the latter for he takes "any measures as he may deem necessary". The special powers are not necessarily provided for by law. He is the only judge of its opportunity, what specialists qualify "constitutional dictatorship".

## II. The legality of exception

This implies the adaptation of the law to the exceptional circumstances. Even when there is neither disorder nor a threat to order, a regular norm (above all as regards its motives and targets), can become un–adapted, even illegal with the change in context. In this case, the administrative authority is obliged to make useful modifications on the request of the concerned (see C.E. 10 January 1930 *Despoujol*). There can be a change of law or a fact (context), which were unforeseen and upsets the basis of the decision or contract.

When there is a threat to order, the administrative authorities have provisional and exorbitant powers. According to Montesquieu, the guarantee of liberty is in law but there are moments we have to cover liberty as we hide the statue of God. During crisis, it happens at times that it is impossible to conform entirely to the law of normal times without compromising the life of the nation.

If attempts are made to respect the principles and ensure the continuity of the public services, violence will triumph and the state will be condemned "to die". When the normal law or individual freedoms and the superior interest of the state are in conflict, the latter is usually favoured. So legality in normal times is different from legality during exceptional periods. Does legality of exception constitute a limit or an eclipse to the principle of legality? The answer of this question is controversial

## A. Controversy on relationship between exceptional circumstances and legality

The renowned authors and judges have adopted various positions regarding the relationships between exceptional circumstances and the principle of legality.

### 1. Positions of Legal writers

Some authors like André de Laubadere, Joseph Binyoum and Momo Bernard cite exceptional circumstances among the limits of the principle of legality. They hold that certain administrative decisions which would have been illegal in normal circumstances become legal due to the necessity to ensure public order and the smooth functioning of the public services.

Another group of authors notably Mathiot, Dupius and J.C. Kamdem hold a different view. According to André Mathiot, it is not a period when law is deprived of its obligatory force. The exceptional circumstances theory is constructed even on the basis of the principle of legality, in consideration of the general duties of the public authorities. It is simply admitted that the content of this principle and the administrative obligations cannot be invariable. To George Dupius, exceptional circumstances does not imply an eclipse of legality, since in each case the judge does a profound control of the existence of the exceptional circumstances and the extent of powers that possess the administrative authorities in such situations.

These authors are saying the same thing in different ways. The first group talks of certain decisions not all. At least one author of the second group holds that the principle of legality is not invariable. There is control during exceptional circumstances depending on the context, but the fact is this control is different.

## 2. Positions of the Judges

The opinion of the judge depends on the circumstances at hand and should not be generalized. At times, they attempt to bring out general rules.

In line with arrêt *Heyries* (C.E. 28/6/18) the rule of law which governs administrative activity in normal period changes the judicial regime during exceptional period. This can be illustrated with some cases where there was violation of individual liberties (C.E. Feb. 1919 *Dames Dol et Laurent*) non respect of the rules of procedure (*Heyries*) etc. The judges however generally agree that they have to control the moment, target and means used.

The nature of measures taken on the basis of exceptional powers has different regimes depending on the matter. If the matter is found on the legislative domain, it is a legislative act against which appeals are not possible. If on the statutory domain, it is an administrative act of which appeals are possible on the basis of abuse of power. (*C.E. Rubin de Servens*). So generally, legal controls are possible though can be done in a different manner.

## B. The control by the judge

In the French arrêt *Andreani et Desfont* the judge Chardeau declared that we should not give the administration complete liberty on the pretext that circumstances are exceptional. It is necessary with the extension of administrative powers that control be stricter.

## 1. The Domains of control

The control of the administrative judge is on three essential points: the moment, target and means used. As regards the moment, the judge appreciates the duration, the abnormality of the situation (C.E. 19/06/53 *Houphouet Boigny*), the necessity of exceptional powers (CFJ/CAY 27/1/70 *Obama Eteme c/RF du Cameroun*. The Target must be for the safeguard of public interest, any diversion of powers lead to annulment (see *Andreani et Desfont* precité). Finally, measures must correspond to the target. The authorities should not arbitrarily choose the means on the pretext of crisis.

### 2. Limits of legal control of the measures of crisis

Certainly, there exist legal control of administrative action during exceptional circumscribes, but this control is limited. The control of the judge is a posteriori (that is after the crisis) when the damage has been done, but this is not however, peculiar to the period of crisis. In general, the limits depend on the hypothesis in question. As regards article 9 (2), decisions to use exceptional powers which are measures taken in the legislative domain called legislative acts are not controlled. Where there is a state of emergency, the competence of the military jurisdiction is applicable according to the rules governing the military. In such a situation it is difficult for the defence rights of the citizens to be respected. To impose on the administration the respect of the legal order, regular controls are necessary.

## 8.5 Control of the Administration

As a law of politics "responsibility follows power" the alternative is uncontrolled and uncontrollable government bureaucracy. The administration has to be accountable, liable, answerable or responsible for their actions. The very permanence of bureaucrats gives them considerable power, consequently the necessity for control. The controls respond to three main preoccupations– control of regularity, control of opportunity and control of productivity and efficacy. Administrative law specialists distinguish between "endogenous and exogenous controls" "preventive and repressive controls" and "administrative, political and legal controls". As an introductory work, there is simply a distinction between internal and external controls of the administrative system.

### I. Controls by actors inside the administrative system

These are controls by agencies or authorities that form part of the administration. These are mainly administrative and financial controls which have been treated in detail elsewhere.

### A. Administrative controls of the administration

According to Debbasch Charles, the administrative control is exercised by the administration on itself. It is a form of auto–control destined to ensure the smooth functioning of the administration, its regularity and its efficacy. With this control one can verify whether the administration has accomplished its mission in conformity with the legal, technical, human means put at its disposal.[102]

This control can be hierarchical or supervisory. According to Kamdem J.C., "hierarchical control is that of superiors over the subordinates. This control is for the interest of power, to safeguard its unity, authority and efficiency."[103] If controls are generally to check or limit the powers of the authorities, this control aims at ensuring authority. This control is above all necessary at the summit of the State.

As discussed under decentralization, with supervisory control (tutelage) there exist two moral persons of public law. It gives right to the authorities of the central or deconcentrated levels to see to it that decentralized or specialized institutions (authorities) function according to the law.

## B. Financial controls of the administration

In Cameroon, accountants, state inspectors, finance controllers, play an important role at their respective domains. These controls are placed under the double responsibility of the Minister of Finance and the Minister Delegate of Supreme State Control under the supervision of the President of the Republic.

### 1. Control exercised by the Minister of Finance

This control is done by finance controllers and the special units found in this ministry (See Chapter Four). The control was regulated by Decree no. 77–41 of 3rd February 1977. According to this decree, finance controllers constitute the external service of the Ministry of Finance and belong to the Department of the Budget[104]. These controllers are found in all ministries, diplomatic and consular missions, public establishments, local public entities and any other public persons. The fundamental characteristic of this control is that it is hierarchical, preventive, and regular.

---

[102] Debbasch, 682.

[103] Kamdem, Institutions Administrative et Droit Administrative, T1, 63–64.

[104] Article 12 of Decree No. 77–41 of 3rd February 1977.

If the control of regularity is the principle, the controllers at times control the opportunity of expenditure. The control of regularity generally permits to verify whether the administration has accomplished its missions, in accordance with certain textual imperatives or prohibitive stipulations. It concerns not only financial operations but all legal acts. Here, it is simply verification whether financial norms on engagement of expenditure have been followed. The control of opportunity by controllers is exceptional but exists. In this case, the controller has very great latitude of appreciation of the action of the controlled. He is not as in the control of regularity, confined to precise rules, but to general rules of good management.[105] The permanence of the controller renders this possible. This control is supplemented by those of specialized units (brigades) of their ministry. They are intermittent, episodic or i*mprompto*. In addition to their control, there is also that of the state control department.

## 2. Control by the Supreme State Audit Services

Decree N° 69/70 of 2nd February 1969 created the General State Inspectorate (IGE) which replaced the Federal Court of Audit. The inspectorate was placed under a minister delegate and later was amalgamated with the public service.[106] By 1992 it regained autonomy as Supreme State Control and is responsible for: auditing, at the highest level, public services, regional and local authorities, public and semi–public enterprises... at the administrative and financial levels... Controlling and auditing accounts of the State's budget. In this respect it shall make conformity and regularity, financial, performance, programme evaluation, environmental and specific controls. The following divisions concern the public service directly (See Chapter Four).

The Inspections Division has a team of technical and administrative personnel. Under the authority of a division head, it is responsible for the setting up, the execution and the general supervision of roving audit missions.[107] It has to maintain close contact with internal audit services in the various ministries whose reports it studies in conjunction

[105] Debbasch, 682–683.

[106] Article 12 of Decree No. 77–41 of 3rd February 1977.

[107] Art. 19 (1) of Decree N° 97/47.

with the Studies and Legal Affairs Division. Unfortunately, this institution has become a "cemetery of elephants" where superordinates at "mid–distance" or at the end of their careers are dumped.[108]

The Roving Audit Missions are organized by a special decree, and comprise of State inspectorates and controllers assisted by auditors–in–training. Within the framework of their duties, members of the roving audit missions are completely independent of the services and the bodies being audited and have unrestricted powers in respect of investigation.[109] They have to follow their professional code of ethics especially obligations of reserve and professional secrecy. The main objectives of these missions are to assess the quality of management, establish breach and violation of regulations or the principles and rules of sound management, and to evaluate and appraise efficiency.[110] After every mission, there is a report, stating the findings, opinions and where necessary recommendations which are subject to written requests for explanation.

The Budget and Finance Disciplinary Board is responsible to determine the penalties relating to the liability of authorizing officers and vote holders of the State and the State enterprises .The Disciplinary Council for the Implementation of the Budget[111] was replaced by the Budget and Accounts Disciplinary Board[112] (CDBC) which now is called the Budget and Finance Disciplinary Board. It is organized by a special decree.[113] The seizure of the Board is not a prejudice to the exercise of the disciplinary or penal sanction.[114] It is a complementary and not a substitutional action. The board is not a court;[115] it is an administrative organ[116] which has witnessed some "judicialization". From this standpoint, it has pre–established procedures characterised by its

---

[108] Lekene, 327.
[109] Decree N° 97/48 of 5 March 1997 relating to roving audit missions.
[110] Art. 15, decree N° 97/48.
[111] Instituted by article 11 of the 1962/63 Finance Law.
[112] Created by article 42 of Decree N° 69 (DE) 265 bis of 30/06/1969.
[113] Decree N° 97–49 of 5 March 1997/49; Organization and Functioning of the Budget and Finance Disciplinary Board.
[114] Art. 18(1) Decree No 97–49.
[115] Contrary to the opinions of Bidias, 856 et s, and Lekene, 339.
[116] Kamdem, Institutions Administratives... T1, 70 – 71.

inquisitorial and written nature, the right to judicial assistance and self–defence. From the inception, it was called a board and not a court and replaced a council and not a court. Further, the decision of the board can be attacked or followed–up before the administrative bench of the Supreme Court. The administrative jurisdiction in Cameroon is at two and not three levels.[117]

The control of administrators (authorizing officers) and public accountants has no raison d'être if those found guilty are not punished. According to ordinary law, all regimes of responsibility are founded on the notion of fault as stated in articles 1382 and follows of the Civil Code.[118] The Cameroonian legislator, has therefore, defined the infractions susceptible to engage their responsibility and their corresponding sanctions (See Chapter Four). If the administrations can auto–control, this control is limited for the agents here are at the same time judge and parties"[119]. The administrative controls are necessary but not sufficient, thus complemented with external controls. `

## II. Controls by Actors outside the Administrative System

These controls can be on the administration as a whole or the personnel within it. The administration is part of the executive, mindful of the sacrosanct principle of the separation of powers; it has to be controlled by the other powers. The public, the real holder of the sovereignty, also need an account from their rulers. If the controls by the legislative and public are largely preventive, the excesses are repressed by the judiciary.

### A. Socio–Political Controls of the administration

In addition to the parliament, some societal groups do not remain indifferent to administrative activities. From this perspective, there exist societal and legislative controls.

---

[117] The consultation of the board can lead to the by–pass only of the pre–litigation complaint.

[118] See Hubrecht C., *Notions Essentielles de Droit Civil* (Sirey, 197), 141–142.

[119] Debbasch, 684.

## 1. Societal Controls

The citizens in general control the administration periodically through elections. In democratic countries, failure in elections is seen as a sanction of maladministration. There are also formal and informal actions of societal groups that limit administrative power.

There exist also institutional and associational interest groups as political parties, trade unions, churches, ethnic groupings, regional groups and class groups. It is an exaggeration to say that preaching on moralization in churches does not affect bureaucrats. The meetings of churchmen are commonplace which usually end with a pastoral letter pinpointing ills of the government. The main ethnic groups in Cameroon have associations which defend their interest, and raise an alarm once there is some cheating against them. With the advent of plurality, many trade unions or labour organizations have come up, even for the civil servants, to defend their interests which have helped to check administrative arbitrariness. Furthermore, with the emergence of multi–partism, through campaigns, rallies, radio and television programmes, the opposition parties have helped to criticise the government in power. The mere fact that the crimes of the administrators are being noticed can affect their attitudes.

The mass media plays a very important role in unmasking the administrative misdeeds. The elite have played no small role. The writings and exposés of the elite during seminars, workshops and conferences have been very instructive. They help to orientate the government through their actions. All these lead to the sensitization, education and politicization of the public, making the citizens more committed to the running of state affairs. To an extent, pluralism serves as an eye–opener and riots, demonstrations are not uncommon.

## 2. Legislative Controls

One of the fundamental characteristics of classical constitutional law writes Jean Gicguel is the presence in governments of censors, who by their questions their interpellation, parliamentary commission, among others oblige the government to justify its policies, to explain why it has taken a particular decision and not the other. The administration thus constitutes the organ of execution of the political power; it is the place of the latter, holder of the exercise of sovereignty to control the administration. This formula presents the advantage of conferring to the power which enacted the rules of the fundamental law the possibility of seeing to it that they are respected. [120]

The parliament legislates and controls the actions of government. The legislators can vote laws which can enhance administrative effectiveness or limit the powers of administrators. The control of the government can be through questions or commissions. The parliamentarians can ask the minister oral and written questions relative to their domain. Each legislator who wants to ask a question must deposit it with the president of parliament who communicates the competent minister. The written character depends on how the minister is expected to answer.

The law No. 73–1 of 8 June 1973 provides for many commissions. These are commission of inquiry, special commissions, ad hoc commissions, finance commission and general commissions. For example the Commission of Inquiry is to examine administrative, financial and technical management of the public services and inform the parliament. The Finance Commissions deal with public expenditure controls.

The parliament has enormous budgetary powers. The parliamentary budgetary authorizations have compulsive character and the government has no right to change the object, destination or duration of credits. Through questions the legislators control the budgetary execution. If the government happens to adopt amendment finance laws, it is obliged to offer explanations for such modifications. The government is also obliged to submit periodical reports to the Finance Committee. If attempts to prevent or react to administrative ills prove futile, the citizens have the right to take the administration to court.

### B. Judicial Controls of the Administration

The discussions here are mainly on the general legal controls, the peculiarities of the Cameroonian system are dealt with on the last chapter, Administrative Justice. The judge intervenes as last resort. The judges

---

[120] Debbasch, 668.

are law specialists and have to ensure its implementation. The administrative judge is the common/ordinary law judge of administrative matters in Cameroon. The administrative jurisdiction follows a particular procedure especially with the obligation of preliminary administrative complaint (RGP). The administrative contention comprises of the appeals on annulment for abuse of powers, and payment of damages. Indeed, the examples of maladministration that need legal redress are various and many. Really as Finer observes;

> The possibilities of official misbehaviour are myriad. Power may not be used when it should be used. An official may go beyond the powers granted by law, power may be deliberately or unconsciously, perverted to ends having nothing to do with the public service. Accidents may happen in the course of proper use of power to the detriment of citizens quite detached from the event. Improper procedure may be adopted in the practice of official judgements. Or commands and prohibitions may be uttered without basis in law. Against these, the citizen demands a defence and remedies.[121]

There are two main remedies of maladministration. One remedy is annulment of the injurious act (recours pour excés de pouvoir) or/and if the act causes injury, there is action for indemnification (plein contentieux).

## 1. Cases of Annulment: Abuse of Powers (*recours pour excès de pourvoir*)

There exist complaints against the administrative acts on the grounds of *utra vires (*beyond powers*)*. There are three fundamental conditions that warrant the receivability of abuse of power appeals:

- Petitions should be exclusively on administrative acts;
- Such an act should be a unilateral decision;
- The plaintiff must have been injured personally.[122]

---

[121] Finer, 919.

[122] Kamdem Jean Claude, Contentieux Administratif (UNIYAO: FDSE, Cours polycopie 19585–1986), 339 –349.

In addition, there are issues regarding whether a public person is involved, respect of conditions of form and procedure, and absence of parallel petition. From the standpoint of these rules of receivability, the concern is on the basis and the effects of appeals.

### a. Internal and external illegality

With the fulfilment of these conditions, the judge verifies, the basis of legality evoked by the plaintiff. The question is whether the act is legal or not. There are two main types of illegality; the external and the internal. Under external illegality, the judge asks two fundamental questions: Has the act been done by a competent authority? Have formalities and procedures prescribed by the regulations in force been followed? External illegality, therefore, focuses on the incompetence and non–respect (vice) of form and procedure. The violation of any of these leads to annulment. As regards the competent authority, many hypotheses are possible. There can be "usurpation of powers' which is when the authority does not possess the power to decide, or possesses but intrudes in the domain of other authorities. Also discussed under administrative acts, the competence of the authorities is limited in time, area and content, the violations of which can lead to incompetence. As regards the forms and procedures, it is the violation of substantial (not indicative) formalities that lead to the cancellation of the administrative acts.

The judge also appreciates internal legality, by verifying two important questions: Has the author of the act searched for a different target than that assigned by the law? Has he committed an error in the choice of the judicial rule or violated one of these rules? In the first case, the illegality is termed "diversion of powers" which is when the administrative authority accomplishes an act on its competence, but with a target other than that legally prescribed.[123] In the second case, the authority might have acted without paying attention to the rule or interpreted it erroneously.

---

[123] Confirmed by court rulings: CFJ\CAY arrêt *Fouda Mballa C/ Etat du Cameroun Oriental.,Bilaie Jean C/ Etat du Cameroun Orientale.*

### b. Effects of the appeals

As regards the effects of the appeal, it depends on whether the judge sees the act as regular or not. In the first hypothesis, the process stops. It implies that the appeal has been rejected for one reason or the other. The attempt to control the administration has been a failure. In the second hypothesis, the administrative act is cancelled. The effects of this cancellation have to be retroactive or retrospective[124] and "*erga omnes*."[125]

We can conclude with Owona that,

> the appeals against abuse of powers constitute an instrument par excellence of guarantee for the principle of legality. It is the appeal of the oppressed against the oppression of the administrative bureaucracy on the liberties and rights of the administered.[126]

If the annulled illegal administrative act causes damage to the victim, the legal process is supplemented with the responsibility or liability of the State.

## 2. Cases of Responsibility: Payment of Damages (*plein contentieux*).

At times the functioning of the administrative services causes damage to the administered. These causes of damage are very varied in nature; illegalities, loss of objects, excessive sluggishness, inexact information and various accidents. The days of administrative irresponsibility are passed. But the responsibility of the administration is "neither general nor absolute,"[127] it follows special rules. There exists the responsibility of the State as well as those of the state agents. There is responsibility or liability for fault and that without fault which leads to the payment of damages.

### a. Responsibility for Fault and without fault

Legally, there are conditions and foundations of each system of responsibilities. The Cameroonian judge defines personal fault as the

---

[124] At times it is not only impossible but unfair to put things as they were or they ought to be e.g reconstitution, of career.

[125] The effects are on everybody, even third persons.

[126] Owona, *Droit Administratif Special..*, 238.

[127] See T.C lst February 1873– arrêt *Blanco*.

totality of facts, of action whose gross irregularity makes them to lose their administrative character or the totality of acts or facts manifestingly insusceptible to be attached to the exercise of power belonging to the administration.[128] As regards the system of responsibility with fault, three necessary and sufficient conditions must be fulfilled;[129]

- There must be a damage or prejudice suffered by the victim;
- This damage should be as a result of the service fault;
- The causal link between the fault and damage.

In this case, the basis of responsibility lies on the fact that the administration has not performed its function as it should. The administration with or without excesses, has adversely and singularly affected individuals.[130]

Unlike private law, there is a system of responsibility without fault. This is generally in favour of the victims against the all–powerful State as the conditions are easily fulfilled: The damage has to be abnormal and special.[131] The basis here is that the individuals should not suffer any special or abnormal damage due to the activities of the State.

### b. Responsibility for the payment of damages

The responsibility for the payment of damages depends on some parameters especially the type of fault whether personal or service. Appeals against the agents are done by the victims who seize the judicial jurisdiction or by the administration before the administrative jurisdiction. In these two cases, there is the existence of a personal fault. In the case of personal fault the agent is directly responsible to the administration or victim. Unlike the service fault, the personal fault is that which is detached from the exercise of the administrative function. There are two hypotheses:

---

[128] See arrêt No 8 of the CFJ\AG *Max Keler Ndongo* of 16 October 1968 and arrêt No 10 of the CFJ\AG *Mve Ndongo* of 17 October 1968.
[129] Kamdem, Contentieux Administratif, T II, 366– 373.
[130] Prejudice can be material, physical or corporal.
[131] Kamdem, Contentieux Administratif, TII, 38.

- This detachment can be material, that is, committed outside the exercise of the function and with no link to it.
- This detachment can be psychological, when the fault committed in the service, reveals not an "administrator more or less subject to error" but man with his "weaknesses, passions, imprudence." [132] When the judiciary judge intervenes, he applies the rules of private law, but the public person substitutes as a full right the agent's responsibility.

The responsibility of the agent to the administration is seen from at least three hypotheses: First, in the case of a personal fault, the agent must pay for the damage he has caused. If the victim attacks the agent, the public power substitutes his responsibility, and takes a "recursory action" against the agent before the administrative court for the benefit of the administration. The Administration also issues an order of receipt against the faulty agent. Second, when there is accumulation or coexistence of personal and service faults, there is division of responsibility. On the one hand, if the appeal was made against the State, it pays the damages but turns towards the agent to repair his personal fault. On the other hand, if the appeal was against the agent, after the paying damages, he can turn towards the administration to pay its own due share corresponding to the service fault. One can conclude with Owona that there can be segregation of responsibilities as well as discrimination of faults.[133] Finally, as ruled by the Cameroonian judge "the property of the State, which is lost or depreciated by holders or users, during or outside the service, are subject to an imputation of their value on the remuneration of the concerned."[134] In such a situation, a receipt order is issued against the agent.

Appeals against the administration can be made by the victims or the agent with the intervention of the judicial and administrative judges depending on the situation. The victim, who suffers from damage due to action or inaction of the administration, can sue the administration in order

---

[132] Owona , 232.
[133]Owona, 233–234.
[134] See arrêt No 187\CFJ\CAY *Mdedez Norbert C/ République Fédérale du Cameroun* 24 Mars 1972.

to protect his rights. The competent judge can be the judicial or administrative. The agent can appeal against the administration through the administrative judge. This can be to ensure his right of substitution or contest an order of receipt against him.

In cases of responsibility, the judge must conciliate the traditional preoccupation to preserve public property with the legitimate rights of the administered to obtain substantial reparations. The principle is the "integral reparation of the prejudice (material, physical, corporal) suffered, all the prejudice and nothing but the prejudice. All in all, there is controversy regarding the relationships that exist between public and private liability.

### c. Private and public systems liability

Kamdem J.C in *Contentieux Administratif,* Tome I (5–10) vividly compares private and public systems of liability in his attempts to demonstrate the autonomy of administrative law. He poses the fundamental question whether rules of law applied by the administrative judge are original in comparison to the principles of civil law. He examines the dissident opinions of Eisenmann (*Sur le degré d'originalité de la responsabilité extra–contractuelle des personnes publiques*) and R. Chapus (*responsabilité publique et responsabilité privée*). According to these authors, the liability of the public power is not veritably autonomous because the differences that separate them from the private liability remain secondary. Without doubt, there is no identity, nevertheless reciprocal and profound resemblances exist.

According to Eisenmann, two observations dominate the debate. First, the domain of real application of private law to the problems of liability in the functioning of public services is very significant. It is neither an exception nor an abnormality to application of "special law" (administrative law). Second, the comparison of the two liabilities from the two primordial points of foundations and functions (finality) of these two systems shows without doubt that there are differences, but resemblances are essential.

Kamdem, however, argues that as regards the first point, it is true that due to the multiplication of private management, the judicial judge has become regularly competent in matters concerning public liability. In these hypotheses, it is probable that he applies rules of private law, but that is not automatic. However, the crux of the matter is, when the administrative judge is competent, does he apply a radically original law? Regarding the second point, Kamdem questions whether the two points of comparison (foundations and functions) are well chosen. Certainly, the two liabilities have as finality principally economic compensation (reparation of damages) with no penal correlation, but this is common to civil liability. Besides, the double foundations accorded by the author viz– in private law, fault and correlation between advantages and charges; and in public law correlation between advantages and charges, equality of citizens before public charges are controversial.

Chapus thesis is based on two arguments. First, that the reciprocal influence of the two liabilities is above all remarked in road accidents and the techniques of reparation. Second, the author uses concepts such as liability due to the action of third persons and that due to action of things which do not correspond to the spirit of administrative case law.

Kamdem therefore argues that the dominant opinion holds that the administrative law of liability remains fundamentally different and autonomous from the rules of private law. To argue for the originality of public liability does not entail the refusal of reciprocal influence between administrative and judicial cases, nor contest that there is the judicial intervention in the liability of the public power. Besides, as regards causality and rules of indemnification, the autonomy of administrative law is not very clear. But then, there are very strong arguments in favour of autonomy. The first argument takes into consideration the decisions of the administrative and the judicial judges. To the administrative judge in the now reputed French case of C.E 6 December 1855 *Blanco–Rotschild*;

> Considering that the liability which can be imposed on the State for damages caused to individuals by the actions of persons employed in the public service, cannot be regulated by the principles which established the civil code, for the relations between individuals... That this liability is neither general nor absolute; that it has special rules which vary depending on service needs and the necessity to conciliate the State with the private rights.

Following the same line of reasoning, the judicial judge himself, the French Cour de Cassation in arrêt *Giry* ruled that the judicial courts, when competent to appreciate the liability of public service, have the "right and duty to apply the rules of public law"

Second as regards the conditions for application of liability, the fundamental notions of service fault, personal fault, liability without fault, substitution, abnormal and special damages etc do not have clear equivalence in private law. The administration is expected to render services, the nature of these services and the manner in which they are ensured is determined by laws and regulations.

Thus in general terms, the spirit of the two disciplines are different, and by implication administrative law is original and autonomous. It is necessary for the control of the administration and to balance the exigencies of authority and freedoms. With the rampant administrative malpractices, the worry is whether those who violate the laws of the administration are effectively sanctioned by the courts.

# Chapter Nine
# Administrative Litigations

In contemporary world, the suing of government and public officials has been subject to much debate. Arguably, officials can find themselves in chains for decisions always hurt someone. This can lead to too much caution, administrative inefficiency and ineffectiveness. Indeed, given the pervasive and all–powerful nature of contemporary public administration, it should be held responsible for blatant neglect, exploitative and malicious actions. There are many formal and informal mechanisms of administrative control, but the judicial system is expected to provide the best authoritative vehicle or last hope for checking administrative abuses. The issue is that the scope of administrative acts is controversial for negatively it is defined as all acts that are not legislative, governmental, judicial or private.

In the Anglo–Saxon countries, jurisdictional monism is applicable where the judicial judge is competent to rule on all cases. In France, there are three types of courts; criminal, civil and administrative. The *Tribunal de Conflits* exist to solve conflicts between ordinary civil courts and administrative courts. The French practice jurisdictional duality where different jurisdictions handle public and private law matters. There is dichotomy between two court orders, *les jurisdictions de l'ordre administratif* and *les jurisdictions de l'ordre judicaire* with corresponding two types of trials le *contentieux administrative* and *le procès civil.* There is a Supreme Court (*Cour de Cassation*) for private law matters and another (*Conseil D'Etat:– Administrative Supreme Court*) for public law matters. Sure, different rules and procedures may be applicable; however there exist commonness of finality which is justice, mutual influences and interactions as what divides them is not a line but a zone. In normal circumstances, reciprocal or concurrent intervention should be authorized by texts. The peculiar status of the State, and the rules that forbid the judiciary tribunal to hear the acts of the administration, justifies the necessity to have a particular law and specialized jurisdiction.

## 9.1 The Evolution of Administrative Jurisdiction in Cameroon

The evolution of administrative jurisdiction in Cameroon is a reflection of environmental changes notably the political dynamism. It reflects the evolution from colonization to independence, from the unitary to the federal form of state, from the one–party system to the democratic tendencies. From these standpoints, three periods can be distinguished: before 1972, after 1972 to the 1990, and finally since the 1990s.

## I. Administrative Jurisdiction before 1972

The Anglo–Saxon tradition does not distinguish between administrative and other jurisdictions. All the litigations in which the administration is party are resolved by the judicial judge, in conformity with common law. This jurisdictional unity is what obtained in the former west Cameroon. As such, development of the early stages is centred on the administrative jurisdiction of former East Cameroon. Before 1972 it was dominated by three institutions successively *le Conseil du Contentieux* (CCA), *le Tribunal d'Etat* (TE) and *le Cour Federal de Justice* (CFJ).

### A. *Le Conseil du Contentieux Administratif* (CCA)

The Council of Administrative Justice was the first administrative jurisdiction in Cameroon. After the defeat of Germany during the First World War, and in line with articles 32 and 119 of the Versailles Treaty, Cameroon was divided between France and Britain. From 1920, France extended to its own portion jurisdictional duality implying a specialized system for administrative matters. This was instituted in Cameroon by the French Decrees of 14 April 1920 and 8 July 1952. These texts were an extension to Cameroon of the French regulation applicable in the overseas territories and colonies. The organization and attributions of this institution are examined.

### 1. The Organization of the CCA

The CCA was presided by a magistrate, two administrators from France and a government commissioner. As Henri Jacquot in *Le*

*Contentieux Administratif au Cameroun* remarked, at the beginning the CCA could be confused with the Administrative Council of the Territory. Certainly, there was functional separation between the two, but in practice this did not exist from the organic point of view. He, therefore, addresses two criticisms to the CCA: It did not respect the principle of separation of administrative and judicial jurisdiction. In addition, it did not respect the principle of separation between the administrative jurisdiction and the active administration. The CCA remained anchored in the administration and in litigations the administration was always judge and party.

## 2. Attributions of the CCA

The CCA was not competent on matters of complaints against power abuse which were taken directly to the French *Conseil d'Etat* (CE). The public service complaints of the French Republic (known as State public service) were out of its jurisdiction. The CCA had an ordinary law competence limited to local services. It was an attribution judge in matters of electoral disputes and the application of the status of local functionaries. The decisions of the Council were susceptible to appeal before the French C.E. This structure was modified with the accession of Cameroon to internal autonomy and independence.

## B. *Le Tribunal d'Etat* (TE)

The evolution of the political status of Cameroon by the accession to internal autonomy on 10 May 1957 and independence proclaimed on the 1st of January 1960 implied the change in the organization of administrative justice. The preoccupation of translating its sovereignty into practice entailed that the new State has to reform its jurisdictional structure in administrative matters by substituting the CCA with the State Tribunal (TE). Logically, as comments Owona Joseph, the abuse of power of an independent state cannot be appreciated by a foreign jurisdiction.

## 1. Organization of T.E

The members of T.E (president and two assessors) were appointed by the Prime Minister and they did not necessarily need to be specialist of law. The textual provisions of competence changed from unlimited to assigned duties. The Decree of 4 June 1959 enumerated the matters under administrative jurisdiction: power abuse, administrative contracts, public domain, rights of public agents, liability, legality and those expressly attributed by the texts. The exceptions were classical concerning irregular dispossession of property (*emprise*) and gross violation of rights (*voie de fait*).

### 2. Procedure before the T.E

According to the Decree of 1959, the T.E decides in the first and last instance. It possessed neither the jurisdiction of appeal nor that of annulment (cassation). The aggrieved persons had only a single instance of jurisdiction in administrative matters. It was an innovation of 20th June 1961 that instituted a double instance of jurisdiction. Article 2 of this 1961 law gave competence to the Supreme Court of the Republic of Cameroon to review the orders of the T.E. Besides, this law made the Supreme Court, the judge of conflicts of jurisdictions, as performed by the *tribunal des conflits* (T.C) in France.

## C. *La Cour Fédérale de Justice* (CFJ)

The T.E was an ephemeral jurisdiction and disappeared with the reunification of the two Cameroons and the formation of a federal form of State. It was therefore substituted by the Federal Court of Justice which was the first administrative jurisdiction to receive constitutional consecration in Cameroon (Article 33 of the federal constitution of 1st September 1961). It was later organized by Ordinance No 61–OF–6 of 4 October 1961. The CFJ was a supreme federal institution, with controversial contribution to Cameroonian administrative law and justice.

### 1. The CFJ as Supreme Federal Institution

Due to the federation, there were some changes regarding the competencies and organization of the CFJ.

#### a. Competencies of the CFJ

According to article 33 of the 1961 constitution, the CFJ was a "federal administrative judge" responsible for matters concerning federal authorities. Law No 65–LF–29 of 29 November 1965 and 14 June 1969 made it a "national judge" extending its competencies to federated states, other units and establishments of public law. In addition to its administrative jurisdiction, the constitution attributed powers to the CFJ as constitutional judge and regulator of conflicts between the highest jurisdictions of the federated states.

### b. Composition of CFJ

The architecture of the CFJ was similar to that of the C.E. The Law of 14 June 1969 created two sections baptized administrative benches situated in Yaoundé and Buea. These benches were judges at first instance of administrative litigations of federated states. Their decisions were susceptible for appeal before the plenary assembly.

The CFJ continued to borrow personnel from the judicial order and the active administration. Certainly as affirms Jacquot, this system was more economical. Besides, mindful of the small number of litigations, it did not make sense to create a corps of administrative magistrates exclusively charged to accomplish this function. But this affirmation is contestable. First administrative law is case–law, and its evolution depends on the quality of judges. Second, judicial judges will have the temptation to apply the rules of private law. Third, a specialized magistrate corps will play a "consultative function" in helping to prepare legislative texts. [135]

## 2. Contribution of CFJ to Cameroonian Administrative Justice.

Evaluations by legal scholars of the 12 years existence of the CFJ are controversial, while some have positive opinions, others disagree.

### a. Positive Opinion

According to Owona Joseph,

> The authority and work of CFJ have been great in the birth of a specifically Cameroonian administrative law…this authority has been in the sense of the national adaptation of praetorian rules traced by the prestigious French C.E and the French administrative jurisdictions. [136]

---

[135] Kamdem, Contentieux Administratif (UNIYAO : FDSE, T.1, 1988/1989), 26–27.

[136] in Kamdem, Contentieux Administratif, T1, 28.

He notes that there are two attitudes of the Cameroonian judge. They adopt the positions of principle of French case–law or a national and original principle.

### b. Negative position

Alain Bockel observes that;

> It is the magistrates of the judicial order trained uniquely in view of their principal mission, who accessorily pronounce on problems sometimes delicate of administrative law. But then, we know the importance of court rulings in the formation and development of this law. Without doubt, the reading of certain court decisions witness the preoccupation of borrowing methods of reasoning and classical principles adopted by the French administrative law judge, but behind this façade, one notices, and some rulings prove this clearly, that judges cannot undo their training. We can certainly think that this will have an impact on the purity of administrative law. In spite of the specificity of problems posed within the framework of administrative justice…The Cameroonian administrative law cannot avoid being influenced by the techniques and methods of reasoning of private law. The duality of jurisdictional order as conceived in Cameroon seems less favourable to the affirmation of administrative law…[137]

Kamdem observes that this argument of Bockel is mainly on the quality of the judicial judge. They have a spirit, technique and method of reasoning based on their training.This might have explained the inertness and docility of the Cameroonian administrative judge marked by extreme prudence, lack of audacity and courage which block innovation. But then the countries that operate jurisdictional monism are not necessarily bad. However, this problem was dealt with by the creation of a specialty in the National School of Administration and Magistracy (ENAM) to train specifically administrative judges.

In 1972 Bipoun–Woum Joseph–Marie observed that an examination of decisions made by the administrative jurisdictions show that in a spontaneous manner they are based on the principal rules of the

[137] Kamdem, Contentieux Administratif, T1, 32.

French administrative law. In 1973, Marcel Nguini, the president of the Supreme Court of the United Republic of Cameroon, declared that as judge of the administration, most of the decisions of the CFJ have been "greatly influenced by the conceptions inspired by the French C.E rulings." These decisions are therefore not adapted to the political, economic and social realities of Cameroon.

The second remark by Bipoun–Woum is that, at the present moment (1972) contrary to what obtained in the formation of administrative law in France, the rules of law applicable to the administration, in the States of French expression, are above all legislative. Kamdem holds that this observation is exact, but should not be exaggerated because no matter the extent of the legislation, this cannot exhaust the law and the judge has the power of application and interpretation of texts, a determinant role in the adaptation and creation of the law.[138]

## II. Replacement of CFJ by the Supreme Court in 1972

1972 saw the replacement of the federal form of state by the unitary one which affected the administrative jurisdiction. At this time, the evolution was based on the adoption of three main texts which abrogated the former ones: The Constitution of 2 June 1972 which created in its article 32 the Supreme Court; The ordinance No 72–6 of 26 August 1972 fixing the organization of the Supreme Court modified by law No 76–28 of 14 December 1976; and finally law No 75–17 of 8 December 1975 fixing the procedure before the Supreme Court in administrative matters. These texts fixed clearly the structures of the administrative jurisdiction which can be evaluated.

### A. The Structures of the Supreme Court in Administrative Matters

The reform of 1972 placed the administrative jurisdiction entirely anchored within the Supreme Court. According to the 72–6 ordinance, in its article 10, the Supreme Court comprised of the administrative bench

[138] Kamdem, Contentieux Administratif, T1, 32–36.

which judges at first instance, and the plenary assembly which judges on appeal. This was a regression, for the two administrative chambers of CFJ were replaced by one situated in Yaoundé. The organization was different but the Supreme Court had functional independence due to its specific competencies.

### B. Competence of the Supreme Court in Administrative matters.

Article 9 of the 72–6 Ordinance clearly stated what comprised administrative disputes: petitions for annulment of the basis of power abuse; actions for indemnification of prejudice caused by administrative acts, litigations concerning administrative contracts and public service concessions, litigations on public domain and those expressly attributed by the law.

The 1996 constitution transformed the judiciary authority to power and stated the composition of the Supreme Court. Law No 2006/016 on the organization and functioning of the Supreme Court and law No 2006/022 on the organization and functioning of Administrative Courts made more clarifications that will be seen subsequently.

## 9.2 The Competent Judge in Administrative Matters

The administrative judge is the common/ordinary law judge of the administration in administrative matters. The main source of inspiration is the general rule of competence, which generally is clarified by texts and judicial practices.

### I. The General Rule of Competence

The legislative definition of competence of the administrative judge can lead to the misconception that the administrative jurisdiction is the exception and rigid limits will be incapable of absorbing new circumstances. It is from this standpoint that texts present elastic formulae, some principles of distribution. There are some guiding principles that determine competence notably the distinction between public and private laws, separation of powers between State organs, separation between administrative and judicial authorities or functions, and the judge action is that of exception.

This rule holds that it is the law applicable to the litigation that determines the competent jurisdiction. When the solution to the dispute entails the use of public law, it is the administrative judge that is competent. If it raises a question of private law, it is the judicial judge. This rule is determined by the parties involved (organic criterion) or by the object (material or functionalist criterion) of the litigation. The analytical method (based on the question or act) or the synthetic method (based on activity) can be used.

## A. Rule determination based on Parties

In positive law, there are three presumptions with corresponding three eventual possibilities. First, the litigations between private persons are as a general rule, the competence of the judicial judge. The administrative judge is not competent because the legal acts of individuals and their activities are not generally part of public law. This principle admits two derogations: when a legislative text expressly provides for administrative competence, and when the litigious operation occurred during the execution of a public service.

Second, litigations concerning two public bodies are in general, the competence of the administrative judge. In line with the conclusions of Romieu in the French *Terrier case*, "all the actions between public bodies themselves are based on the execution, non–execution and poor execution of a public service are of administrative competence." This, however, except with legislative stipulations to the contrary notably accidents caused by administrative vehicles and acts in the private domain of the state. Third, it can happen that the litigation concerns both private and public persons. In this case, there is a mixed process, the rules of public and private laws applied respectively.

## B. Rule determination based on Object

Following the analytic method, the object (aim) of the litigation is fixed in reference to the determined legal act which led to the lawsuit. For instance the administrative competence is accepted when a contract contains exorbitant clauses to common law, when the unilateral administrative act possesses prerogatives of the public power or character of public service.

In the French *Epoux Bertin* case, it was ruled that the determinant factor is the execution of public service which confers rights and obligations of public law. In his conclusion in *Vingtain and Affortit*, Chardeau brought out that the notion of public service determines by itself the application of the public law regime. This line of reasoning was made more explicit in the decision of *Ministre de l'Agriculture C/ Consorts Grimouard* which defined public service as comprising of three elements; mission of general interest, intervention of public body, with special prerogatives.

In line with the synthetic method, the object of the lawsuit is determined in function with the global activity by which the process is attached. If it is considered as relevant to the legal regime of public or private law, the competence will be administrative or judicial respectively. Thus in cases of liability of missions of administrative public services, the administrative judge is competent. The judicial judge is competent in matters regarding the management of the private domain, functioning of the judicial services, industrial and commercial services, and acts of private law passed by administrative public services. The general rule of competence has many challenges because of the interactions between the public and private laws.

## II. The Distribution of Competences in Matters of Administrative Litigations

The administrative judge is the common law judge of the administration. This implies that he is the original, principal or main judge in administrative matters. It also entails administrative judge is the ordinary trial judge, is competent as a rule and the other judges intervene exceptionally. While the jurisdiction of the judiciary judge is attributive, that of the administrative judge is without text specifically awarding competence in administrative lawsuits.

### A. Administrative Judge; principal judge in administrative matters

Historically, in the French Case of *Cadot* of 13 December 1889, the *Conseil D'Etat* recognised its quality as the ordinary law judge in administrative matters, competent even in the cases not previewed by texts. In other words, common law judge implies the principle, principal or even natural judge. Needless to say, the intervention of other judges becomes the exception (attribution). The 1996 Constitution, Law No 2006/016 on the Organization and Functioning of the Supreme Court and law No 2006/022 on the Organization and Functioning of Administrative Courts see the administrative judge as the principal judge in administrative matters.

## 1. Constitutional provisions

Article 38 of the 1996 Constitution states that;

(1) The Supreme Court shall be the highest court of the state in legal and administrative matters as well as in the appraisal of accounts.

(2) It shall comprise:

- A judicial bench
- An administrative bench
- An audit bench

Precisely, as concerns the administrative jurisdiction, it states in its article 40 that;

The administrative bench shall examine the administrative disputes involving the State and other public authorities. It shall:

- examine appeals on regional and municipal election disputes;
- give final rulings on appeals against judgements passed by lower courts in cases of administrative disputes;
- examine any other disputes expressly devolving on it by law.

The administrative jurisdiction is therefore endowed by the highest law of the land, the constitution. The administrative bench of the Supreme Court is the highest jurisdiction in administrative matters.

## 2. The Provisions of Law No 2006/016

Before the provisions of this law, it should be noted that Law No 2006/015 of 29 December 2006 on Judicial Organization states in its article 2 (2–3) that “Judicial power shall be exercised by the Supreme Court, Courts of Appeal and Courts.” Judicial organization shall comprise:

The Supreme Court, Courts of Appeal, Lower Courts of Administrative litigation, Lower Audit Courts, Military Courts, High Courts, Courts of First Instance and Customary Law Courts.

Law No 2006/016 of 29 December 2006 to lay down the organization and functioning of the Supreme Court in its article 2 states succinctly that "The Supreme Court shall be the highest state court in judicial, administrative and audit matters." It precise in its article 9 that the Administrative Bench shall comprise:

- a division for civil service litigation;
- a division of land tenure litigation;
- a division of tax and financial litigation;
- a division of public contracts litigation;
- a division for nullification and sundry issues.

Each of these divisions shall hear appeals relating to matters within its jurisdiction.

### 3. The Provisions of Law No 2006/022

Article 14 1) of Law No 2006/022 states, "Save otherwise provided by law, Administrative Courts shall be ordinary trial law courts (common law) with jurisdiction to hear administrative litigations at first instance." With the inspiration from the constitution, law No 2006/022 specifies and precise the Cameroonian administrative jurisdiction. With few modifications this law continues with the tradition of Ordinance 72–6 (art.9) as to what constitutes elements of administrative jurisdiction. Its preliminary stipulations bring out this;

Article 1: The Law No 2006/022 lays down the organization and functioning of the administrative courts.

Article 2: Lower courts for administrative litigations within the meaning of article 40 of the constitution shall be called Administrative Courts.

(2) Administrative courts shall have jurisdiction to determine at the first instance litigations on regional and council elections and at the last instance all administrative litigations concerning decentralized public authorities in accordance with the provisions of article 14 (2) of this law.

(3) Administrative litigation shall include:

(a) Petitions for the annulment for ultra vires, and in civil matters incidental petitions in appreciation of legality. For the purpose of this article, ultra vires constitutes;

- defect of form;
- problem of incompetence;
- violation of the law or regulation;
- misuse of powers

(b) Claims of indemnification for damages caused by an administrative act;

(c) Litigations relating to contracts (excluding those concluded even implicitly under the private law) or public service concessions;

(d) Litigations concerning state land;

(e) Litigations relating to the maintenance of law and order operations.

Most of these components have been treated under administrative action. From this article, one can confirm that the Administrative Court is the main judge in administrative matters. The enumeration of the cases gives the impression that the competence of the administrative judge is attributive or the exception. But arguably, if there are other matters qualified as administrative, then they should be the exception.

## 4. Extension of Competence of the Administrative Judge

There has been progressive extension of the domain of competence of the administrative jurisdiction from the initial one. These extensions are mainly legislative; the decretal and case–law extensions have been controversial.

As regards legislative extensions, article 38 (d) of law No 2006/016 on the Organization and Functioning of the Supreme Court states clearly that administrative bench of the Supreme Court shall be competent in "all other matters expressly attributed to it by the law." This is simply a continuation with the tradition of art 9 of the 72–6 Ordinance which made the same provisions. Certain laws have thus provided the administrative competence regarding human rights and freedoms, electoral and financial disputes.

The democratic wind of change since the 1990s witnessed the adoption of many texts on human rights and freedoms in which the administrative court was awarded competence notably in matters of freedom of association, freedom of political parties and freedom of press. In the *EPC C/ Etat du Cameroun* case (1994), the judge annulled the order of the Governor of the Centre Region prohibiting the activities of the said church. The administrative judge intervened regarding implicit refusal on the authorization of political parties as demonstrated in *UPC Manidem C/ Etat du Cameroun (1992)*. Also the judge has intervened in disputes on the prohibition and seizure of newspapers as seen in the *Le Messager C/Etat du Cameroun Case (*1990).

Article 33 of Law No. 92/002 of 14 August 1992 on the Election of Municipal Councillors, states that all electors and candidates have the right to request for the cancellation of elections before the administrative judge. Article 38 (a) of Law No 2006/016 states that the administrative bench shall be competent to hear "appeals against decisions handed down in regional and council election disputes."

As regards disputes of financial character, article 328 of the General Tax Code holds that in matters of direct and business taxes, the decisions taken by the Minister in charge of Finance on contentions in which the concerned is not satisfied, he can attack the decision before the Supreme Court. The 2005 decree on the regulation of public contracts (*marches publics*) gives the administrative judge the jurisdiction to decide on cases regarding the interpretation and execution of such contracts. The problem is whether regulations can be qualified as law. From the broad sense, law is all the rules that govern the administration. But from the strict sense, law is voted by the parliament following the procedure previewed by the constitution. However, this decree can simply be seen as an application of Ordinance No 72–6 (article 9) and later 2006/022 law (article 2(3c) thus giving jurisdiction to the administrative judge in matters of public contracts.

The administrative judge when interpreting laws, ruling on cases and with legal loopholes can extend his proper competence. But as seen under the assessment of the administrative jurisdictions, there is controversy among scholars regarding the establishment of an autonomous Cameroonian administrative law and justice.

## B. The Competence of the Ordinary Courts in administrative matters

In the countries that practise jurisdictional duality, there is always the fear that the administrative judge is tempted to rule in favour of the administration. There are, therefore, provisions for the ordinary courts to intervene in some disputes. According to article 3 of law N° 2006/022;

(1) The ordinary courts shall have jurisdiction under the private law over all actions or disputes brought against any of the public persons referred to in article 2, the said bodies being vicariously liable for the acts their employees committed in the course of their employment.

(2) They shall further have jurisdiction in respect to irregular administrative dispossession of immovable property and grave violation of fundamental liberties and property rights and issue orders to end them.

However, the administrative bench of the Supreme Court shall rule on any preliminary objections made in respect of these matters.

Many texts have awarded the judicial judge the competence in administrative matters, notably expropriation for public use. As discussed under liability, the administration usually substitutes the public agents in cases where they cause damages to the individuals. The most popular interventions of the judicial judge concern rights and incidentally, the appreciation of the legality of administrative acts.

### 1. Disputes regarding administrative violation of fundamental and property rights

The competence of the judicial judge in matters of irregular administrative dispossession of immovable property (*Theorie de l'emprise*) and grave violation of fundamental liberties and property rights (*Voie de fait)* is founded on the conception that he is the defender of fundamental freedoms and property rights.

#### a. Irregular administrative dispossession of immovable property

Three conditions must exist to ensure the intervention of the judicial judge. First, there should be veritable dispossession by the administration which has as consequence the privation of the proprietor from the enjoyment of his property. Second, the dispossession should be on immovable property. Finally, it should be irregular; it is founded on illegal title or material conditions. If the seizure is based on legal title, it is the competence of the administrative judge.

Under Cameroonian law, at first the judge decided that the judicial judge had the exclusive power or competence in matters of irregular dispossession in CFJ–CAY 23 March 1971 *Medou Gaston.* Arguably, the judicial judge is not competent to appreciate the legality of administrative acts. That is why the administrative judge in CS–CA 30 November 1979 decided that the administrative judge is competent to appreciate its regular or irregular character. The judicial judge fixes the amount to be paid for the damages and takes measures to put an end to it (CS–CA 23 march 1979 *Baba Youssoufa C/ Etat du Cameroun*).

### b. Grave violation of fundamental liberties and property rights

This comprises of three elements: First, these are circumstances where there is material execution of the decision by the administration. Second, the act should be grave, manifestingly insusceptible to be attached to the execution of a legislative or regulatory text; the power belonging to the administration (CFJ–AP 17 October 1968 *Mve Dongo/Ngada Victor*). It is finally a violation of fundamental liberties and property rights.

As regards the extent of the power of the judge, article 9 (4) of Ordinance No 72–6 gave powers to the former Plenary Assembly and later article 3 (2) of 2006/022 Law gives competence to the Administrative Bench for the establishment of these grave irregular acts. Before the judicial judge, the establishment constitutes as a consequence a prejudicial question. Also, the fixing of the reparation is the exclusive competence of the judicial judge who appreciates the damages caused and determines the amount of money to be paid as damages by the administration (CS–CA 29 March 1979 *Atangana Ntonga Sylvestre C/ Etat du Cameroun*). Besides, as stated above it is the judicial judge who looks for ways to force or provide injunctions to the administration to end the irregular act.

## 2. Interpretation and Appreciation of legality of administrative acts

The interpretation and appreciation of administrative acts by the administrative judge does not pose any problem. Article 15 (2) of the 2006/022 Law precise that;

> The administrative court of the area where the office of the authority that took the challenged decision is located shall also have jurisdiction to determine actions for damages in respect of injuries suffered as a result of the challenged decision. Furthermore it shall entertain matters relating to the interpretation and appreciation of the legality of the litigations referred to it by the ordinary law courts.

Following the general rule of competence it is illogical that the judicial jurisdiction should be competent to appreciate the legality of administrative acts or interpret their significance. The power of the judicial judge to interpret administrative acts, puts in conflict on the one hand the principle of separation between administrative and judicial authorities and on the other the principle according to which the "judge of action is the judge of exception."

However, during the court process, in trying to resolve the principal litigation, incidental or accessory questions may arise. In such complex situations two solutions are envisaged. In the first hypothesis, the general rule of competence is seen as an inconvertible dogma that must be respected scrupulously. This entails that the incidental question will be considered to be prejudicial, thus the accessory question will be sent to the natural judge (administrative) to resolve. This approach is logical, but then it is long, inconvenient and costly. The second hypothesis therefore applies the adage, "The judge of action, is the judge of exception." The judicial judge will be competent but this implies the violation of the principle of separation between the administrative authority and the judiciary. These two solutions are extremes, it depends whether it is interpretation or appreciation.

Interpretation implies that the administrative act is obscure or unclear thus the need for precision. The repressive jurisdictions have identical powers with the civil ones. As regards the regulatory acts, the judicial judge have the right to determine the sense and significance as confirmed by the TC decision in the now celebrated case of *Septfonds* (1923). The justification is that, ordinary courts interpret the law, and the regulatory acts resemble the law by their general and impersonal character. On the contrary, the interpretation of non–regulatory or individual decisions entails defining the situation or rights of the administered thus directly infringing in the administrative functioning. As such, civil and repressive judges do not have the power to interpret and have to refer it to the administrative judge as a prejudicial question.

In principle, the civil jurisdictions do not have the competence to appreciate the legality of administrative acts. This rule, however, is subject to some exceptions. When the administrative act is non–existent, there is judicial competence on the administrative matter and when the act gravely violates the inviolability of the private domicile, fundamental liberties or property rights. The repressive judge has the power to appreciate if the administrative act serves as foundation for penal pursuits or constitutes a means of defence.

### C. Resolution of Conflicts of Jurisdiction

The complexity of the distribution of competences in contentious matters between the administrative and judicial jurisdictions can lead to conflicts. In some legal systems conflicts are resolved by parity bodies comprised of an equal number of magistrates from both jurisdictions. In others, there is a supreme jurisdiction which can be judicial or administrative. It can also be an autonomous institution in relation to both jurisdictional orders as the case of TC in France. In Cameroon, formerly, in line with Ordinance 72–6, this role was played by the Plenary Assembly of the Supreme Court. Presently, Article 41(1) of Law No 2006/016 states that, the panel of Joint Benches resolves conflicts of jurisdiction.

### D. Exemption from administrative jurisdiction: Acts of government

As discussed earlier, exceptional circumstances render the control by the judge problematic. Under the section on administrative acts, it was pinpointed that private person acts, legislative acts, judicial authority acts and acts of government are not unilateral administrative acts, thus not under administrative jurisdiction. However, the laws clearly emphasize on the acts of government. The 72–6 Ordinance in its article 9(5) exempted acts of government from judicial review. In continuation with the tradition, after the stipulations of competences in articles 2 and 3, article 4 of Law No 2006/022 states that "No court shall have jurisdiction to review acts of government." The Cameroonian legislature has not expressly defined acts of government; this according to Henri Jacquot is an attempt to avoid very violent crises between powers. But Alain Bockel criticised this attitude claiming that it encourages arbitrariness in the most delicate sector. Even decisions emanating from Law No 64–LF–16 of 26 June 1964 on the fight against terrorism were qualified as "specific act of government of a new type."[139] In spite of some confusion, the Cameroonian administrative judge has been consistent as to what is act of government.

The acts of government are those which though taken by the government enjoy general and absolute jurisdictional immunity. That is their legality cannot be attacked before the court of law. Maurice Kamto distinguishes this notion from acts of the government which comprises of the totality of acts taken on the basis of regulatory power whose execution is susceptible to be attacked before the competent court. It is not also the "reason of the state" which holds that decisions on political questions are not susceptible to be petitioned before the judge. He argues that in the absence of a normative definition, it is the judge who has attempted to provide one under Cameroonian law. The judge pronounced on this notion in some cases: CS–CA 1979 *Kouang Guillaume Charles C/Etat du Cameroon*; 1980 *Essomba Marc–Antoine C/ Etat du Cameroon*; 1980 *Monkam Tientcheu David;* 1980 *Essougou Benoit C/ Etat du Cameroun.*

The first three cases concerned the designation of traditional rulers and the state representatives held that the Administrative Bench of the Supreme Court where the respective plaintiffs tabled their petitions was incompetent to decide on the litigations, the reason being that the incriminated acts are government and benefit as such from total immunity of jurisdiction. In the three decisions the court was consistent, declared its

[139] Owona, Joseph : L'Institutionnalisation de la Légalité d'Exception dans le Droit Public Camerounaise.» *Revue Camerounaise de Droit,* No 6, Juillet–Décembre 1974

competence and provided details as regards the domains of intervention of the acts of government. These are only acts regarding the relations between the government and the parliament and the relations between Cameroon and foreign governments in the international and diplomatic domains. This implied the rejection of the vague notion of political questions.

In the *Monkam Tientcheu* case, the judge created some confusion by declaring that; "even in the hypothesis where a law stipulates that a given act cannot be an object of any administrative or judiciary petition, this stipulation cannot be interpreted as excluding the petitions for abuse of power which is open, even without text, against all administrative acts that cause injury and which has as effect to assure conformity with the general principles, the respect of legality. Kamto comments that this ruling is revolutionary as can be interpreted as a pure and simple suppression of the acts of government under Cameroonian law.

Besides, the consistency and the rule of precedent in the above cases was challenged in the *Essougou Benoit* case where the judge defined the act of government as an act having essentially political character whose decision belongs exclusively to the government. It is also an act attached to the exercise of the executive power in government matters. According to Salomon Bilong, this position of the administrative judge is troubling from three perspectives: First, the judge did not precisely define the content of political questions. Next, the decision challenged the consistency, "pacificism" that has existed for a long time in the domain, putting to question the state of law. Finally, this position is reactionary in relation to the French C.E which since the *Napoleon case,* has definitively abandoned the theory of political questions. He concludes that the worry is, however, relative because this case has not been followed by other court decisions, it is isolated.[140]

## 9.3 The Procedures Governing Administrative Jurisdiction

It is necessary to distinguish between the form and the procedure. In order to understand this distinction, it is advisable to start with the

---

[140] Bilong, 197–200.

notion of act which signifies two things. First, it is the content which is taken into account, what the law prescribes, what the judgement decides, what the contract previews. Second, act signifies the procedure to be followed. This act–content is known as the "factum" what is done, and the act–operation is the "facere" the action to do. The form concerns the written, *instrusmentum*, the date, visas, motives, and executory formulae. The procedure concerns the how or the normative operation, the *negotium*, the totality of facts and behaviours of the author of the act and the plaintiff, the delays to be respected, the competent authorities, rights of defence and the form of judgement.

In Cameroon, laws determine the administrative jurisdiction processes and modalities of: filing petitions before the judge, how the judge intervenes, how the trial is done and how the ruling is made. These laws are Law No 2006/002 fixing the Organization and Functioning of the Administrative Courts and Law No 2006/016 organizing the Supreme Court. The procedure starts off with administrative hearings, an indispensable pre–trial phase (recours gracieux préalable). It is after the rejection of this, that there is a trial phase proper, with the intervention of the judge.

## I. Pre–Trial Complaint

Otherwise known as pre–litigation complaint, these are administrative hearings before the matter is taken to the court. Article 12 of Ordinance No 72/6 states that "The petition before the Supreme Court is not acceptable except after the rejection of a pre–trial petition addressed to the competent minister or the authority statutorily habilitated to represent the public body or establishment concerned." Article 17(1) of law No 2006/022 continues with the same obligation when it states that "Petitions may be made to the administrative court only following rejection of a complaint made to the authority that issued the challenged act or the authority empowered by the statutory instrument to represent the public body or public establishment concerned." This pre–litigation compliant has a compulsory character, handled by specific authorities and subjected to clear time limits.

### A. The Compulsory Nature of Pre–litigation complaint

The pre–litigation complaint has an imperative character and it is a means of public order. It is imperative because the petition to the administrative judge is not acceptable if this phase is not respected. In the case of *Ekindi Joel C/ Etat du Cameroon* (1968) the judge stated in clear terms that "the pre–litigation complaint is obligatory, on the pain of foreclosure." It is a means of public order which entails that its non–observation or violation can be automatically raised by the judge, even if none of the parties to the lawsuit invokes it (CS/CA 1978, *Item Dieudonne C/ Etat du Cameroon, Atangana Essomba Protrais C/ Etat du Cameroun).*

However, there exist some legislative and judge made exceptions to this principle of compulsory character. Some of these exceptions were instituted in 1990 in matters of human rights and freedoms. Regarding the political parties, Law No 90/56 of 19 December 1990 states that the explicit or implicit refusal of authorization to create a political party is susceptible for petition by a simple complain before the president of the Administrative Bench. This is also the case with measures of automatic suspension of the activities of a political party on the basis of grave threat to public order or the decision of the Minister in charge of Territorial Administration to dissolve a political party for the same reasons. In addition, Law No 90/052 on Association precise in its article 13 that the decisions of the MINAT on the suspension or dissolution of an association can be done before the president of the Administrative Bench. Law No 92/022 of 14 August 1992 states clearly that all electors or candidates can petition for the cancellation of the electoral operations in the court. This contestation can be done by simple complaint before Administrative Bench, thus exempted from the pre–litigation complaint (article 34). The laws also expressly state that decisions of some quasi–jurisdictional institutions such as the budgetary and account discipline can be directly petitioned before the Administrative Bench.

As regards case–law exceptions, classically, when the judiciary judge is petitioned by mistake, the pre–litigation complaint is no longer required if the same case is later tabled before the administrative judge. (CS–CA 1982 *Dzietham Pierre C/ Etat du Cameroon*).

## B. Competent Authority for Pre–litigation Complaint

With the notion of "competent minister" in its article 12, the Ordinance 72–6 created a lot of confusion and uncertainty regarding the competent authority. Yet the sanction on the mistake of the competent authority was very severe. Generally, the authority petitioned by mistake had neither the obligation to respond nor the obligation to orientate the complaint to the right person. As a consequence, the plaintiff is declared foreclose as the mistake does not suspend the time–limit, or the complaint is declared not receivable before the administrative judge for default of pre–litigation complaint. Many litigants, historically have been victims of this confusion remarkably *Essomba Ntonga Gabriel* (1978), and *Onana Jacques Didier* (1978) C/ *Etat du Cameroun.*

Law No 2006/022 clearly precise that the competent authority is the author of the decision or the head of the public body or public establishment. Hopefully, this will increase access to justice, for the confusion of the competent authority has been a fundamental blockage to the complainants.

## C. Time Limits for Pre–litigation complaint

The pre–litigation complaint is subjected to some time limits which are imperative in character, which poses the legal problem on how to fix these limits. In line with article 17(3) of law No 2006/022 the time–limit depends on the nature of the complaint. Thus the pre–litigation complaint, under the pain of foreclosure is done:

a) Within three months from the date of publication or notification of the challenged decision;

b) In the case of request for indemnification, within six months from the date of the realization of the damage or its knowledge;

c) In the case of abstention of the authority who is legally bound to act and fails to do so, four years from the date of which the said authority failed to act.

This time–limit can be increased by one or two days depending on where the complainant lives. If the complainant lives outside the country, there is corresponding prolongation of the time–limit based on distance.

This is one month if the complainant resides in Africa, and two months for the rest of the world. Certainly, this is indispensable for decisions that are not known are not opposable.

The computation of the time can begin the same day or the following day as ruled by the judge in various decisions. In the first hypothesis, the time begins when the aggrieved person is informed or gets knowledge about the decision through publication or notification. The time–limit is fixed from the *dies a quo* (date of publication or notification) to the *dies a quem (*day of time limit) (CFJ–CAY 1971 *Alai Belobo Nestor C/ Etat du Cameroun*). Exceptionally, the time begins to run from the date the concerned had acquired knowledge. This entails that there is no regular publication, but the complainant in one way or the other got knowledge regarding the existence and content of the decision. This theory of acquired knowledge is applicable for instance when the concerned was present when the decision was signed, requested the decision to be interpreted or when the decision is based on an anterior one. Another hypothesis applied by the judge is counting next day from the date of publication or notification (*délai franc*) (CS–CA 1978 *Ngongang Richard C/ Etat du Cameroun; Essomba Ntonga Gabriel C/ Etat du Cameroun*).

### D. Assessment of Pre–trial petition

The pre–trial petition has two essential objectives; information and linkage, however because of its obligatory character and the complications attached to it, it has helped to block administrative justice.

#### 1. Information of the administration

The preoccupation of the legislator is that the administration be preliminarily informed about all petitions against it before the court process is launched. From this standpoint, it offers the possibility of reconciliation between the parties. At least theoretically, it offers the possibility of each party to present her views, appreciate those of the other party and if possible reach a negotiated solution. If this is done, the process ends at this level.

#### 2. Linkage to the litigation

The pre–trail petition provides the basis for the litigation. As it starts off the process, it provides the court with a precise, determined and delimited dispute. The litigant cannot submit before the judge a different complaint than the one presented before the administration. In line with the principle of immutability, there should be identity of the complaint presented before the administration and the judge as regards the cause and object of the litigation.

### 3. Blockage of litigations

The pre–trial petition has some latent and perverse effects, that of limiting administrative litigations. Its use entails knowledge in administrative law as regards competent authorities and time limits. The *Guiffo J.P* case demonstrates that even law lecturers can fall prey to this imperative, then what more of the common man. Many complaints have been declared not receivable by the court due to faults regarding the pre–litigation complaint notably time limit, competent authority and identity (Examples include CS–CA 1976 *Edimo Jean Charles C/ Etat du Cameroun*; 1983 *Ngondi Dieudonne C/ Etat du Cameroun.*

## II. The Procedure before the Court

The litigation begins when the plaintiff introduces or tables the complaint before the judge. It is after this that the substance of the case is examined in court. In other words, the judge makes a probationary examination of the case before proceeding to the substance of the case.

## A. The Introduction of the Litigation

The introduction of the case follows a number of rules aimed at avoiding unnecessary litigations. The fundamental legal problem of this introduction is to examine whether the case is receivable. This entails the examination of the acceptability of the complaint in court. The ruling on the case can only start if the judge has preliminarily and positively resolves the problem of whether the complaint is receivable. This is examined from the personal, temporal and material dimensions.

### 1. Personal dimensions of the petition

The law distinguishes between physical and moral persons. The corporate bodies can be private or public. The rules governing these bodies usually indicate the persons who are expected to represent them. To be accepted in court, the body must exist legally. However, the judge always accepts the factual existence in the cases of default of legal formality of creation. All persons who can sue must have the capacity, an interest and quality.

### a. Capacity to sue

The capacity of physical persons comprises of three dimensions: physical, legal and moral. As regards the physical capacity, the complainant must exist, born and living at the time of the case. A complaint cannot be tabled by an imaginary person. Legal capacity obliges that the plaintiff should be 21 years at the time of the litigation. Besides, she must be in possession of her rights. Moral capacity concerns the possession of reasoning faculties. He must be capable of discernment, a mentally deranged, crazy, mad person lack the capacity and lucidity to engage in a legal process. The law consider them incapable and takes measures to protect them.

### b. Interest to act

Interest is another condition for a petition to be receivable in court. Interest has a double foundation. First, prejudice or grief suffered by the plaintiff. This implies that the situation or the litigious fact causes trouble and the judgement solicited can put an end to it. Second, it is the expected benefit or advantage (material, pecuniary or moral) that justifies the interest of the complainant. Thus the maxim that "no interest, no action" which signifies that if action is not susceptible to offer a utility to the person who takes the initiative, the complaint is not acceptable.

This interest must possess certain characteristics; concretely two conditions have to be satisfied. The interest must be certain, that is, it must be born, should exist and must be actual. Besides, it must be personal, that is the complainant should be a victim; she should be directly and personally touched.

### c. Quality to sue

The quality is the legal title which serves as basis for the engagement of the process. It is a title which gives a legal situation on the basis of which one can act in justice on his behalf or as representative. This entails that a person is an actor of the legal system determined by his role and situation. The law emphasizes on certain roles, situations by which it gives special protection. In each case, the law determines who has/have the power to act in justice. The quality marks the coincidence between the actor and the role. For instance, it is only spouses that have the quality to request for a divorce. Some legal scholars have created confusion between the notions of interest and quality, this may be due to the complementary relationship between the two.

## 2. The temporal dimension of the petition

This entails the time limits that run after the pre–litigation complaint. These time limits which are also imperative depend on the attitude of the administrator regarding the pre–litigation complaint. However, these time limits can be extended in some circumstances.

### a. Time limit varies in function of administrator's attitude

Article 18(1) of Law No 2006/022 states that "Petitions against administrative decisions shall be barred where they are not filed within a time limit of sixty (60) days as from the date of the decision rejecting the administrative hearing provided for in article 16 above." The rejection can be implicit or explicit and if the time limit is not respected, the case is foreclosed, thus the petition not acceptable. The prescribed time limit runs as from the day following the notification.

### b. Extension of the time limit

Article 19 (1) states that the above prescribed deadlines can be extended where the petitioner in the meantime:

a) files an application for legal aid;

b) brings an action before a court that lacks jurisdiction;

(2) In such a case, it shall be proper to file the petition within sixty (60) days following service of decision on legal aid or on the issue of jurisdiction."

The legal aid is necessary to protect the indigent and illiterates, to ensure equality before the law. If the plaintiff petitions before an incompetent jurisdiction, the problem is that, this may take a long time for it to pronounce judgement and in which case the petition remains acceptable before the administrative judge.

### 3. The Material dimension of the petition

The petition starts off the jurisdictional process. It has content; it is an act, a document, an *instrumentum*. The petition is written, stamped and signed by the petitioner or his attorney. Those who are illiterate and do not have representatives can use the thumbprints. If the petition is directed against a decision of an administrative authority, the said decision is attached. In addition, all introductory requests are done with a deposit of 20.000 FCFA. A complementary deposit can be ordered by the president of the jurisdiction in the case of necessity. The corporate bodies of public law are exempted from the deposit.

The petition must present the object (purpose of the complaint), facts (details) legal arguments (cause, means) and the conclusion (solution) of the request for justice. The facts are the elements that generated the contentious situation situated in time, space and gravity. The cause is the legal foundation of the petition; the principle of law that explains and justifies it. The legal means is the foundation of the petition too but at an inferior and secondary level. For instance, as regards litigations on legality, there are two causes internal and external legality. The diversion of powers, incompetence, vices or non–respect of form and procedure are the means which are attached to one or the other cause. The object otherwise known as the conclusion is what the petitioner wants to obtain, this is what is expected to be seen at the end of the ruling; annulment, damages, cancellation of a contract etc. The cause, means and conclusion form what Charles Debbasch calls 'judicial syllogism": major (cause), minor (means) and conclusion (object).

## B. The Examination of the Petition in Court

At this level, the judge has declared the petition receivable and has to rule on the substance of the litigation or contestation. The judge is expected to make investigations before the final phase of the judgement.

### 1. Investigations and Judgement

Investigations form the dynamic phase of the administrative jurisdiction, the judge uses all the legal means possible to search for the elements that can clarify the case and lead to the discovery of the truth.

Once the material conditions have been fulfilled and the petition registered, the president appoints a rapporteur, who shall under his authority, direct the examination of the matter. When these conditions have not yet been fulfilled the rapporteur shall call upon the petitioner to regularize the claim within 15 days of notice under pain of inadmissibility of the petition (article 37). The role of the rapporteur is primordial for he is the one who prepares all the work. He examines the admissibility, determines measures of investigation, exchanges and establishes the report.

In normal times, the investigation is governed by a number of principles. The judge charged with the investigation must ensure the contradictory character of the litigation, which gives him important inquisitorial powers, however within a prescribed limited time. The contradictory process implies that the judge must during the investigations use the method that ensures the contradiction of parties. Regarding the inquisitorial character, once the judge receives the petition, he informs the defendant, and from this moment there is exchange of defences and replications. The judge has the right to request for any information that can help find the truth and resolve the case. Where the petition is admissible, the rapporteur orders that the defendant be served, who has thirty (30) days to file his defence. The order states the time limit within which the respondent shall file his defence (article 38, law no 2006/022). Within fifteen (15) days of service of the statement of defence, the petitioner files the reply to which the respondent may in turn file an answer within the same time limit (art. 40).

The principal measures of investigation include; visit of the *locus in quo*, the examination of the parties, interrogation of witnesses, inspection of documents and expert evidence (arts. 56–93). The hearings are generally public and all judgements are delivered in open court. The State Counsel submits on every issue tabled before the court. Judgement is delivered after deliberations and in accordance with the opinion of the majority of the members of the panel.

During the process, incidental or interlocutory proceedings (Chapter V) which are supplementary claims that intervene in the litigation procedure can occur. These may be counter claims, interruptive, restart of process, jurisdictional and extinctive claims. Any person having interest in the result of the case is entitled to intervene. Besides, withdrawal and acquiescence are permitted on condition that they are accepted by the adverse party (art. 98). In addition, any judge can be challenged for any reason likely to make it difficult for him to render impartial judgement. In general terms, after the hearings, the judge appreciates the whole situation and renders judgement. Besides the normal procedure, the investigation and judgement phase can at times be that of urgency.

### 2. Urgent procedures of judgement

The sluggishness of the administrative litigations can lead to irreversible and irreparable damage on the plaintiffs. Consequently, as Law No 75–17, Law No 2006/022 contains two measures of urgency: summary judgement (*référé administratif*) and stay of execution (*sursis a execution*).

The summary judgement is where the judge decides based on preliminary elements to immediately resolve the case in order to avoid irreversible damages before subsequently rules following the normal procedure. In urgent cases, the president of the court or the judicial officer sitting for him, may on application and if the applicant shows proof of having filled a complaint, summon the parties, and after submissions to the legal department, by a ruling make any orders that he deems necessary, without prejudice to the substantive matter (art. 27). The court rules on such applications in chambers and such rulings are served to the parties within 24 hours. The said ruling is subjected to appeal before the Administrative Bench of the Supreme Court. But, it is enforceable notwithstanding the appeal.

The stay of execution is an urgent measure which stops the execution of an administrative decision contested in the court of law. As a general rule, petitions filed against administrative acts shall not suspend execution thereof. Exceptionally where "the execution is liable to cause irreparable harm and the challenged decision does not affect either public order or security, or public peace, the president of the administrative court may, after notifying the respondent and the submissions of the legal department, order stay of execution." The order of stay of execution is served to the parties within 24 hours and the administrative decision is suspended as from the date of service.

## C. Petitions against Court Rulings

These are complaints to oppose the ruling, third party oppositions, appeals to quash the ruling, redress patent errors or review it (articles 107–118). Oppositions can be made to set aside judgements in default. Notices of appeal against judgements delivered by administrative courts shall be lodged by the petitioner personally, his counsel or by an attorney. The third parties can also oppose the rulings governed by the provisions of ordinary law. Where the judgement contains patent or material errors, the interested party may lodge an application of rectification or redress before the president of the said court. There can also be a complaint for the review of judgment if it is wrong; this is heard by the court that delivered the vitiated judgement and according to the procedure before the said court.

The judgements delivered by the administrative courts at first instance or as court of last resort are subjected to appeal before the Administrative Bench of the Supreme Court in the manner and time laid down by the law on the Organization of the Supreme Court (art. 116).

## D. The Content of the Judgement

According to article 54 of Law N° 2006/022 every judgement of the administrative court commences with the words "In the name of the people of Cameroon, the administrative court" and the findings of the court divided into paragraphs are preceded by the words "decides". It shall state the following: the composition of the court, the names of parties and their submissions; the main legal provisions cited, a statement that the rapporteur, the parties, their attorneys or counsel and the legal department were heard; a statement that it was delivered in open court, after examination of all the documents in the file and after deliberations; whether it was delivered after full hearing or in default. It shall be reasoned and dated.

The legal imperatives of administrative jurisdiction rulings are visas, reasoning (motivation) and the action and conclusion (*dispositif*). The visa is the texts or the rules of law that the judge applies; the antecedent facts which serve as grounds to justify the case. The reasoning contains the court's attempts to justify its decision. It is what the judge follows, the totality of legal and factual elements that explain and serve as basis for the decision. At the end there is the decision and action. The decision simply provides no and yes answers to each issue. It is the result of the visas and reasoning. It is a conclusion of the syllogism of which the contestation constitutes a major part. It is the adoption of a position by the judge on the matter submitted to the court. The action of the court usually appears at the end of the court's written opinion. It directs that something should be done.

## 9.4 Assessment of the Cameroonian Administrative Jurisdiction

The Cameroon administrative jurisdiction has been facing problems, obstacles and limitations from its inception. These problems have been the dependence on the active administration, the judicial judge and the reliance on the French administrative judge. They have also been organizational with the centralization of the administrative jurisdiction in Yaoundé. However, in recent times especially with the democratization processes since the 1990s, there have been many reforms on the administrative jurisdiction. The 1996 Constitution upgrades the judiciary as a whole from an authority to power (Part V). New laws have been enacted on Administrative Courts and the Supreme Court. As discussed above, the constitution and these laws provide the administrative jurisdiction organic (structural) and functional (competence) autonomy. The creation of administrative courts in the regions and the creation of a section in ENAM to train specialized administrative judges have mitigated some problems. Some problems still remain as can be assessed from the autonomy to the active administration, judiciary judge, French law and number of litigations.

### I. Autonomy of Administrative jurisdiction in relation to active administration

This implies that the magistrates have to manage the administrative jurisdiction independently of other powers. The 1996 Constitution states that the judiciary power shall be exercised by the courts and shall be independent of the executive and legislative powers (article 37, 1–2). But ends up stating that;

> The President of the Republic shall guarantee the independence of the judiciary power. He shall appoint members of the bench and legal departments
>
> He shall be assisted in this task by the Higher Judicial Council which shall give him its opinion on all nominations for the bench and on disciplinary action against judicial and legal officers...

The Higher Judicial Council which is supposed to manage the magistrate corps is an administrative body which depends on the executive. Its members are not only magistrates but also parliamentarians and a personality appointed by the President of the Republic. It is presided over by the President of the Republic and the vice president is the Minister in charge of Justice. Certainly it is advantageous that the first personality of the state protects the judiciary; however, it is paradoxical that he personally guarantees the independence of another state power.

## II. Autonomy of Administrative jurisdiction in relation to the French

The commentaries of Alain Bockel, Bipoun–Woum, Nguini Marcel in the 1970s and later Kamdem J.C, Biyoum Joseph, Momo Bernard and Kamto Maurice about the dependency of the Cameroonian jurisdiction on the French are still relevant today. Most of the definitions of concepts and decisions of the Cameroonian administrative judge are inspired by the French. At times court decisions are inundated with French laws and cases. Some scholars have even highlighted court decisions where 18 or more French cases have been cited by the judge in one ruling.

The consequences are that the Cameroonian judge is inert or docile and does not take decisions mindful of local realities. The extreme prudence, lack of audacity and courage of the Cameroonian magistrate are constraints to innovation. As a corollary, the Cameroonian administrative jurisdiction is more receptive and legislative than case–law based. In the elaboration of the rules, the legislative power emphasizes on its political choices, and with the lack of required knowledge, it copies the French texts.

## III. Scarcity of petitions on administrative matters

The effectiveness of the submission of the administration to the law is measured through the petitions made by the public against the administration. Besides, in administrative law and justice, case–law plays a very fundamental innovative, nurturing and even existentialist role. Case–law is dynamic and can play a pivotal role in the adaptation of rules to national realities. But in spite of the multiplicity of administrative malpractices, there are few petitions against the administration. Quantitatively, the numbers of litigations are few, and qualitatively they concern mostly the public servants and the public service.

This can be explained by procedural complexities and environmental challenges. The rules of administrative jurisdiction are complex and the procedure complicated, regionalized (distance) and costly. The political, economic, social and environmental factors make administrative justice difficult. The political regime in reality is presidentialist, with the concentration of powers and the almightiness of the administrators. In addition, the citizens are not very combative, probably explained by their illiteracy and poverty. Law is a difficult science to master; citizens generally do not know the laws or their rights. As Bipoun–Woum rightly holds, the problem of education is an obstacle to administrative control and legality in general.

Even when the decisions are taken by the administrative judge, there is no guarantee that they will be executed. The judgements have the "*autorité de chose jugé*", they have absolute authority, "obligatory and executory force" but in reality enforceability depends on administrative good faith. The administrative decisions have the privilege of "*autorité de chose décidé*" which is manifested at two levels: preliminary or provisional execution and privilege of automatic execution. The procedures of suspending incriminated decisions until the court judgement are exceptional and difficult. As a demonstration of bad faith, the administration can "abuse the procedure." It can refuse to execute the decision on the pretext of lack of budgetary endowments. There has been considerable growth in the administration's power of law–making which can be used to block justice. Sometimes, the executive requests the intervention of the legislative to validate administrative decisions, whose annulments have been pronounced by the judge. Due to the fact that judges cannot contest the law, legislative validations are good instruments for blocking the execution of court sentences. Another block to enforceability is the state's monopoly in the use of force. From this standpoint, contrary to common law there is no means of forced execution against the administration. The enforcements of some judgements are therefore paralyzed.

## Conclusion of part four

Administrative law is of no essence if violations of the law are not punished. Generally, litigations about administrative action fall in the domain of Administrative justice (Contentieux Administrative). The administration has to act in line with the law else its acts be cancelled, and at times it has to pay damages (see the principle of legality). The effectiveness of the administrative law and justice in Cameroon is bedevilled by internal and external factors. Internally more reforms are needed regarding the organization and functioning of the administrative jurisdiction. The environmental factors have to be made favourable to enable the flourishing of the administrative jurisdiction. It is necessary for the national situations to be respected in the procedures and consequently rulings. The misconception that private law is the common law and administrative law is the exception should be discarded. The administrative jurisdiction needs to be granted more autonomy where dependence is detrimental to its evolution. It is only under these conditions that the administrative jurisdiction will play the role incumbent on it.

# General Conclusion

The legal approach provides a solid beginning and foundation for the study of the Cameroonian public administration. This introductory work provides the guidelines for future more detailed legal studies on the aspects of public administration. Besides, the legal approach is challenged by informal actors, influence of other factors and organisational and societal dynamism. First, the formal organisation is all that is official, written and formalised. The informal is neither written nor official but exists. The informal actors are not provided in the blueprint of the organisation. But the formal order of organisational procedure and techniques are constantly outmanoeuvred and threatened by the reality of informal processes. Second, beyond the institutions there are other political, social and economic factors that intervene in the functioning of the administrative machine. Thirdly, law is supposed to be a dynamic science in order to meet with the internal and external changes. Institutions have to adapt to economic, political and social changes. Sometimes institutional arrangements cannot cope with societal dynamism. Institutional rigidity renders rules and structures obsolete and irrelevant when objective conditions have changed. According to the systems theory, institutions are open systems; they do not exist in a vacuum. They are affected by the intra–societal and the extra societal environments. From this standpoint, from the developmental approach, the legal environment constantly faces issues related underdevelopment as there exist reciprocal relations between the two. The challenge is whether the Cameroonian administration in its organization, functioning and justice has what it takes to constantly and reliably protect human rights and freedoms against administrative arbitrariness and abuse of power.

From the forgoing and legal writings, one can make observations regarding the Cameroonian administrative law. First, it is more receptive than innovative. The constituent powers; legislative, executive, and judiciary of Cameroon usually copy or imitate the fundamental principles of French administrative law. Alain Bockel observes that, "the principal concepts, the great theoretical constructions, as particular techniques are identical." With the French importation, one therefore, doubts the autonomy of Cameroon's administrative law and consequently it effectiveness as found in a different context. As Montesquieu had warned, laws are always specific to their contexts and it will be a miracle if those of one country can fit in another.

Second, it is more legislative than "judge–made". In the western world, notably United States, Britain and France, administrative law is largely based on legal decisions or judgements. But the French experience has simply been codified in Cameroon (inflation and incorporation of texts in nearly all domains). The scarcity of administrative cases in Cameroon to nourish the administrative law can either be explained by the lack of courage of the judges, or the unfavourable environment which surrounds this system or the justice system itself. Consequently, administrative law is not really developing naturally as it does not really exploit or is not really inspired by the day to day experiences or the local realities. Thus the fundamental role that administrative justice is expected to play in nurturing a specific administrative law for Cameroon in concordant with national realities.

# Bibliography

## Published Books


Aman, Alfred C. *Administrative law in a Global Era.* USA: Cornell University Press, 1992.

Aman, Alfred C., Mayton, William T. and Aman, Afrec C. *Administrative Law: Hornbook Series*. USA: West Publishing Company, 2nd ed., 2001.

Anyangwe, Carlson. *The Cameroonian Judicial System.* Yaoundé: CEPER, 1987.

Asimow, Michael R. *Gilbert Law Summaries: Administrative law.* USA: Harcourt Legal and Professional Publications, 13th ed., 2002.

Azfar Omar, Kähkönen Satu, Lanyi Anthony, Meagher,Patrick and Rutherfor Diana. *Decentralization, Governance and Public Services: the Impact of Institutional Arrangements, A Review of the Literature.* University of Maryland: IRIS Center,College Park, September 1999

Bayart, Jean Françoise. *l'Etat au Cameroun.* Paris: Presses De la Fondation Nationale des Sciences Politiques, 2e ed, 1984.

Beget, J.M. *Les Institutions Administratif,* Paris: Economica, 1985.

Bozeman, Barry. *All Organizations are Public: Bridging Public and Private Organizational Theories.* San Francisco: Jossey–Bass Publishers, 1987.

Beget, Jean–Marie. *Les Institutions Administratives*. Paris: Economica, 1985.

Burns, James MacGregor; Peltason, J.W.; Cronin, Thomas E.; Magleby, David B.; O'BrienDavid M.; Light, Paul C. *Government by the People: National, State and Local Version.* New Jersey: Upper Saddle River, 2004.

Cann, Steven J. *Administrative Law*. USA: Sage Publications, 2005.

Champagne, Gilles. *L'Essentiel du Droit Constitutionnel: Théorie Générale du Droit Constitutionnel.* Paris: Montchrestien, 2006.

Chapus, René, *Droit administratif général*. Paris: Montchrestien, tome 1, 2000 et tome 2, 2001.

Cheema, D. S. & Rondinelli, D. A., eds. *Decentralisation and Government*, Beverley Hills CA: Sage, 1983.

Chevallier, J.J. et Loschak D. *Science Administrative; Théorie Générale de l'Institution Administrative*. Paris : LGDJ, T1. 1978

Davis, Kenneth C. *Discretionary Justice: A Preliminary Inquiry*. Westport: Greenwood Press, 1980.

Debbasch, Charles. *Science Administrative: Administration Publique*. Paris: Dalloz, 5^e ed, 1989.

Dwivedi, O.P and Keith, Henderson, eds. *Public Administration in World Perspective*. United States: Iowa State Press, 1990.

Dye, Thomas R. *Understanding Public Policy*. New Jersey: Upper Saddle River, 2002.

Easton, David. *A Systems Analysis Political Life*. New York: John Willey, 1965.

Finer, Herman. *The Theory and Practice of Modern Government*. London: Methuen and co. Ltd, 4th ed, 1961.

Georgopoulos, Constantin.L. *La Démocratie en Danger*. Paris: L.G.D.J, 1977.

Gladden, E.N. *An Introduction to Public Administration*. London: Staples Press, 1961.

Gellhorn, Ernest and Levin, Ronald M. *Administrative Law and Process in a Nutshell*.Washington: West Group Publishing, 4th ed. 1997.

Goodnow, Johnson. *Comparative Administrative Law: An Analysis of the Administrative Systems, National and Local, of the United States, England, France and Germany*.USA: Lawbook Exchange, 2006.

Hall, Daniel E. *Administrative Law: Bureaucracy in a Democracy*. USA: Prentice Hall, 2001.

Hubrecht, G. *Notions Essentielles de Droit Civil*. France : Sirey, 9è édition. 1973.

Jacobini, H.B., Melone, Albert and Kalvelage, Carl. *Research Essentials of Administrative Law*. USA: Palisade Publishers, 1983.

Jacobini, H.B. *An Introduction to Comparative Administrative Law*. New York: Oceana, 1991.

Jameux, Claude. "Organisation du pouvoir, pouvoir de l'organisation" in *Economies et Sociétés–Sciences de Gestion*, 147–178.

Jreisat, Jamil E. *Comparative Public Administration and Policy: Essentials of Public Policy and Administration*. United States of America: Westview, 2002.

Jürgen, Harbich. "State Supervision of Local Government Authorities", *Bayerische Verwaltungsschule*, UDK: harbich,351.9(045),53–56.

Hall, Daniel E. *Administrative Law: Bureaucracy in a Democracy*. USA: Prentice Hall, 2001.

Kamto, Maurice. *L'urgence de la Pensée: Reflexions sur une Precondition de Dévéloppement en Afrique*. Yaounde : Editions Mandara, 1993.

Kamto, Maurice. « Dynamisme Constitutionnelle du Cameroun Indépendante » *Revue Juridique Africaine*, numéros 1, 2, et 3,(1995) :7–49.

Laubadere André de. Venezia,Jean–Claude; Gaudemet Yves. *Traité de droit administratif*, LGDJ.

Legrand,André *Initiation au Droit Public: Formation Administration Concours*, France :La documentation Française, 2003.

Levine, Charles; Guy, Peters and Frank, Thompson J. *Public Administration: Challenges, Choices, Consequences*. Illinois: Glenview, Scott, Foreman/ Little,1990.

Levin, Gellhorn. *Law in a Nutshell: Administrative law and Process*. USA: West's law in aNutshell, 4th ed., 1997.

Lombard, Martinc. *Droit administratif*, « Cours », Paris: Dalloz, 2001.

Long, M. Weil, P., Braibant, G., Delvolve. P.,and Genevois, P. *Les grands arrêts de la jurisprudence administrative*, Paris : Dalloz, 2001.

Lynn N.B. and Widavsky, A.eds:. *Public Administration. The State of the Discipline*. NewDelhi: East–West press (EWP) pvt Ltd, 1992.

MacIver, R.M.. *The Modern State*. Oxford: Oxford University Press, 1962.

Michalon, Thierry. *Quel Etat pour L'Afrique?* Paris: L'Harmattan, 1984.

Mintzeberg, Harry. *Structure et Dynamiques des Organisations: Tendances Actuelles*. Paris: Les éditions d'organisation, Traduit de l'américain par Pierre Romelaer, 1982.

Molitor, André. *Les Sciences Sociales dans l'Enseignement Supérieur: Administration Publique*. Paris : UNESCO, Imprimerie Atar SA Genève, 1958.

Morand–Deviller, Jacqueline. *Cours de droit administratif*, Montchestien, 2001

Muna, Bernard. *Cameroon and the Challenges of the 21st Century*. Yaounde : Tama Books, 1993.

Nicholas, Henry. *Public Administration and Public Affairs*. USA : Prentice Hall 10th ed., 2006.

Nlep, Roger.G. *L'Administration Publique Camerounaise. "Contribution à l'étude des systèmes Africains d'Administration publique."* Paris : L.G.D.J, 1986.

Owona (J): *Droit Administratif Spécial de la République du Cameroun*. Paris : EDICEF, 1985.

Owona, Joseph. *Droit Administratif Spécial de la République du Cameroun.* Paris: EDICEF, 1985

Owona, Joseph. Contentieux Administratif de la République du Cameroun Paris : L'Harmattan, Collection Droits Africains et Malgache, 2011

Owona, Josep h, La Décentralisation Camerounaise, Paris : L'Harmattan, Collection Droits Africains et Malgache, 2011.

Rhonda, Diane; Longley, Ronda. *Administrative Justice: Central Issues in the UK and European Administrative Law.* New York: Cavendish Publishing 1999.

Rivero, Jean and, Waline, Jean. *Droit administratif*, France :Dalloz, 2000

Rosenbloom, David H. *Administrative Law for Public Managers.* USA: Westview Press, 2003.

Schuck, Peter H. *Foundations of Administrative Law.* USA: Foundation Press, 2nd ed., 2003.

Salomon, Bilong. *Approche Méthodologique du Droit Administratif.* Dschang: Presses Universitaires de Dschang, Editions Clés, 2005.

Sawadogo, A. A. *L'Etat Africain face à la décentralisation.* Paris: Editions Karthala, 2001.

Stillman, Richard. *Public Administration: Concepts & Practices.* USA: Houghton Mifflin, 6th edition, 1996.

Warren, Kenneth F. *Administrative Law in the Political System.* USA: Westview Press, 4th ed., 2004.

Wunsch, J. S. & Olowu, D., eds. *The failure of the Decentralised State and Self Governance in Africa.* Goulder: Westview Press, 1990.

## Articles

Budine, J. 'La distinction entre collectivité locale et collectivité territoriale. Variationsémantique ou juridique?', *R.D.P.,* 1992.

Cheka, Cosmas, "The State of the Process of Decentralization in Cameroon." *Africa Development,* Vol. XXXII, Number 2, Council for the Development of SocialScience Research in Africa(CODESRIA), (2007): 181–196.

Debbasch, Charles; « Le Droit Administratif, Droit Dérogatoire au Droit Commun ? » *Mélanges René Chapus,* Droit Administratif, Paris : Montchrestien, (1992) :127–133.

Djuitchoko, Sietchoua Célestin. « Perspectives Ouverts à la Juridiction Administrative du Cameroun par la Loi No 96/06 du 18 janvier 1996 portant Révision de la Constitution du 02 Juin 1972. » *Juridis Périodique* No 31, Juillet–Septembre (1997):60–66.

Dongmo, Guimdo Bernard Raymond. « Le Droit D'Accès à la Justice Administrative au Cameroun : Contribution à l'Etude d'un Droit Fondamental. », *R.R. J* (2008) : 453 498.

Ewang, Andrew Sone; Moye Godwin Bongyu; and Bunyuy, Juliette Suliy. "The Judge and the Protection of Human Rights and Freedoms." *Cameroon Journal of Democracy and Human Rights*, December 2009.

Ewang, Andrew Sone; Moye Godwin Bongyu; and Bunyuy, Juliette Suliy. "The Capability of the Judiciary to Protect Human Rights in Cameroon." *Annals of the Faculty of Law and Political Science, Tome 14, (2010): 171–190.*

Goulongo, Mbara Gueurandi. Décentralisation Participative et Gouvernance Spatiolocale au Cameroun. *Cameroon Journal on Democracy and Human Rights,* Vol. 2, No 2, Décembre (2008): 44–58.

Guimdo, Bernard Raymond. 'Les bases Constitutionnelles de la décentralisation au Cameroun', *Revue Générale de Droit*, 29, Université d'Otawa, (1998) : 79–100

Jürgen, Harbich, State Supervision of Local Government Authorities, Bayerische Verwaltungsschule, UDK: 351.9(045), harbich□ bvs.de, 53–56.

Kamto, Maurice : « Dynamisme Constitutionnelle du Cameroun Indépendante » *Revue Juridique Africaine, n*uméros 1,2,et 3,(1995) : 7–49.

Kaufman, H. "Major Players: Bureaucracies in American Government." *Public Administration Review,61 (2001):*18–42.

Mescheriakoff, Alain–Serge. « Le Décline de la Fonction Administrative Contentieuse au Cameroun, *R. Jur. Pol. Ind. Coop.,* Paris : t. 34, No 4,décembre (1980) : 746–870,

Momo, Bernard : « Réflexions sur le Système Communal Camerounaise : Contribution à l'étude de la Décentralisation Territoriale au Cameroun » *Juridis Info* No 24, Octobre–Décembre (1995) :81–92.

Ngimbog, Laurent–Roger. « La Justice administrative à l'épreuve du phénomène de la corruption au Cameroun » *Droit et Société 51/52–(2002 : 301–323.*

Olinga, Alain– Didier : « L'Exigence de la Prise en Compte des Composantes Sociologiques de la Circonscription en Droit Electorale Camerounaise », Juridis Périodique, No 23, Octobre–Décembre (1996) :67–72.

Owona, Joseph . « L'Institutionnalisation de la Légalité d'Exception dans le Droit Public Camerounaise. » *Revue Camerounaise de Droit,* No 6, Juillet– Décembre 1974.

Sindjoun, Luc : « Identité nationale et 'révision constitutionnelle' du 18 Janvier 1996 : Comment Constitutionnalise–t–on le 'Nous' au Cameroun dans Post–unitaire ? » Polis, Vol. 1, Février 1996.

Tchapnga, Keutcha Célestin et Teubou, Barthelem.y « Réflexions sur L'Apport du Législateur Camerounais a L'Evolution de la Procédure Administrative Contentieux de 1990–1997. » *Revue Internationale de Droit Africain EDJA*, 45,Avril–Juin ( 2000) : 61–75.

Tchapnga, Keutcha Célestin. Mutations Récentes du Droit Administratif Camerounaise, *Afrilex (*2000/01) :1–22.

Tchapnga, Keutcha Célestin. » La Reforme Attendue du Contentieux Administratif au Cameroun. » *Juridis Périodique*, No 70, Avril–Juin (2007) : 24–29.

World Bank, Cameroon. *The Path to Fiscal Decentralization: Opportunities and Challenges, Poverty Reduction and Economic Management,* Report N° 63389–CM, September 2012.

## Official Documents

Law N° 74/23 of 5 December 1974 to Organise Councils and subsequent amendments thereto.

Decree N° 74–138 of 18 February 1974: General Rules and Regulations of the Public Service.

Decree N° 77/418 of 24 October 1977 Creating and Organising the Local Government Training Centre (CEFAM).

Decree N° 82–100 of March 3, modifying Decree No 78–484 of November 9, 1978 fixing the common provisions applicable to State Employees governed by the Labour Code.

Réforme Administrative: République du Cameroun, Recueil de textes, Imprimerie Nationale, Edition 1984.

Decree N° 84/388 of 2nd June 1984 on the Organization of the Ministry of Public Service.

Decree N° 88/105 of 2nd August 1988 on the Organization of the Ministry of Public Service and State Control.

Décret N° 92/244 du 25 Novembre 1992 nommant le Premier Ministre.

Décret N° 92/245 de la 26 Novembre 1992 portante Organisation du Gouvernement.

Instruction Générale N° 005 du 27 Novembre 1992 relative à l'Organisation du Travail Gouvernemental.

Décret N° 92/245 du 26 Novembre 1993 portant organisation du Gouvernement, modifié et complété par le décret no 94/135 du 21 juillet 1994.

Decree N° 94/199 of 7 October 1994 on the New Statute of the Public Service

Décret N° 94/160 du 16 August 1994 portant Réorganisation du Ministère de la Fonction Publique et de la Réforme Administrative.

Décret N° 94/199 du 07 Octobre 1994: Le Nouveau Statut de la Fonction Publique de l'Etat.

Law N° 96/06 of 18 January 1996 to amend the Constitution of 2 June 1972 supplemented by Law No 2008/001.

Decree No 2000/365 of December 11, 2000 modified by Decree No 2006/182 of 31 May 2006 on the Re–organization of the Special Fund for Equipment and Inter communal Intervention (FEICOM).

Decree N° 2002/216 of August 24, 2002 to Reorganize the Government of Cameroon.

Decree N° 2004/320 of 8 December 2004 to Organize Government, as amended by Decree No 2007/269 of September 2007.

Law N° 2004/17 of July 22, 2004 on the Orientation of Decentralization

Law N° 2004/18 of July 22, 2004 to lay down Rules applicable to Councils

Law N° 2004/19 of July 22, 2004 to lay down Rules applicable to Regions

Decree N° 2004/320 of 8 December 2004 to organize the government, as amended by Decree N°2007/269 of September 2007

Decree N° 2005/086 of 28 March 2005 to Organize the Ministry of Public Service and Administrative Reforms.

Decree N° 2005/104 of 13 April 2005 to Organize the Ministry of Territorial Administration and Decentralization.

Decree No 2006/182 of May 31, 2006 Re–organising Special Fund for Equipment and Intercommunal Intervention (FEICOM).

Law No 2006/004 of July 14, 2006 to lay down Conditions Governing the Election of Regional Councilors.

Law N° 2006/016 on the Organization and Functioning of the Supreme Court

Arrêté N° 130/CAB/pm du 6 octobre 2006 portant Création, Organisation et Fonctionnement d'un Comité de Concertation pour la mise en œuvre de la Decentralization.

Law No 2006/022 of 22 December 2006 to lay down the Organization and Functioning of Administrative Courts

Law No 2006/015 of 29 December 2006 on Judicial Organization

Law No 2006/016 of 29 December 2006 to lay down the Organization and Functioning of the Supreme Court

Decree N° 2007/268 of 7 September 2007 modifying and completing certain provisions of Decree No 2004/230 of 8 December 2004 on the Organization of Government

Law N° 2007/2006 of 26 December 2007 relating to the Financial Regime of the State

Decree No 2008/013 of 17 January 2008 on the Organization and Functioning of the National Council on Decentralization.

Decree N° 2008/376 of 12 November 2008 on the Administrative Organization of the Republic of Cameroon

Decree N° 2008/377 of 12 November 2008 fixing the Attributions of the Heads of Administrative Circumscriptions and the Organization and Functioning of their Services.

Decree N° 2008/377 of 12 November 2008 fixing Attributions of the Heads Administrative Circumscriptions and determining the Organization and Functioning of their Services

Law N° 2009/011 of 10 July 2009 on the Financial Regime of Decentralized Territorial Entities.

Law No 2009/019 of 15 December 2009 on the local Fiscal System.

Decree N° 2011/408 of 9 December 2011 to Organize the Government.

Law No 2011/28 of 14 December 2011 to set up a Special Criminal Court

Decree N° 2011/412 of 9 December 2011 on the Reorganization of the Presidency of the Republic.

Law No 2011 of 14 December 2011 to amend and supplement certain provisions of law No 2006/15 of 29 December 2006 on Judicial Organization

## Case and Text Commentaries

Aba'a, Oyono Jean–Calvin: : CS/CA Mama Biloa C/Université de Ngaoundere, Decembre 2000 http://www.afrilex.u–bordeaux4.fr, 213–243 ( A student holder of a fake Chadian baccalaureate, rector decides to cancel registration, direct petition to the judge on the basis of urgency, violation of judge of time limit for self–defense, award of stay of execution to the detriment of the public power).

Djuitchoko, Sietchoua Célestin : CS /AP Aff. Guiffo Jean–Philippe C/Etat du Cameroun (MINEDUC) *Juridis Periodique,* No 65, Janvier–Mars (2006):39–49 (dismissal of an assistant lecturer of the University for academic insufficiency, legality of the decision, abuse of power).

Guimdo, Bernard: CS/PCA/91–1992 Union Nationale Camerounaise (Stanley Akwote Akondi C/ Etat du Cameroun(MINAT) *Juridis*

*Info*, No 19, Juliet–Septembre (1994): 27–33 ( refusal of legalization of a political party, petition for abuse of power, absence of legal base, liberty of association, acquired or implicit knowledge).

Tchapnga, Keutcha Célestin et Tonnang, Edouard Gnimpieba : Ordonnance No 05/CS/PCA du 05 Octobre 1992 portant sursis à exécution. Affaire Sigho–ko Abraham C/ Etat du Cameroun (MINSANTE), Juridis Periodique, No 68, Octobre Decembre, (2006):115–120 (implicit administrative authorization, stay of execution, non–respect of the public minister, award of stay of execution)

Tchapnga, Keutcha Célestin et Djuitchoko, Sietchoua Célestin : CS /CS Jugement No 29 du 03 Mai 1990, Mbarga Symphorien C/ Etat du Cameroun(MFPE), Jurisprudence Administrative, *Afrilex* 2000/ 01(notification must be done in written form?)

Tchapnga, Keutcha Célestin : CS/AP arrêt du 16 aout 1990, Albert Ono Ngafor: C/Etat du Cameroun, http://www.afrilex.u–bordeaux4.fr, pp 269–284 (the protection of property rights against administrative infringement)

Tchapnga, Keutcha Célestin : Le Regime Juridique du Sursis à Exécution dans la

Jurisprudence Administrative Camerounaise, *Juridis Periodique*, No 38, Avril–Juin (1999):83–91.

## Unpublished Works

Abdoulie, Fye. Effectiveness of Decentralization in The Gambia. University of Yaoundé II: Masters Dissertation in Governance and Regional Integration Institute of Governance, Humanities and Social Sciences, Pan–African University, 2014/2015.

Anyangwe, Carlson. Introduction to Law and Legal Systems, UNIYAO: FLES, 1987/1988.

Biyoum, Joseph. Droit Administratif, Université de Yaoundé : Cours polycopie de 2eme année de licence, 1984.

El–Beherry Ibrahim R□faat Mohamed. *Théorie des Contrats Administratifs et Marches Publics Internationaux,* Doctorat en Droit, Université de Nice Sophia–Antipolis Institut du Droit, de la Paix et du Développement (I.D.P.D.), 2004.

Ferretti, Raymond. Cours de Droit Administratif, l'Université de Metz, 2002.

Kamdem, Jean Claude. *Contentieux Administrative*. Université de Yaoundé : Faculté de

Droit et Sciences Economiques, cours polycopie, T.1, 1988/1989.

Kamdem, Jean Claude. Cours de *Contentieux Administrative*. Université de Yaoundé : Faculté de Droit et Sciences Economiques, cours polycopie, T.2, 1985/1986.

Lemen, Nlinga Armel Brice. The Transfer of Competencies and Means to Councils in Cameroon. University of Bamenda: Dissertation, Department of Law, Higher Technical Teacher Training College, 2014.2015.

Morand–Deviller, Jacqueline. *Cours de droit administratif*, Paris : Montchrestien, 2001

Nlep, Roger Gabriel : L'Accès aux Juridiction Camerounaise de Droit Public (no source)

Reuben, Yohana Kiwambe: Institutional Arrangements in Tanzania Local Government Authorities (LGAs) and Good Governance. University of Yaoundé II: Masters Dissertation in Governance and Regional Integration Institute of Governance, Humanities and Social Sciences, Pan–African University, 2014/2015.

Tsessue, Daniel. *Droit Administratif*, Yaounde: Ecole Nationale D'Administration et de la Magistrature(ENAM,), cours polycopié 1981

Yuliani, Elizabeth Linda, Decentralization, Deconcentration and Devolution: What Do They Mean? Paper presented at the Interlaken Workshop on Decentralization, Interlaken, Switzerland: 27–30 April 2004.

Zufferey, J.B. *Cours de Droit Administratif*, IUR II / UNIFR 2006–2007

Zufferey, J.B. Cours de Droit Administratif Général, Documents d'Appui, Université de Fribourg: Faculté de droit, Suisse, Année académique 2010 – 2011,

## Websites

World Justice Project's (wjp@wjpnet.org) accessed on 30 January 2016

Prime Minister's Office: Government Portal; Laws and Statutory Instruments, www.spm.gov.cm accessed February– May, 2016

*www.unifr.ch/droitadministratif* accessed February 20–25, 2016

http://www.ciesin.org/decentralization/English/General/Different_forms.html accessed in 2016

# About The Author

Moye Godwin Bongyu is an Associate Professor of Governance in the faculties of Law and Political Science of the Universities of Dschang and Bamenda. He is holder of a First Degree in Public Law, DEA and Doctorat de 3é Cycle en Science Politiques from the Universities of Yaoundé I and Yaoundé II. He obtained a PhD in Public Administration and Policy from Jackson State University in Jackson, Mississippi (USA). He has authored some books notably *African Public Administration: The Effective Management of Personnel, Debt–Poverty Trap: A Political and Economic Analysis, and African Public Administration: A Systems Approach.* He is interested in and has published articles on governance, public administration, law, development, politics, health, transport and security.

www.ingramcontent.com/pod-product-compliance
Lightning Source LLC
LaVergne TN
LVHW010621300926
849162LV00001B/23